Pai Gavioli

Thirty-six Years of War
and Finally Peace
with My Impossible
Brazilian Father-in-Law

A MEMOIR
BY JIM MARTIN

Of course, he would
never consider his life
to be a story, as in a book,
for example.
This is because books drift
toward art, and art drifts
toward fairy tale. For him,
life is no fairy tale. It's hard
as stone. It hurts like a
stick in the eye. He wastes
no time on books.

Pai as a young man during the Great Depression.

With love to Daisi,
who has enriched my life beyond words.

Proceeds from the sale of this book will be donated
to Educandário—Centro de Reabilitação São João Batista.
The nonprofit agency, which began in 1939 serving children with polio,
now provides free clinical as well as educational services to children
and adolescents with multiple disabilities. Located in Porto Alegre,
the agency serves families with low incomes throughout Rio Grande do Sul.
It is maintained primarily by donations from individuals, corporations
and public-private partnerships, as well as volunteer workers.

Educandário—Centro de Reabilitação São João Batista
www.educandario.org.br

Scan code to go to Educandário site.

Copyright © 2014 ♦ All rights reserved
ISBN 978-0-692-02632-8

ACKNOWLEDGMENTS

The chapter, "March to Berlin," was previously published
in the March-April 2009 issue of *Minnesota* Magazine,
the alumni magazine of the University of Minnesota.

Engravings, pages 35 and 100, reprinted by permission
of the Lutzenberger family

Photos of Pai and Marcus, page 73, and
Pai and Jim, page 122, by Brick Chapman
Outside back cover photo by Christian Eipeldauer

Book design, Barbara Koster

CONTENTS

A Note from the Author 9

OCTOBER 1, 1970: Family Citizenship 10

AUTUMN 1968: Leaving Guyland for Daisi 14

JUNE 1969: Marriage 18
HE WEEPS LIKE A CHILD 21

JULY 1970: Journey to Brazil 22

OCTOBER 2, 1970: Three Years in Brazil 31
MEAT 34 ◆ SARAH 38
THE HOUSE 41 ◆ THE CITY 44
THE PEOPLE'S TONGUE 46 ◆ GAUCHOS 51
THE CLOSET 54 ◆ BORN IN MONTENEGRO 57
A FOREIGN THREAD 58 ◆ ABSTINENCE 60
A HIGHER VOLTAGE 61 ◆ SHAMED 63
A VOW OF PROSPERITY 65 ◆ GLASS SKULLS 67
ROOTS 69 ◆ A FAMILY MEETING 70
A BIRTH 72 ◆ WITCHCRAFT 76
A FINANCIAL SYSTEM 77 ◆ SEPARATION 78

1973-1977: Transplanted 83

JANUARY 1977: A Torrid Welcome 84
THE PINNACLE 86 ◆ STREET SCHOOL 91

FEBRUARY 1981: A Painful Chat 93
A SIMPLE WEDDING 97 ◆ HIS BELOVED BANKS 99
DRIVING WITH GOD 101 ◆ LIKE FATHER, LIKE SON 102
RELENTLESS RECTITUDE 104 ◆ SWEET REVENGE 105
CLIMBING THE LADDER 108 ◆ PESSIMISM 110
MENSTRUATION CEREMONY 111

JANUARY 1986: Penetrating Granite 112
HOW TO EAT CHICKEN 114

DECEMBER 1990–JANUARY 1991: A Soaring Hero 117
COMBATTING THE GOVERNMENT 118

JUNE 1993: An Eating War 120
KEYS 120 ◆ INTIMACY 121

FEBRUARY–MARCH 1995: Driving Lessons 124
ATTACKING THE DRAGON 126 ◆ FURTHER WITCHCRAFT 126
LOVE MADE VISIBLE 127 ◆ DEAD GIRL 130

SUMMER 1997: Dona Sarah and the Two Josés 133

MARCH 1998: A Slice of Salami 140
ONE MAN, TWO FATHERS 140 ◆ INHERITANCE REJECTED 142
AN OPEN WOUND 143 ◆ CALMA, CALMA 143

MARCH 1999: Preserving Patrimony 146

FEBRUARY 2000: March to Berlin 148
TURNING GOLD IN AUTUMN 151 ◆ HIS TRAGIC VOICE 152

JANUARY 2001: A New Wariness 154
BANKS GET DEFENSIVE 154

MARCH 2002: Fathers Poles Apart 155
A SHRUNKEN DOMAIN 157 ◆ TALKING WITH STRANGERS 159
LOCKING UP 161 ◆ FERRYBOAT CAPTAIN 162

JULY 2002: Temperance 163
SLEDGEHAMMER 165 ◆ VENUS 167
SLUM DRAMA 167 ◆ HERE IT IS! 168 ◆ TO REMEMBER IS TO LIVE 170
THE LAST PIECE OF BREAD 173 ◆ ALWAYS ECONOMIZE 175

DECEMBER 2003: A Year of Losses 178
A MILESTONE 180

JUNE-JULY 2004: Quietness 182
ABANDONMENT 183 ♦ DISTANT THUNDER FROM VENUS 184

MAY 2005: No One's Home 185
TOUCHED BY THE STARS 186 ♦ THE RAIN THAT NEVER COMES 187
LOOKING FOR CAPTAIN CORNUCOPIA 191
THE BITTER TIMES HAVE NOT YET ARRIVED 191 ♦ PULLING OARS 193

SEPTEMBER 6, 2005: The Phone Rings 194

OCTOBER-NOVEMBER 2005: The Wreckage 195
THIS IS HOW I AM NOW 198 ♦ CALL THE MANAGER 202
TRANQUILITY 204 ♦ PICKLE JARS 205
THEY'RE TAKING MY LIGHTS 206 ♦ TRIUMPH 207
DEFEAT 209 ♦ HARD BARGAINS 211
FAREWELL TO THE KITCHEN 212

MARCH-APRIL 2006: If I Were to Die This Morning 217
A TORN CAPE 220 ♦ LEAVING HIM 221
BURIAL 223

FEBRUARY 2007: They Belong to the Grass 224
EPILOGUE 225

APPENDICES 226
RULES HE LIVES BY 226 ♦ MAP 227
CHRONOLOGY 228
SIX GENERATIONS: THE GAVIOLI-MEDEIROS FAMILIES 230
INDEX 232

> When an old person dies,
> we say a library has burnt down
>
> —PROVERB FROM GABON AFRICA

A NOTE FROM THE AUTHOR

No one writes a book alone. Seven years ago, a group of women accepted me into their writers' group. They nurtured my first draft, and with warmth and encouragement, mercilessly slashed and burned its overblown verbiage and uncontrolled metaphor.

Following that, my close friend Rosa Maria dela Cueva Peterson spent hours poring over my second draft, and gracefully told me its problems outweighed its virtues. I trusted her, because she knows writing and understands the Martin and Gavioli families perhaps better than I.

The third draft went to my sons, Marcus and André, as well as to my good friends Brick Chapman, Richard Cornell, Scott Johnson, and Phil Lundblad. They advised me to keep at it.

The angel sitting on my shoulder all this time, who initially inspired me to write this book, is my dear Peace Corps friend and author Peggy Anderson. I gave her the fourth draft, which she gently destroyed. It took me a year to recover, producing draft number five. It's been her invaluable wisdom, humor and unfailing moral support that have kept me going.

I'm deeply indebted to my close friends Barbara and Brian Koster. Barb, a graphic designer, did an elegant job of turning this sow's ear into a silk purse. Brian went beyond the call of friendship, providing encouragement, practical advice, and volunteering many selfless hours to create a Gavioli family tree and map of Rio Grande do Sul.

I'm also grateful to my editor Laura Silver and proofreader Karen Reid, whose sharp eyes, intelligence and ear for tone have elevated the story.

It's impossible to repay my debt to the Gavioli family, who, with an openness characteristic of Brazilians, helped shape my understanding of Pai and Brazil. Special thanks to Pai's half brother, José Augusto Gavioli, who shared with me his knowledge of Pai's early family history.

I am also grateful to several authors. My appreciation of Pai was deepened by Robert Bly's great book, *Iron John*, which renewed my understanding of what it is to be a man. Similarly, I gained greater understanding of how Brazil is changing from Larry Rohter's book, *Brazil on the Rise—The Story of a Country Transformed*. I also wish to credit Luis Fernando Veríssimo, a popular Brazilian humorist from Porto Alegre. I have taken the liberty of borrowing his impossible notion of transforming Brazil into a Scandinavian country from his collection of newspaper columns, *O Mundo é Bárbaro*. Also, thanks to Bernard Cooper for his honest and humorous book, *The Bill From My Father: A Memoir*, which resonated with my perception of Pai.

Finally, my greatest debt is to Daisi. She allowed me into her remarkable family, only to endure the hours, days, months and years I spent at the computer attempting to honor them. I hope she'll forgive me.

Jim Martin // June 2014

OCTOBER 1, 1970

Family Citizenship

I can hear my heart beating. My wife, Daisi, has nervous stomach cramps. For nearly two years, we've imagined this day.

Our plane lands in a gray Brazilian rain around lunchtime. We're a week earlier than expected, having cut short three months of travel from Saint Paul, Minnesota, to Porto Alegre.

We get out of the cab in a baptismal downpour. Daisi rushes into the home she left two years ago. I lean our backpacks against an old scrub tree and extend my hand to the cab driver, palm up, offering several baffling bills whose numbers are inflated into the tens of thousands. Delicately, he lifts several wet bills from my open hand. He seems honest. At this point I don't care.

From inside the house, I hear a shriek, then pandemonium.

The cab drives away over glistening cobblestones, packed tightly like thousands of loaves of bread. I turn to the house, which looks like a little German cottage, home to Hansel and Gretel. A modest two-story house, it has a wood exterior painted blue, and a steep roof of dark orange tiles made from Brazil's iron-rich earth. In one corner of the miniature front yard, hardly bigger than a king-size bed, is a tree with leaves as big as snow shovels. The house fits snugly between two small neighboring wooden houses, separated by whitewashed concrete walls about chest high. All the houses on the street, crowded behind iron fences or brick walls, are set close to the sidewalk. I bend down to pick up my backpack and discover Daisi's father next to me. Already soaked in the downpour, he bends over her backpack, wondering where to grab it. Seems he's never seen one before. We lug them over a bumpy sidewalk, through his gate and into his house.

Dripping wet in the cramped living room, I dump my backpack on the carpet. Shouting, hugging, and jumping are exploding everywhere. Daisi's father hugs her for what seems an eternity, then breaks into tears. Moments later, he points to a small couch and tells me to sit down and be comfortable, impossible amid this jubilation. Portuguese, which I don't understand, hits me like machine-gun bullets from all directions. I grin insanely, nodding my head, approving everything, comprehending nothing. Euphoria needs no translation.

Until now, the Gavioli family has been a cluster of vague figures in my imagination, like Amish dolls with no faces. Suddenly here they are, flesh and blood, seemingly quasi-real, bumping up against me in this tight living room. Everything has the unstable quality of a dream.

PAI GAVIOLI
Thirty-six Years of War and Finally Peace with My Impossible Brazilian Father-in-Law

I accidently bump into a curtain that covers a corridor leading to the inner regions of the house. The curtain falls over my head, putting me completely in the dark. Uproarious laughter from the Gaviolis. I lift it off my head, wanting to apologize, but have no words for it. More hilarity. Excellent work, Jim. In your first moment on the Gavioli stage you're the bungling fool. You've made your first impression.

The exultation subsides. Daisi's father summons me into an adjacent small bedroom. On each side of the bed is a small table. Looming in one corner, a mammoth television set dominates the room. There's no space for a chair. Senhor Gavioli motions me to sit on the bed he shares with his wife. Daisi's eldest brother, Sidnei, who speaks some English, is also here, to translate. Senhor Gavioli shuts the door. He stands above me, examining me. The bedroom is quiet.

Short, bald, and rotund, he resembles Winston Churchill without the cigar. Unlike Sir Winston, though, he wears thick glasses that magnify his blue eyes nearly to the size of quarters. His glasses are utilitarian, with heavy plastic frames that lack style. They're designed solely to position the lenses squarely before his penetrating eyes, which are sharp, deep, and intense.

He has a straight nose and strong laugh lines curving at the corners of his mouth. He's wearing an ordinary short-sleeve shirt and everyday gray slacks. There's not a thread of ostentation anywhere about him. He looks like an immigrant with more urgent things on his mind than clothes. He could be any ordinary fifty-five-year-old guy on the street, except for a palpable voltage of raw energy radiating off of him. For an uncomfortably long time his magnified eyes bore into mine, sizing me up, until I can't take it anymore and look away.

He breaks the silence in a declamatory voice, as if making some sort of proclamation: "*Nossa família é sua família. Nossa casa é sua casa.*"

I turn to Sidnei for the translation. "Our family is your family. Our house is your house."

A tingle runs up my spine. The small room grows larger. He looks down at me, waiting for my reply. I don't know what to say, or how. Never have I ever been so swiftly, unconditionally, and decisively accepted by anyone with absolutely no effort on my part.

I look up at him standing over me. I get the feeling I'm part of a soap opera, one in which I don't know my lines. No, wait, not a soap opera. Maybe I'm part of a makeshift ceremony in which I've just been awarded Gavioli Family Citizenship. I'm confused. Things are happening too quickly.

OCTOBER 1, 1970
Family Citizenship

His alarming gaze continues to drill deep into my eyeballs. He wants to know whether I have any questions. "*Me pergunte qualquer coisa.*" Sidnei translates: "Ask me anything you want." It's beginning to appear that I'm engaged in a serious conference with a serious man.

What does he want? Should I formally request his daughter's hand, a request now two years out of date? The moment calls for something impressive. I feel an urge to appear learned, to be curious about important things.

"How do Brazilians manage to handle high inflation?"

He hears Sidnei's translation. Then his eyes narrow. He measures the question. He begins a reply, but seeing my blank expression, he stops.

"*É um mistério*" (It's a mystery). Brazil is full of them, he adds. He'll be happy to explain it to me later when I know more Portuguese. His tone seems slightly patronizing. Nonetheless, I'm grateful to escape a lesson in economics, especially in Portuguese. Why did I choose the dismal science of economics, about which I know nothing? That was stupid. Maybe, in this our first encounter, I'm just being courteous, granting him the upper hand. That's probably it.

No, that's not it. Maybe I'm scared of him. C'mon Jim, get a grip.

Then he does an odd thing. He leaves the room and returns with a bright-yellow felt vest. It sags beneath the weight of multiple meritorious pins earned from his Lions Club.

I don't get his drift. Why is he showing this to me? What is he saying about it and these weird pins? There's something comical about the vest. Yes, this is a joke, and now that I'm part of the family, he's sharing with me. I bet he collected them as a prank. He's putting me at ease by showing his fun side. I'm about to go along with the joke and laugh at this preposterous vest. But wait. Now he's pointing to each pin. I think he's explaining each one. Most are for perfect attendance, I think. He might be serious. Yes, without a trace of irony. It looks like he's proud of the vest, and apparently proud to be a loyal Lion.

I've heard of Lions Clubs, but have no idea what they do, or why. Evidently, as I tried to impress him—widely missing the mark—he's trying to impress me. Also missing the mark.

Good thing I didn't laugh at his bizarre vest, which would have jeopardized my admittance into the family. Whew, close call.

The tiny bedroom is hot and humid. He's standing very close, waves of body heat rolling off his girth onto me. I'm getting tired. I don't understand anything he's saying. My eyes are glazing over. But he's just getting started. He's still talking to me, gently tapping my chest with his thick finger, or gently touching my elbow. A tapping and touching fortified with lots of penetrating eye contact.

He's looking me over, examining me up and down, measuring me, as if buying a horse. He's commanding my undivided attention. He's gazing into my face, searching for my reactions. This examination is far from the fleeting, deferential glances common in Scandinavian Minnesota. He's sizing me up as a possible friend, or enemy, not some abstract cog in a remote economic wheel, which can pass for identity in Minnesota. With him so close to me, I'm beginning to feel more real, more aware of myself, more connected to my body, which, by the way, is still being touched, poked, jabbed, and embraced.

Yes, embraced! He wraps me in a sweaty embrace. I'm almost lifted off the floor, hanging like a piece of meat off the curve of his large belly. All this fleshiness and physicality in this tiny bedroom is distressing for a guy raised in the touchless Scandinavian style. The embrace goes on and on, as though sealing my membership in the family.

Whew. At last I'm back in the little front room, liberated from his claustrophobic presence. I can breathe again. Our backpacks, slumped in a heap on the floor, look obsolete, something from a different age. Our trip through Central and South America is melting away, trickling down into memory's subsoil. Minnesota, our home just three months ago, barely exists. Rushing in to replace everything are the Gaviolis. And Brazil.

Brazil, which two years ago was a meaningless green blob on the map. Now here I am in this exotic country, which produced Carmen Miranda, the Brazilian Bombshell, who sang and danced with grapes and bananas in her hairdo. Jim, let's try to wake up here a second, OK? You're in Porto Alegre, city of a million and a half people, the capital of Rio Grande do Sul, nearly six thousand miles from Saint Paul as the crow flies. Meanwhile, you have no idea where you are. Which is part of the thrill. Gotta be lost before you're found.

Yes, I'm thirty and I'm lost. Let me count the ways. Do I have a job? No. A home? No. A car? No. Children? No. Am I a man? No. Actually, I'm still a boy. Sort of a Peter Pan, flying innocently, far above ground like a bird, free of worldly possessions. No keys. No status. No tangible skill or craft. No acquaintance with metal or wood, like plumbing or carpentry. But now things have changed. My soaring, innocent life has landed in this small house, in the lap of this highly real Gavioli tribe. Thank goodness I'm married to Daisi. She's my lifeline. I trust her, and maybe even her family. A radiance shines out of them, flowing from somewhere, perhaps Brazil itself.

In this modest house, in its small rooms, its small front yard, and with these almost-incandescent people, is where life begins anew, a far cry from what it was two years ago.

OCTOBER 1, 1970
Family Citizenship

AUTUMN 1968

Leaving Guyland for Daisi

Flash back two years. I'm living with three other guys in a sprawling, run-down Victorian mansion with mice and squirrels and birds in the walls, in a deteriorated area of Saint Paul near the cathedral. I'm living in Guyland—a world of beer, Frisbees, touch football, parties, and no entanglements with women. I haven't had a date in two years and I'm deep into the unexamined life. But I have an excuse. I'm recovering from setbacks.

The first setback was Harvard College. I entered Harvard Yard as a freshman thinking I'd be a doctor, like my father, and his father before him. I quickly managed to nearly flunk math and chemistry. I decide to trade medicine for the nebulous and perhaps merely decorative field of English literature. Dad is disappointed, but he never actually tells me. He and I are not in the habit of discussing life's major decisions, a silence that I interpret as trust. So while my classmates are attending lectures and diligently preparing for greatness, I'm playing basketball, football, volleyball, and billiards—interrupted by dreamy hours in the library reading novels, philosophy, and sociology I don't fully understand. Four years later, I'm awarded a diploma I feel I don't deserve.

Inspired by President Kennedy, I join the Peace Corps in 1962. I'm sent to Niger, West Africa, one of the poorest nations on the planet. I am to teach English in a French-run high school in Zinder, a dry Islamic town on the southern edge of the Sahara desert. I arrive eager and full of midwestern idealism. But things do not go well. The headmaster, a short, stocky former French colonist who resents the Peace Corps as American interference in a country that only two years earlier was a French colony, makes sure I have virtually nothing to do in his school. Lacking the inner resources to come up with a substitute project useful to this impoverished part of the world, I sink into beer and debauchery.

After a year of less-than-exemplary performance, the Peace Corps director angrily transfers me to another town and another school. Things improve. I actually manage to teach for a year.

Still disillusioned, I return to the US, and Washington, DC, where I join a project teaching English in a black inner-city high school. I barely manage to last the year.

Thus end seven years of education in personal limitations, which are greater than I had imagined when I left high school. My wings, which soared back in high school, are cut. I am fallen to earth, sometimes ashamed, quite unsure of who I am or could be. The solution: stop pitying myself and try harder.

A private school for boys in Saint Paul hires me to teach English. For the next three years, life improves.

But enough about me.

In the fall of 1968, one of my housemates meets a Brazilian woman. After a couple of dates with her, he invites me and a third housemate to meet her over a beer. Note that this is the sixties, a loose and open-ended time when three buddies on a date with a Brazilian woman is totally within the bounds of normal.

She gets in the front seat and finds me and another guy in the back seat. She seems baffled to see us back there. She's blond, short, and wearing high heels, way out of fashion in the sixties. Her halting English is charming, and dwarfs my nonexistent Spanish, which is not a problem because Brazilians speak Portuguese, another of my nonexistent languages. She's in Saint Paul, she tells us, as part of an international work-study program for social workers.

We take a booth in the tavern and order beers. She sits across from me and lights a cigarette. She gestures with the cigarette in front of her face, as if she wants to appear sophisticated. None of us guys, straight shooters in the tobacco department, smokes.

"Oh, so you're a smoker," I say.

"Yes," she says. Then she adds, in candid broken English, that smoking gives her time to think what to say. Hmm, actually not a bad idea.

Johnny Cash is twanging away on the jukebox. "Doesn't Brazil have the Amazon River down there?" I ask innocently over my beer. She smiles, perhaps pleased to find someone curious about her country. But then skepticism crosses her face as she weighs my question for stupidity. Yes, it turns out that Brazil does have the Amazon down there.

"Doesn't Brazil have a military dictatorship down there?" With this, my knowledge of Brazil hits bottom. Another pause as she probes my face for the true depth of my ignorance. Finally, she smiles, apparently pleased to illuminate this dark corner of my mind:

"Yes, the military has ruled Brazil for four years."

Fine, I think, four years ago I was in Africa, and no one told me about it. No way I could have known.

This ends my inquiries about Brazil, a green shape on the map. I'm gratified, however, that my questions, regrettably clueless, actually highlight a virtue—boyish innocence. It's pretty hard to serve up boyish innocence without a shovelful of ignorance to go along with it.

Through the noise, smoke, and music, I detect something un-sixties about her. For one thing, she doesn't slouch. She sits erect, as taught in grade school.

AUTUMN 1968
Leaving Guyland for Daisi

There's something wholesome and optimistic about her, like a fresh sheet of paper.

She laughs easily. She wears a pleasant smile, probably false, as she's doubtless baffled by our brilliant and amusing bar chatter. Now she's quiet, lost in thought. Her face has a vacant look. She's no longer listening to us. She hardly touches her beer.

She has an intriguing name: Daisi, the flower that in Old English is called "Day's Eye," a primitive symbol for the sun, a useless tidbit picked up in English literature. The spelling of her name, ending with an *i*, seems distinctive. Her last name, Gavioli, rhymes with "ravioli," easy to remember. Altogether, she radiates a bright, morning-in-the-meadow air, dazzling in the tavern's gloom.

Then it hits me. She's not like us. She's uncontaminated by our national calamities. We're living in a scary year, 1968, a horrible year. Martin Luther King and Robert Kennedy have been assassinated. My cousin, a Marine platoon leader, was killed in Vietnam this year. I bet no one's ever given Daisi the finger, like a blue-collar worker recently gave me when I was chanting anti-war slogans in a peace march in Minneapolis. I was pumped, energized by the marchers surrounding me, full of the rage and disaffection of our generation. I could have punched the guy in the face, except I'm now studying for a master's in English and I'm out of shape, and he looked tough.

This refreshing woman hasn't felt our turbulence, civil rights protests, the Beatles' *Magical Mystery Tour*, marijuana, riots at the Democratic National Convention in Chicago, Nixon's pathetic victory for the "silent majority," bearded hippies with braless girlfriends . . . no, none of this. She's unpolluted.

Me, I'm soaked in the sixties. I harbor a careless contempt for government of all kinds. Mass production of hamburgers and billions of pounds of soulless, evil plastic depress me.

What moves me are the Beatles, and Bob Dylan's raspy-voiced prophecies —"The times they are a-changin'." I feel a revolution coming. It will sweep away materialism, greed, and the pathetic bourgeois obsession with acquiring THINGS! Youth is rising, transforming the world! We will bend everything toward love and flowers! We're entering a New Age!

> *When the Moon is in the Seventh House*
> *And Jupiter aligns with Mars*
> *Then peace shall guide the planets*
> *And love will steer the stars*
> *This is the dawning of the Age of Aquarius . . .*
> –The Fifth Dimension, from the musical *Hair*

My spine tingles at these words. But for Daisi, they're probably meaningless. It's not her fault she's from another planet. And despite her high heels, her hair pulled straight back, her eye shadow, her nylons—all this unsixites varnish—she's unjaded. And appealing.

My housemate has already dated her a couple of times. Exercising the freedom of Aquarius, I inquire whether it's okay to ask her out. No problem, he says. Then he inquires whether it's kosher for *him* to ask her out, if a future need arises. Hey, no problem, I say. We agree completely, because this is the Age When Love Will Steer the Stars, a time in which hard reality has melted into a free-flowing, liquid form. All problems have easy solutions now—except for the old-fashioned ones of war, greed, and other misconduct by people ignorant that Jupiter has aligned with Mars. For us, all is groovy.

I phone Daisi. She's foreign, so I speak slowly. I remind her who I am—one of the three guys in the bar two weeks ago. Silence on her end.

"I'm the one with wire-rim glasses. Like John Lennon." More silence on her end. How could she not know John Lennon? Maybe she doesn't understand me. Telephones are tough for foreigners. I quit the dillydally and go for pay dirt:

"Do you want to go out on a date?"

A really long silence this time. I bet she's wondering which of us is calling.

Okay, she doesn't remember me. She doesn't know me. She doesn't know my housemate is a great friend. She doesn't know he gave permission to ask her out, that it's my turn. Maybe she thinks women here get passed around like nickels and dimes. Jeez, I hope she doesn't think this.

There's a long, long silence. Have we been disconnected? Then I hear a single word: "Okay."

When I pick her up she's made up in South American style: high heels, nylons, flawless lipstick, bronze makeup and hair pulled back like the Girl from Ipanema rising from the sea. Venus in a tight skirt.

Her natural beauty camouflaged under this shellac, she's like a rose dipped in gold paint. Highly produced and ultra-feminine, she's out of step with sixties simplicity. She'd alarm the feminists burning their bras in bonfires.

I decide to show her Saint Paul's prime piece of Americana: Mickey's Diner. This simple little eatery looks like a lone train car from the Great Depression that somehow got lost and ended up downtown. It's got all the classic diner trappings:

AUTUMN 1968
Leaving Guyland for Daisi

a stainless steel counter, a dozen red-cushion stools, and two booths armed with jukeboxes.

Actually, Mickey's is a greasy spoon. The regulars are mostly bums and drunkards, indispensable to Mickey's charm. This is the real deal here, perfect for bourgeois slumming. It's best to arrive with rock-bottom expectations.

I hold the door open and she enters, a South American goddess, radiating an exotic tropical aura that turns the heads of derelicts slumped over coffee cups. Perfect!

We take a booth. I order for the two of us the absolute pinnacle of our national cuisine— burgers, fries, cokes, and malts—the best nourishment money can buy at Mickey's. She surveys the ambiance with a touch of unease on her face. She works on her burger in silence.

Maybe I shouldn't have chosen Mickey's.

We exchange furtive glances. Long stretches of no talking are interrupted by embarrassing attempts to communicate. We're reduced to hand signals, like the deaf, with exaggerated facial expressions and reassuring smiles. The gulf between us is huge. I ask whether she'd like to smoke some grass with me and my friends. She's surprised. Turns out she comes from a strict home and has barely had alcohol. She's noncommittal on the grass, still untouched by the spirit of the sixties. Maybe she thinks I'm straining to impress her. Which I am.

I wonder who she is. Do all Brazilian women dress like this? I seem to recall they wear pineapples and bananas in their hair. I wonder what her family is like.

Out of the jukebox drift the Beatles: *"Love Is All You Need . . . Love Is All You Need . . . "*

JUNE 1969

Marriage

I continue living with the guys in the mansion, while Daisi lives about a mile away in a tiny bungalow at the Home of the Good Shepherd, where she helps counsel troubled teenage girls. We continue seeing each other, parties, dinners, listening to Joan Baez in her bungalow. As time passes, she seems to like me and my friends more and more.

This is a golden time. I think about her constantly. I can't wait to see her. She's happy to see me. We click together, despite the cultural barriers, which seem to be falling week after week.

After four happy months, we hit turbulence. It occurs at a family Christmas party at my cousin's house. Knowing no one, lost in family chitchat,

Daisi clings to me. A strangely wicked need to get away from her comes over me. I disappear down the basement to smoke a cigar with the men. I never smoke cigars. Minutes later, through the smoke, Daisi appears, looking lost and forlorn. Annoyed, I go back upstairs with her to my family's embarrassed smiles, small talk and futile attempts to communicate. I have a vague sense of wrongdoing.

Back at her bungalow, I park the car and turn off the motor. She announces that she needs some time away from me. Perfect. I need some distance from her, too.

A week goes by. I get lonely. I ask her to dinner. She accepts. We're both relieved and delighted to be together again, talking, laughing, exuberant—far from our struggles at Mickey's months ago.

A month later, on our way to meet friends, driving through a light snowfall, a fancy, a strange giddiness, arrives out of nowhere. Without thinking, I blurt out that maybe we should get married.

Stunned, Daisi goes quiet. Snowflakes are striking, then melting, on the windshield. Whoa, did I just say this? What an idiot! I haven't even thought this through.

I change the subject, pretending I never said it.

A week later we quarrel again, so angry that we stop seeing each other. Ten days pass. Missing her terribly, I call and ask if she'll see me. Maintaining a certain dignity and independence, she accepts this time, too. I'm pretty sure now that I'm falling love with her, and possibly—but I'm not sure—she's in love with me.

In March we plan a nine-day Colorado ski trip for early April. She's never been on skis before. It'll be great. One week before we're to leave, we fall into our worst quarrel ever. I have no idea why this is happening. It's becoming clear that we each have a complete and unique personality that has survived a lifetime without the other. A disturbing thought occurs to me: maybe we don't need each other.

After four days of angry silence, I call and ask whether we should call off the trip. Oddly, we decide to go ahead with it on one condition: we will absolutely never mention the quarrel on the trip!

It works. We drive to Colorado the best of friends, and now best of lovers, always keeping a firm embargo on the quarrel. We have a great time. We ski, we see friends, we drink wine before a fire, we sleep together, and then, as we return to Saint Paul, now about twenty miles from home, a huge silence drops down between us like a wall. The quarrel is back. Excruciating minutes pass, each a small eternity, until we finally reach her doorstep. She steps out of the car and, without looking back, walks to her front door, opens it and disappears.

Two agitated weeks pass. Then, one evening in May, I stand in my parents'

JUNE 1969
Marriage

backyard looking up at the stars. Time is running out. Daisi is set to return to Brazil in fifteen days. For the hundredth time, I weigh the pros and cons of asking her to marry me. I've even penciled out a ledger with two sides, "yes" and "no," both locked in maddening gridlock. On the "no" side are hard realities that would need attention. Where would we live? If Brazil, could I survive there? What would I do? Would her family accept me? Above all, do I really know her? Finally, would she marry me?

And what about the "lightning-bolt" theory of love, espoused by one of my housemates? In this electro-romantic theory, love is supposed to come crashing into the soul with all the force of a thunderstorm. The guy who doesn't feel this isn't really in love.

Gazing into the starry heavens, I see in my mind's eye her small body walking out onto the tarmac toward the plane that will carry her away from me forever. This image plays over and over in my head. An intolerable sadness comes over me.

Then, a strange emptiness. The rock bottom of a long, tedious argument in my head has dropped open. I look around for all the familiar reasons not to marry her. They are gone. All that's left are scores of "yeses" running around like excited children released from school.

We are married on June 7, 1969, in the Unitarian Church in St. Paul.

For the first time in two weeks, I call and ask to see her.

"Why?"

"I want to ask you something."

"Like what?"

I can tell from her flat tone of voice that her patience is at an end. She wants absolute clarity in our relationship, otherwise she's ready to kill it and move on. This is one of her strengths, a scary decisiveness.

"It's important," I say.

After a long silence in which I can hear her wheels turning, she agrees to see me.

Two days later I knock at her door. It opens a few inches, and stops, revealing only half her face. For several long seconds, one solitary eye coldly studies my face for clues of what's coming.

"May I come in?"

Without a word, she lets me in. In silence, I hand her a tiny box. Sitting cross-legged on the dining room table, she quietly opens it.

Then she opens her arms and wraps me in a long embrace. She slips off a ring from her aunt Cecilia and replaces it with her engagement ring. Another embrace and a long, life-changing kiss.

Moments later, we look for Aunt Cecilia's ring. It's gone. Vanished into thin air. Something gained, something lost.

As we're about to leave for a celebratory spaghetti dinner, Daisi remembers something. She dashes off a note and tapes it to the front door.

Rodrigo, I'm not here. Sorry. I'm engaged to marry. —Daisi

Some guy named Rodrigo was her date tonight. No way did she intend to be alone tonight. I wonder what poor Rodrigo will feel reading this note. Moments later, guess what. I don't care.

HE WEEPS LIKE A CHILD

Two days later, we send a telegram to Daisi's parents in Porto Alegre. Keeping it under ten words to save money, she crafts a concise marriage announcement. It's dense, free of punctuation that would increase the cost, and, as it turns out, almost unintelligible.

CASO JIM JUNHO SEGUIRMOS DE CARRO BRASIL FELIZ DAISI

The literal translation is: THE JIM CASE JUNE WE FOLLOW BY CAR BRAZIL HAPPY DAISI

What it means is this: "Following my marriage to Jim in June, we'll be coming to Brazil by car. Happily yours, Daisi."

JUNE 1969
Marriage

One week later, in my parents' bedroom, she calls her father long distance. Within one minute she's in tears, waving me out of the room. This is between her and her father. I'm not needed. Okay fine, but why the tears? Marriage announcements are supposed to be joyous. Something must be wrong.

After some long minutes, she emerges from the bedroom.

"My father," she says heavily, as if speaking from thousands of miles away, "gives his permission. He wept like a child."

This drops me down a depth. I know almost nothing about this guy. Daisi says he's tough, strict, from a poor family. Okay, but tough guys don't cry. That's odd. Oh well, whatever. He's *her* father, not mine. It's none of my business.

And yet, I begin to wonder who he is. And who the others are—her mother, her sister, her two brothers. I know nothing about them, either.

Nine months ago, when she left Brazil for the United States, her father gave her this instruction: *Não case com um gringo* (Don't marry a North American).

Contrary to his prudent and sensible advice, we get married in a Unitarian church in Saint Paul, on June 7, 1969. No one from her family can attend, which is painful for Daisi. Too short notice, too many miles, too little money.

Our marriage ceremony is wrong, of course. Normally, her father and mother would be here. And, according to custom, I'd have faced him and asked his permission to take his daughter from him in marriage. But he's too far away. I can't speak his language. He probably can't speak mine. He's losing his daughter to some foreigner and can't do a thing about it.

What sort of welcome in his home awaits me, I wonder. I hope he's a good guy.

JULY 1970

Journey to Brazil

Thirteen months later, my graduate school finally completed, and buoyed by the free spirit of the age, we leave on a hitchhiking voyage to Brazil. We'll be checking out the Americas along the way: Mexico, Central America, Colombia, Ecuador, Peru, and Bolivia. We expect to live in Brazil for at least two years, after which time Daisi can legally reenter the country. Then we'll decide: live there or return here.

We're pumped. The trip promises new worlds. New languages. New cultures. New foods. New insights on our new marriage. Everything will be new and improved.

For our parents, this is a monumentally brainless idea. Mine are against it. Daisi doesn't even dare tell her parents. The problem is simple. They're all old.

This is the dawn of a New Age, a Global Youth Culture. The old are more clueless and out of touch than at any time in world history. Case closed.

Friends drive us to Winona, Minnesota, where they share our last meal as members of the middle class. They bid us farewell and leave us, fortified with a thousand dollars in travelers checks, standing at the edge of a highway leading to the southern hemisphere, wearing the uniform of the age —T-shirts, jeans, sandals, and backpacks. We look poor. Perfect.

With Daisi in front of me as bait, we stick out our thumbs. The very first vehicle stops! It's a Volkswagen van, headed to Iowa. We couldn't have dreamed this any better.

Never have we been so free. Nothing ties us down. We have no keys, no car, no house, no picket fence, no dog, no children, no jobs. Our subscription to the middle class is discontinued. All we own is on our backs.

I delight in our newfound poverty, our escape from tedious middle-class predictability. I'm tired of pea-brained consumerism, rigid punctuality, and the absurd notion that bigger is better. Forget that. Small is beautiful. Simple is divine. The poor have authenticity. They're noble. They deserve to be imitated.

Actually, I don't know any poor people. But Daisi does. In Brazil, some of her neighbors were poor. However, in her opinion, poverty isn't that noble. She

Daisi and Jim embark on a three-month hitchhiking journey to Brazil in 1970. From left: Daisi, Jim's father Dwight, Jim's mother Evelyn, Jim's brother Jeff, and Jim.

JULY 1970
Journey to Brazil

sees it as a burden, an injustice. It lacks romance. There may be some truth in these charming notions, but I find them sadly misguided. We have a little spat over this, which surprises and disappoints me.

All goes well until we reach the border at Laredo. A burly Mexican customs official denies me entry into his nation. My hair is too long. Mexico doesn't allow hippies, he says. Fortunately, a barber is located only a few feet away. Within five minutes my locks are shorn, at a shocking cost, which apparently is the price of admission into his country.

Next morning at breakfast I order what an elderly Mexican gentleman—at a table a few feet away, still wearing his hat and looking authentic—is eating. It's menudo, a crystal-clear oil containing pieces of gray, rubbery cow intestine. I can't swallow it. I request a bowl of Corn Flakes.

We forge ahead, sleeping in gloomy Catholic churches, humble homes, simple schools, infirmaries, on trucks, and in sleeping bags beneath the stars. I'm surprised at how the world at night is transformed into a vast bed, no reservation required. I have a friend in Saint Paul who has traveled like this for years. His motto is simple: never pay to sleep. This makes stunning good sense.

One evening, a Mexican priest says we can bed down—not in the church—but behind it, in a windowless shed, on top of a pile of bricks and rubble, in pitch darkness, in intense heat, together with mosquitos, spiders of unknown size and toxicity, and a family of bats squeaking and swirling about our heads. This is when Daisi begins to doubt my friend's good sense.

"Daisi, just think of how much character we're building," I say, half in jest. She chooses not to dignify this with a reply.

One afternoon in a spacious square in Mexico City, pigeons fluttering about, an old woman, curved and bent down by the weight of years, dressed in black, offers us a few coins. I am stunned by her generosity. Our disguise as impoverished travelers—sandals, dirty sunburned feet—*is working*! Nor is she the only one. Others offer us fruit. Or show us their city. Or take us in for a night then give us breakfast. We're getting charity from some of the poorest people I've ever met. I certainly wouldn't expect this from the middle class in the US. My admiration for poverty grows.

Freedom is thrilling. One evening, an eighteen-wheel trailer truck stops for us. We climb inside its long covered trailer, standing on seven tons of boxed-up margarine. Night falls. Engulfed by darkness and the swaying motion of the truck, we soon find ourselves locked in a most intimate embrace. No one has done this before on margarine! *We're pioneers!*

Our parents are wrong. This trip is the most brilliant thing we've ever done.

Next morning, urgently needing a toilet, we bang on the cabin window, but the driver can't hear us. The truck keeps barreling down the highway. We can't wait any longer. We grip each other's shoulders for balance on the lurching crates of margarine, and relieve ourselves in plastic sandwich bags. More pioneering!

As the days go on, there's always a need for toilets. Some are clean. Others are located at the wrong end of the fragrance spectrum. My belief, which I once again dare voice to Daisi, eloquently, I think, is that confronting stale urine, and filth generally, is the price one pays to build strong character.

I must have picked the wrong moment to say this.

In my love of liberty and the pursuit of poverty, I rarely think of my parents. In fact, I've neglected to notice how this journey, like a rope, is actually tethered to *my* parents at one end and *hers* at the other. They are the ones upon whom we depend to hold the rope up. The key thing though, which I do notice, is that we're like dogs that have slipped their leash—crazy free. We're like the great South American condor, soaring high, experiencing new worlds, while our parents, sadly, like old trees, are rooted deep in the ground. Whew, glad I'm not like them.

One day a bronzed-skinned Mexican truck driver named Carlos, showing a sinister scar zigzagging down one side of his face and neck, stops for us. No, I should say he stops for Daisi, because without her, few would stop for me alone.

As we bounce along on his stiff cabin seat, the two of them chatter away in Spanish I don't understand. Now they're laughing together. I begin to feel jealous. I begin to wonder whether this is the man my friends warned me about, the one who would rape Daisi, steal our money, and kill us both.

Later, she tells me he's unmarried, but has many children living along his truck route. He's also paying his sister's way through college, which he never had the chance to attend.

"Yeah, okay fine, but what were you two laughing about?"

"He told me he was worried that we might rob him! Ha, ha."

Okay, pretty funny, but not that funny. Actually, I'm annoyed. Maybe I should have learned Spanish.

※ One hot and humid morning in Guatemala, standing next to a steamy grove of banana trees screaming with mosquitos, we wait for a ride. Four hours drift by. By now it's already noon, and hotter than ever. An olive-drab Ford pickup truck carrying guerrilla-hunting soldiers stops and offers us a lift. We're uneasy, but okay, let's try it.

Daisi sits in the cabin between two soldiers. I'm relegated to the back of the pickup, joining fifteen passive-looking adolescents with copper-colored Indian faces. Each carries a massive rifle with bayonet, and, slung over the shoulder, a belt of bullets the size of toothbrushes. They eye me suspiciously. As the floorboard pounds my ass numb, and with no small talk in Spanish to jolly things up, I begin to imagine the evil they could do us.

Abruptly, for no apparent reason, in a remote area, the pickup comes to a stop. I am told to get out. *This is it!* They're going to enjoy my wife in the jungle and then butcher me.

Then I'm ordered to sit up front in the cabin, next to Daisi.

"What's happening?" I ask her.

"I told them we're married."

It dawns on me how incredibly lucky I am to be married to Daisi, especially in Guatemala. But not just in Guatemala.

Our relationship has undergone a surprising flip-flop. Now *she* does all the talking to people we meet. She makes all the big decisions. She has a good feel for Latin America, and I don't. She's in charge, and I'm taking orders. For the first time in our relationship, I depend on her for everything. She's carrying me on her back. I'm no longer the affable, easy-going guy I was in Minnesota. I have lost myself, as if I've had a lobotomy.

※ We've had some setbacks. In Mexico, while sleeping in a room with five men, seventy dollars in travelers checks quietly disappeared. Strolling in a crowded market in the Guatemalan mountaintop village of Chichicastenango my wallet was lifted from my jeans. In a boarding house in Colombia, one of our towels, drying on a line, went missing.

To sum up, I give humanity an A-minus for Goodness. My idealism remains intact.

We encounter romantic types, whose view of the world is sharp and narrow. One, whom we meet in Mexico City, is a political exile from northern Brazil, a professor with dark, burning eyes who advocates radical, violent action against the repressive Brazilian military dictatorship. I find this alarming.

Another, a French hippie possessing a floppy sack of belongings and dusty feet with long toenails sticking out of his sandals, wears a giant straw hat whose brim slopes down from its pointed crown like Johnny Appleseed. "Indians," he tells us, gave him "magic mushrooms" to eat, which put him in "complete harmony" with the trees, the village, the mountains, the earth, the Indians themselves, and his girlfriend.

Another time, on a cold day in Colombia, riding in the back of a vegetable truck, we meet two adolescent boys. Shivering in their thin shirts, they tell us they're going to Ecuador and Peru to make their fortunes as bullfighters. To prove their valor, one of them pulls out of a sack a red cape and a primitive wooden sword, as if made by a child, worthy perhaps of Don Quixote. Abruptly, the other boy breaks into a high-pitched, mournful, haunting song. This triggers others in the back of the truck to contribute sober songs from their austere lives. I chip in with "Oh, Susanna."

Standing with our thumbs out beside the road one evening, watching a massive orange Peruvian sun die into the horizon, a young Peruvian doctor and his pretty wife stop for us. We stuff ourselves into the back of their small car, knees against our chins. Soon we're happily rocketing along the Pan American highway, now a gravel road, when suddenly from the opposite direction, a trailer truck abruptly veers across our path toward a fuel station. The doctor hits the brakes. We skid sideways over the gravel toward the truck, tipping up on two side wheels, almost rolling over, narrowly missing a collision. White with anger, the doctor explodes in profanity. We escape bloodshed, or worse.

My parents are right. This trip is idiocy.

A couple of weeks later, we reach La Paz, Bolivia. We're both exhausted, tired of pretend poverty, and impatient to see Daisi's family. With 109 hitchhiking and bus rides behind us, we buy two plane tickets—ending our dream of a road trip all the way to Brazil.

Again, when one thing ends, another begins.

Pai, age 84, paying bills at his desk.

Clearly, Pai is blessed with two outstanding characteristics. One is his passion for provocation, inherited from his Italian ancestors and gaucho warriors of yesteryear. The other is his relentless hammering, a gift from his German ancestors, who may have been blacksmiths.

For gauchos, meat is sacred. It is to be worshipped and consumed communally. Gauchos believe vegetarians are infidels.

"*Jim, podes comer essa carne*" (you can eat this beef).

"No, I can't. I'm a vegetarian."

"Yes you can. . . . this cow ate only grass."

PAI GAVIOLI
Thirty-six Years of War and Finally Peace with My Impossible Brazilian Father-in-Law

OCTOBER 2, 1970
Three Years in Brazil

On my second day in Brazil I'm hungry. I've lost fifteen pounds getting here. This is the day that the Gavioli's housekeeper, Dona Eva, a strong and heavyset black woman who wears an apron and kerchief, resembling Aunt Jemima the pancake queen, serves up a heaping platter of *panquecas* for lunch. These are crepes rolled around ground beef, garlic, onion and parsley. I wolf down five of them, painfully stretching my shrunken stomach. The next day, she makes potato-dumpling gnocchi, fettucini, roast beef with chunks of potato soaked in an orange-colored oily meat sauce, and the Brazilian staple—a puddle of black beans over rice. I'm becoming known as a big eater, which in this family is a virtue.

Late that afternoon, Senhor Gavioli drives us a couple of miles to a brand-new apartment building located on the side of a steep hill. He proudly escorts us into a small, second-floor, two-bedroom unit, which he recently bought for five thousand dollars. Still smelling of fresh cement, the apartment is his amazing gift to us, with a refrigerator and stove tossed in. From its small balcony, we can see downtown a couple of miles away, the core of Porto Alegre's nine hundred thousand people. Its cluster of tall white buildings looks like a miniature Manhattan. Behind it, a large red sun is sinking into the wide Guaíba River, as if marking the end of a chapter in our lives.

Humbled by his generosity, I ask Daisi to remind her father we're jobless, and for now, can't pay him rent. He doesn't seem to care.

Next day he drives me to an open-air market. *"Gosta de laranja?"* I think he wants to know whether I like oranges.

"Sim," I say.

That's nice. He's going to buy me an orange. He hoists up a full bushel basket and dumps them all into his trunk. "Wow, enough, enough," I say in English, thanking him. He immediately pours in another bushel basket. Embarrassed by this excess, I exclaim, "No, no, no. *Por favor*, no more oranges." Ignoring me, he dumps in a third basket, filling the trunk with hundreds of oranges.

He gets a kick out of teasing me, which feels like bullying. Without English, my lifeline to who I am, I'm lost in a sea of Portuguese and can't fight back. My degree in English literature is as useful as a paper oar.

A silent chasm opens between us as we drive home. His teasing has broken into my sensitive self like a rock tossed through a stained-glass window. Who is this guy? Probably a bourgeois bully at the peak of his earning power, and delighted to show it in oranges. No skinny Minnesotan, who married his daughter before proper inspection, will stop him. I fall into a sulk.

Driving straight ahead, not looking at me, he knows where he's going. He's in charge, fortified by an identity apparently carved in stone. Meanwhile, I'm young and directionless, with an identity that feels like a limp leaf of lettuce. And I'm trapped in his car.

I look out the window. The streets are narrow and the traffic treacherous. I feel we're moving too fast, speeding past shops with signs in small print, designed more for pedestrians than moving cars. Crowds fill the narrow sidewalks. A truck directly in front of us roars, bathing us in black exhaust.

A tight knot of vehicles is nearly touching us on all sides. Moments later, Senhor Gavioli aggressively swerves around a slow, horse-drawn cart stacked with cardboard for recycling. Farther ahead, a shirtless man slowly pushes another cart, his neck veins bulging, his feet bare on the hot asphalt. Directly ahead, a bus strikes an overhanging tree branch, which swings violently back and forth from the impact.

Soon the asphalt changes to cobblestone, which thunders beneath our tires. We stop for a light. I notice a wall covered with flowers—hibiscus, jasmine, bird of paradise—like organic souls far from their Amazonian jungle home, serenely oblivious to this traffic jungle, and my hurt feelings.

When she sees the trunkful of oranges, Daisi's mother throws up her arms in dismay. *"Sempre exagerando!"* (Always overdoing it!), she cries. Now she and Dona Eva must squeeze them by hand to make gallons of orange juice before the fruit rots moldy green in the heat.

Later, I tell Daisi that I resent his bullying me with oranges. "I can't talk to him. I don't know how to deal with him," I say.

"Join the club," she replies.

"I think he's a control freak."

"I told you," in a tone indicating she doesn't want to talk about this anymore.

For the next four months we'll be living with Daisi's parents until our apartment is ready. As a new member of the family, I now occupy a place at their table, where I've gained eight pounds in two weeks. I'm getting addicted to the French bread—crusty outside and soft inside—with butter and jam, plus strong coffee mixed with hot milk. Often the whole family gathers here for the noon meal, a generous spread served quietly and efficiently by Dona Eva. Daisi's father loves these occasions. He's loud, jokey, and uproarious. I laugh along with everyone else, understanding nothing. Yesterday at the table, in a political argument laced with flashes of lightning and thunder, he expressed his desire—as a good capitalist—to liquidate Cuba. This is strange, I thought, because Daisi says he's a strong supporter of the collective action of unions and workers' rights. Sarah remained quiet, even though I suspect she has an opinion about Fidel. She smiles rarely, but when she does, it's disarmingly beautiful and reassuring.

All four Gavioli children have English or European names, chosen from books Sarah was reading at the time. Sidnei, thirty-one, is the eldest, four years older than Daisi. He's the responsible first child. He has dark eyebrows, a strong, handsome face, and speaks to me in a clear, basic English easy to understand. A financial auditor, he has the cool manner of an executive, ranking second in financial decision-making behind his father. His wife, Maria-Eunice, has a languid and sympathetic demeanor. She tries earnestly to communicate with me. They have a two-year-old son named Beto.

Davison, twenty-three, attends night school in accounting. He has black hair, sharp features, and speaks fast, slangy Portuguese that flies way over my head. Four years younger than Daisi, he's the maverick, the rebel, a joker like his father. He and his father have a history of conflict, Daisi says. I notice they seem to keep each other at arm's length.

Lori, nineteen, eight years younger than Daisi, is beautiful and excitable. She has a perfectly formed mouth, sparkling eyes, and an infectious laugh. As the baby of the family, Lori got lots of toys from her father, Daisi says. Lori speaks to me in slow, extra-loud Portuguese, as if addressing an infant.

Conversation at the table is my Gavioli classroom, even though understanding them is like standing in a river trying to grab fish barehanded. If I happen to catch a glimmer of understanding, I try to reply. I mentally line up four or five words in a row, like a toy train—maybe a noun I've heard, plus an adjective I've never tried before, plus a couple of other words—all pushed forward by a little verb engine that probably isn't firing in the right tense.

When they're all lined up in my head, I open my mouth and force my clumsy tongue to push my tiny train out onto the tracks. There it goes, carrying my little toy thought out into the world. And then . . .

The family falls silent. They look at me in deep puzzlement. Evidently, while I was assembling my little train, the conversation had moved on to other tracks. Finally someone figures out that I'm several tracks behind. Ha, ha, laughter fills the room. Then they go back to their incomprehensible chatter, leaving me on a side track, going nowhere.

Jim, you've become an idiot. You don't understand jokes or stories, much less tell them. You don't understand radio, TV, and newspapers. You don't even know how to ask a question. You are impotent before this giant Portuguese-language sea monster, which they have tamed, and which they manipulate, with such ease. My clumsy tongue, lagging miles behind the lightning of thought, leaves me confused, embarrassed, and vexed.

Like a chimp behind bars, I'm an amusing oddity. I'm here, and Daisi's family is way, way, way over there. Between us stands an iron language barrier that imprisons me but allows them to roam free. I'm in a verbal cage, through whose bars curious Brazilians peer, and sometimes yell, hoping for contact by turning up the volume.

I find myself retreating to the back of my cage. Maybe this is what Daisi did in Minnesota. While close to me there, she's farther away from me here, largely uncoupled from me, drawn into the orbit of her family.

I ask her simple questions. What did your mother say? Where are we going? Who are these visitors? Sometimes she tires of me, like a mother whose child has too many questions. Other times, she takes pity on me.

"Is my family too much for you?" she asks one day.

"Nah, I can handle 'em," I say, not really sure I can.

MEAT

Of all the food consumed at the Gavioli table, not a small amount of it ends up on my father-in-law's fork. He is the proud owner of a sizable belly. His prominent paunch, positioned on his prow like a grille on a Cadillac, marks him as a well-fed man of means. It proclaims freedom from want. It has middle class written all over it.

On our first Sunday in his home, he prepares a colossal welcome-home feast for us, which, by the way, will help nourish his major-league tummy. It's a celebration made of barbecued beef, chicken, pork, and sausage called *churrasco*. It's a carnivore heaven that South American gauchos have made famous.

Churrasco is a primitive ritual. It's all spears and knives, men huddling together before a fire, roasting meat for their bellies and the bellies of their womenfolk and offspring. It also has the feel of a large, communal embrace.

Chunks of meat, rubbed with rock salt to contain the juices, are thrust through with slender swords a yard long. The meat sizzles on a wood fire, and

Rugged Brazilian gauchos of yesteryear drink strong tea and roast meat over a fire. This drawing, by José Lutzenberger (1882-1951), is taken from his collection of illustrations, *O Caixeiro-Viajante No Rio Grande Do Sul.*

fat drips on the orange-hot embers, releasing a fragrant smoke that waters the mouth, as it did the mouths of our ancestors in Paleolithic times. Gavioli men stare into the embers, absorbing the heat and admiring the meat, exchanging mock insults on how to cook it.

The Gaviolis are urban gauchos. The classic gaucho, however, now found mostly in myth, lives on the vast treeless plains of the South American pampas. This heroic figure slaughters a cow for a great churrasco, and then probably shoots pistols at wild cougars drawn from the forest by the smell of blood. This is not your typical Minnesota corn farmer. Golden Age gauchos of yesteryear stand around an open-pit fire, meat sizzling on spits. They slice off succulent samples and gnaw them off the points of their blades. They pass around, like a peace pipe, a hollowed-out gourd shaped like a woman's breast, containing a hot and bitter infusion of erva mate, a green tea called *chimarrão,* sipped from an ornate silver straw. This communal macho ceremony, rife with teasing, arguing, and laughter, is a far cry from roasting marshmallows.

Clad only in shorts and flip-flops, Daisi's father prepares his churrasco under a hot noonday sun on his brick barbecue pit behind the house. His sun-bronzed tummy shining with sweat and grease drippings, he works several sizzling spits.

Like all true gauchos, he owns a churrasco knife, which is a glorified hunting knife. The handle is carved from the horn of a bull. Its wide blade, engraved with an image of a gaucho squatting next to a fire on the pampas, is sharp enough to slice a hair lengthwise.

OCTOBER 2, 1970
Three Years in Brazil

He knocks a spit forcibly against the brick oven, dislodging rock salt, which falls into the coals. The feast is ready. Rushing into the house, meat-loaded spear in hand, shouting above the family din and chatter, he proclaims: *"Vamos tirar a barriga da miséria!"* (Let's put the stomach out of its misery!)

What misery? My stomach isn't in any particular misery. Evidently, his is. Which, based on its magnitude, seems odd. Whatever. His proclamation sparks a rush to the heavy dark table in the small dining room. Let the Meat-O-Rama begin.

Advancing directly to me first, as if I'm the honored guest, he touches the point of his spear on the center of my plate, and, with his other hand, using the flat side of his knife, he zips a crisp piece of broiled chicken down the shaft of his saber. Moments later, after quickly serving the others, he's back. Down the shaft he slides me a dark red sausage. Serving everyone seemingly at once, he rushes back and forth between the pit and the table, as if he fears the world will end before he can enjoy this moment. By now my stomach is bursting. He rushes up behind me, swings his sword over my shoulder, and slices off a juicy slab of beef.

"Thank you, thank you, but please, Senhor, no more. I'm full."

He's gone without answering. Moments later he's back. Now it's a white slice of pork that he's sliding down the shaft of his weapon. Minutes later he's back again. The meat just keeps coming. He's pushing me, prodding me, teasing me. How silly to think my pathetic protestations can stop this river of food.

Everyone served, he finally sits himself down to eat, driven by the hunger of a man unequaled in the meat department. This, I've discovered, demonstrates one of his many Rules for Living: FEAR HUNGER AS YOU WOULD THE LORD. When he sets a portion for himself, usually it is not too small. He eats with gusto, like he drives a car, too fast. Food flies into him with such velocity that the hairs of his bare chest become sprinkled with a dusting of *farofa,* a white manioc powder designed to absorb meat juices on the plate, not usually on the chest.

There are people in the world for whom the sun, moon, and stars revolve around their stomachs. He is such a person. For him, food is the ground of existence, the source of all meaning. The table must groan under the weight of its eatables, which, by the way, obeys another of his Rules for Living: PUT MORE FOOD ON THE TABLE THAN CAN POSSIBLY BE EATEN. For Senhor Gavioli, churrasco and his family gathering together to consume it are one, as inseparable as a wave is to water. The two—churrasco and family—are as close as the stomach is to the heart.

Among gauchos, consuming large amounts of beef is a point of pride. Some of them—but most definitely not my father-in-law—almost lose themselves in meat. They reward their triumphant bellies, big barrels of hardened lard, by gnawing on a pork rib, for example, ripping off flesh and fat with their teeth, licking their chops with a slippery sound, greasing their faces to a shine, their hands and fingers glistening with fat—easily consuming one kilo (more than two pounds) of beef per meal. Then washing it all down with beer. These are not slender souls who nibble on carrots. These are voracious Brazilian carnivores whose bellies, like champions, are made, not born.

I behold the barbaric appetites of these lords of the table with a mix of awe and fear. They become, at these moments, red-toothed cougars.

But this is not my father-in-law. He's a magnificent eater, but not a savage.

The meal consumed, he smiles broadly and rubs his paunch in triumph, taking sensual pleasure in his own corporality. Like a wounded animal, his belly has been mercifully put out of its misery.

None of this applies, however, to his wife, Sarah.

Sarah at 19

OCTOBER 2, 1970
Three Years in Brazil

SARAH

Sarah, now age sixty, has a strong voice that easily reached the back of her classroom, where she taught for thirty-seven years. Her gentle almond-shaped eyes observe me with quiet directness, and in slow, clear English she says, "If you want something, ask me."

Her eyes do not seek to penetrate my soul, as those of her husband do. Her eyes—honest, sincere, and disarming—consider me calmly, accepting me for who I am.

Her gray hair lies flat, no frills or flounce, with just enough length to cover her ears and the back of her neck. She uses no lipstick and wears an unpretentious housedress that calls no attention to itself. She seems to have no desire to impress anyone. Her lack of nonsense and ostentation gives her a quiet power. Her name, Sarah, aptly means "lady" or "princess" in Hebrew.

She has a comfortably heavy figure, moving slowly with a gait that rocks to the left, because her ankles are turned inward from childhood polio. Her weakened legs and ankles have taught her to be efficient, to plan ahead. She navigates the house slowly, lurchingly, with remarkable economy of movement.

Sarah is not cheerful. She has a streak of melancholy, of longing, a subterranean sadness that draws the family to her. Not at all touchy-feely, she's a fact-based person, informative, objective, rational. She radiates an aura of experience. I trust her completely.

While her extroverted husband sparkles gregariously at the dinner table, Sarah is mostly quiet, in the background. When she does say something, there's not a shred of teasing, irony, or sarcasm in it. Come to think of it, Daisi's like this, too.

One day, when she was seven years old and crippled by polio, Sarah attempted to crawl across some railroad tracks on all fours. Suddenly, around a bend came the train. Unable to cross in time, she managed to crouch down into a depression between the ties just before the locomotive screamed and thundered directly over the top of her. The train passed. Its deafening roar faded, leaving an eerie silence in its wake. For a long time, she lay between the tracks, frozen, unable to move.

That was one of her first early lessons in survival. At age eight, more tragedy struck. She lost her father in the prime of his life to the 1918–1919 Spanish Flu pandemic that killed up to fifty million people worldwide. If this weren't enough, two years later, typhoid fever, a bacteria from contaminated food or water, took her mother.

Orphaned at age ten, physically handicapped and lonely, Sarah was taken in by American Baptist missionaries. Her two brothers and two sisters were scattered, taken in by other families. Attending a Baptist school, she developed into a somber and stoic young teacher.

Most middle-class Brazilian women at that time stayed home, bickering with their housekeepers. In contrast, Sarah worked. She taught high school Portuguese, mathematics, and English, while raising four children.

She and her husband are the backbone of the Gavioli family. He's the one impossible to live with and impossible to live without—a tower of energy and impulse. She's steady and sensible, the earth upon which this tower rests. He's the optimist, she's the pessimist. There have been times when she's told him to stock up on food against revolution, an imminent revolt of the Brazilian masses, which never came. Separately, as youths, they each struggled to survive without family. Married, they created one of their own, coming to know one another's weaknesses and strengths. I admire their strength and wish I had it, but without undergoing the pain it seems to require.

Accustomed to work, Sarah conducts herself with directness and purpose. There's nothing idle about her. She manages the home, working in perfect harmony with Dona Eva.

Sarah's serene, long-serving African-Brazilian housekeeper, Dona Eva, is part of the soul of the Gavioli household. At first glance, she fits a mammy stereotype, a domestic servant of African descent, generally good-natured, overweight and loud. But she's not this. She's a deep, calm, heavy-set, physically

Sarah holds her worn and tattered Portuguese-English dictionary, held together by a string.

OCTOBER 2, 1970
Three Years in Brazil

strong woman of few words, who, as she works, wears a sphinx-like Mona Lisa smile. On one side of her face and neck is a long, wide scar, a burn from a childhood accident in the kitchen. It shines where her skin, the color of dark chocolate, has stretched to heal.

For some in Brazil's middle class, domestic help is a perquisite of higher status, and one of its main symbols. By no stretch of the imagination is this true for the Gaviolis and Dona Eva. For Sarah, who raised four children while teaching full time, all the while struggling with ankles that bend inward, Dona Eva is an absolute necessity.

While most Gaviolis are driven by spontaneous combustion, Dona Eva moves gracefully through the household with the quiet power of an ocean liner. She arrives early morning, as if delivered by the sunrise, and works nonstop all day—cooking, washing dishes, sweeping, scrubbing, and cleaning and ironing clothes—then departs quietly at night. She never speaks to me, unless I speak to her first. She treats me with great deference, calling me Senhor, avoiding me as if I were an object difficult to understand. When the two of us manage a small communication, she smiles, revealing beautiful white teeth. One front tooth is missing.

Though she's like a member of the family, she doesn't live with the family. She lives one or more long bus rides away, in a wooden shack in a poor

Franklin Delano Roosevelt is Pai's favorite US President.

settlement on the outskirts of the city, where her salary supports her children as well as others. Recently while working, Dona Eva began bleeding profusely and fainted from an illegal back-alley abortion. The abortionist failed to remove the placenta, saying it would come out on its own. It didn't. Dona Eva hemorrhaged and became infected. Sarah took her to a hospital, where after three days, she recovered.

THE HOUSE

I wondered what I might learn from a stroll through the house. For example, the small, frugal living room at the front of the house contains only a sofa and an armchair. With my back to the front door, on the left side of the living room is Daisi's parents' bedroom, whose door is always open. Straight ahead is an archway, concealed by the curtain that fell on me, covering a passageway that tunnels into the house and its mysteries.

The passageway leads to an area off limits to visitors, where I assume lie all the secrets of the house, the family, and Brazil generally. Because I'm family now, I'm free to wander behind the curtain into the dark, narrow corridor, whose damp walls exhibit abstract splotches of black mildew, silently feeding on exotic Brazilian nutrients.

Immediately behind the curtain, on the right side of the corridor, is the one and only bathroom. Drooping at a tired angle from a keyhole on the inside of the door is a brass key. This key, touched by every hand in the house several times a day, shines like gold. The bathroom itself is a narrow, gloomy chamber, whose high ceiling reaches about twenty feet to the roof, where a louvered glass shutter opens for ventilation. This opening is just big enough to allow a single angelic, cathedral-like sunbeam to descend upon, bless, and illuminate the occupant sitting prayerfully on the toilet.

Farther down the corridor on the left is Lori's bedroom, which until two years ago she shared with Daisi. A bit farther, located at the foot of stairs leading to the attic, is a little nook, the geographical center of the house. This is where a heavy black telephone sits importantly on a tiny table. It's the only phone in the house. There's a waiting list up to a decade long to get a residential phone. However, because Daisi's father works at the phone company, he gets one. Hanging on the wall above the phone is a framed photograph on yellowing newsprint of President Franklin Delano Roosevelt. When one makes a call, one looks directly into Roosevelt's calm face. "He's my favorite American president," Senhor José tells me, because Roosevelt gave benefits to workers. This resonates with Senhor José, a former union leader who helped gain benefits for workers at the telephone company.

Penetrating deeper into the house, the corridor ends at a small, dimly lit dining room, scarcely big enough to contain its heavy, dark wooden table. This room is a focal point, where the family gathers for food, banter, updates, information, gossip, planning, rebukes, and disputes. It's easily the most entertaining room in the house.

This room has two doors. The one straight ahead is the door to Davison's bedroom. The other, on the right, opens to Dona Eva's domain, a small, narrow kitchen. This steamy chamber of clattering pots and pans is illuminated by a single, hard-working light bulb hanging from the ceiling at the end of a long cord. A small, diligent stove is fueled by bottled gas, as is the shower in the bathroom, the only hot water in the house. Water issues from a concrete storage tank on the roof, fed by a pump that groans in pain at odd hours day and night.

Upstairs is the attic, an inferno thanks to the tropical sun that bakes the tile roof. The attic has two rooms. One is a small guest bedroom with a low ceiling. The other is Sarah's study. This room, which has a slanted ceiling, belongs to her alone. Along one wall are old hardcover books, mostly Brazilian literature. They are among the survivors when Daisi—then age five—gave many of her mother's precious few books away to strangers on the sidewalk. "Take one, my mother has lots of them," she said. Next to the books is a collection of old 78-rpm phonograph records, mostly classical. No samba

"Take one, my mother has lots of them."

here. A nearby glass cabinet contains Sarah's collection of colorful ethnic dolls from various regions of Brazil. Below one of the two windows is a small couch on which, after lunch, Sarah valiantly tries to instruct me in the mysteries of Portuguese grammar. Snug against another wall is a small writing desk, which she graciously lets me use anytime I want. It's where, with little else to do, I seclude myself in privileged solitude, take up a pencil, and draft a lengthy letter to my friends describing our trip.

Daisi is changing. Doors within her, closed in Minnesota, are opening. She seems to know everything, understand everything, enjoy everything. She's like a key, lost for two years, once again turning smoothly in its Brazilian lock.

In Minnesota, Daisi appeared to be an individual, separate from things around her. Here she's a bright thread in the family fabric, with a role, a reputation, a history I never knew. For example, I learn that even as a child, she was an absentminded dreamer. I thought this was merely a temporary defense mechanism she developed to handle Minnesota. I learn that she's the family peacemaker, not an easy role among Gaviolis. I meet people who remember her as the state swimming champion in the 100-, 200-, and 400-meter races. She's a book of which I've read only the first chapter.

I, however, am a foreign thread. A length of rough twine that will take some work to weave into the family.

While she moves gracefully in her culture, I stumble blindly. While she makes plans for the day, I wonder what's happening next. This annoys her. I guess she didn't expect I'd be such a slow learner. I remind myself, again, no gain without pain.

"Why aren't you ready?" she asks one morning.
"Ready for what?"
"The bus station. To get our tickets."
"What tickets? Where are we going?"
"I thought you knew. We're going to Caxias. Some friends will drive us back."
"What's Caxias? What friends?"
"Just get ready."

A dark thought grips me. Now that she's thriving, and I'm a drag, will she lose patience with me? Maybe I'm not the one she thought she married. Maybe she'll find a dark, handsome Brazilian, a shiny lubricated key who easily fits all Brazilian locks. Seems the only locks I fit are in Minnesota. Our young marriage seems ominously turned upside down.

OCTOBER 2, 1970
Three Years in Brazil

THE CITY

After breakfast, I take a walk. Old women in slippers and bathrobes, and old men in shorts and flip-flops, tend their little gardens in their little yards. The neighborhood appears to be a family that's just gotten out of bed. I smell the fragrance from a factory roasting coffee beans. Lush waves of scarlet bougainvillea droop over brick walls like molten candy. In the breeze, red hibiscus flowers nod an up-and-down "yes." Out of their open bell-shaped mouths, they stick out their long stamen tongues, too beautiful to be mocking me, but maybe I'm wrong about this. I'm wrong about a lot here. Flowers are visited by butterflies the size of passports, which, in no particular direction or hurry, bounce soundlessly through the air like drunken fairies from the Amazon.

Accustomed to such beauty, Brazilians walk past it, apparently without noticing.

I expect that around four this afternoon, as nearly every afternoon, cumulous clouds will appear out of a clear blue sky. They'll quickly take shape like giant heads of white cauliflower, cover the sun, turning everything grey. Then they'll explode in thunder and horizontal rain. Wind will bang house shutters and lift the skirts of palm trees bowing submissively.

The excitement will be over as quickly as it began, the sun revealing a dripping wet world in vivid color.

This morning, Porto Alegre is already hot and humid. My sandals sink into the soft asphalt pavement. Whitewashed walls are so bright my eyes water. Humidity makes the summer feel hotter than it already is, and winters colder, I'm told. A nineteenth-century French botanist and traveler, Augustin Saint-Hilaire, in a visit to Rio Grande do Sul, observed: "In this state, there are no residents, only survivors." Good to know.

January is the peak of summer, with temperatures in the mid-nineties. The heat won't last, they tell me. Even winters, whose temperatures are mild, ranging from seventy-five to forty degrees Fahrenheit, can still be disagreeable in houses with no heat, like the Gaviolis'.

Porto Alegre is located on the east bank of the Guaíba River, which is not really a river, but rather a wide lagoon at the convergence of five rivers. The lagoon broadens out toward the Atlantic Ocean in a huge coastal estuary, 174 miles long, named *"Lagoa Dos Patos,"* or, Duck Lagoon.

The city has seventy-eight official neighborhoods. Some of the buses that go there have the following translated names: Tatters, Ragamuffin, Help, Glory, Baby God, Good Jesus, Parthenon, Sadness. I'm tempted to mount these buses and explore their romantic realms, but I might not find my way back.

Eighty percent of Porto Alegre is white, and 20 percent is Afro-Brazilian, descended from slaves. About a third of the population lives in slums, called *"vilas,"* mostly on the outskirts, where Dona Eva lives. Despite visible poverty, the economy of the city and the state this year, I'm told, is relatively strong. Industries include beef, shoes, leather, rice, and soybeans.

Gaviolis rarely discuss politics, which they hold in contempt. For the past six years Brazilians have been living under an unpopular military dictatorship, following a coup in 1964. I have no moral ground upon which to condemn this repression, because my own country enthusiastically backed the coup, fearing Brazil's huge gap between rich and poor was vulnerable to the spread of Fidel Castro's revolutionary gospel. Two years ago, in 1968, the military tightened its grip, giving dictatorial powers to its ruling general, suspending the constitution, dissolving Congress and all state legislatures, and imposing censorship. I picked up a copy of Time magazine and read about human-rights abuses, including abductions and torture of Brazilian dissidents. Meanwhile, press censorship keeps most people from knowing this. Apart from audio tapes I send home, routinely examined by censors at the post office, my life is unaffected.

I head back to the house. I hear a bird—the insistent, never-satisfied *quero-quero,* the official state bird of Rio Grande do Sul. This bird has somehow learned to sing in Portuguese— *"kero-kero-kero"*—which translates: "I want! Iwant! I want!"

Then I hear a different one. This one's singing, *"Beng tchee vee! Beng tchee vee!"* He's the yellow-bellied *bem-te-vi,* who also sings in Portuguese: "I see you! I see you!" This one is like a little spy in the sky, a feathered conscience, keeping Brazilians under constant surveillance.

Tonight, birds will sleep and frogs will wake. The frogs sing a different song, which sounds like, "Why? Why? Why?" These philosophical frogs, pose life's deepest question—this time in English—directly at me. They seem to ask, "Why are you here?"

I reply silently: "To understand the Gaviolis, Daisi, Brazil, and myself."

Next day, I take a bus downtown. People get around town mostly by bus and ubiquitous red Volkswagen taxis, which gather at the downtown bus station like ants at a lump of sugar. I get off at an intersection where alarm clocks, displayed for sale on portable tables that illegally crowd the sidewalks, are ringing incessantly. They're loud, but not loud enough to wake a man sleeping on the sidewalk a few feet away, people stepping over him as if he were a crumpled newspaper.

Fashionably dressed men gather on *Rua da Praia* (Beach Street), a cobblestone walkway in the core of downtown, off limits to cars. They wear crisp clean shirts, creased slacks, and hang their suit jackets with empty sleeves from their shoulders in European fashion. They stand very close to one another, toe to toe, chattering and yammering in unintelligible Portuguese, eyes wide as if in disbelief of what the other has just said. They're constantly touching and poking each other with their fingers, and waving their arms in grandiose gestures. Like Italians, they talk with their hands and their bodies, driving home their thoughts as if the world depended on it.

They don't seem to be talking business. No, I bet they're talking pleasure. This would be soccer, food, and women. Ah, yes, women. It's hard not to notice them, wearing tight stretch blouses, casually displaying dramatic plunging necklines and deep cleavages. Lightly and tightly dressed women strut over the cobblestones in ultra-high heels past the fashionable men, displaying generous amounts of their breastworks—which pop up in a dizzying variety of shapes and sizes: large, small, high, low, firm, flabby. Men lean against walls watching the women jiggle by. Women are nonchalant about their breasts. Sometimes, lost in thought, they'll cup a hand over a breast and forget it's there for several minutes. Guys from cold Minnesota, where women are buried in parkas, notice such things. So does that policeman, standing over there on the corner, casually adjusting his genitals, which here is entirely not against the law.

Distracted by this spectacle of flesh, I accidentally bump someone. "Sorry," I mumble, still not used to saying, *"desculpe."*

I get hemmed in on a crowded sidewalk, brushed and jostled on all sides. People come directly at me then slip past me without meeting my eyes. A man stops in front of me. We try to pass one another. Do I go right? Go left? What's the right move? He veers around me, not touching me, not looking at me, not addressing me, as if not seeing me. Maybe I'm invisible. Perhaps I'm not here. Perhaps I don't exist in this culture and no one told me.

THE PEOPLE'S TONGUE

I've begun taking the liberty of addressing Senhor Gavioli as Pai Gavioli, meaning Father Gavioli. I'm not sure why. It just seems right. His first name, José, would be way too familiar, and besides, no one calls him José. Sarah simply calls him by his last name, Gavioli, as if he were someone she didn't really know that well. His daughter-in-law, Maria Eunice, calls him Seu Gavioli, short for Senhor Gavioli, an honorific showing respect. I probably should follow her lead. But Daisi and the other children call him Pai. Maybe I want to feel part of his family, whimsically placing myself among his children, as if he were my father, my Brazilian father. The family finds this mildly amusing. It produces no reaction in him.

Addressing people in Portuguese can be hazardous. It's easy in English, with only one way, the simple, all-purpose "you." Portuguese speakers find "you" to be a crude instrument. They assume there's not merely one you, but four of them: *tu, você, senhor/senhora,* and *sua excelência.* Choosing the wrong one risks error in delicate issues such as one's age, intimacy, social class, and family rank.

Because I'm living with the Gavioli family, I'm learning to use the most intimate form, *tu,* also used for friends and children. I notice older people use it to address younger people, even strangers. *Tu* is also used to address people occupying a lower rung on the ladder.

Then there's the slightly more formal and all-purpose, *você*. This is used in ordinary settings with peers who don't qualify for the intimate *tu*.

Further up the ladder is *senhor/senhora,* or sir/madam, showing deference or respect. This is the term the Gaviolis use to address Dona Eva, the housekeeper. *Dona* is a term of respect for women, and all the Gaviolis appreciatively call her Dona Eva, just as they call Sarah, Dona Sarah. *Senhor* and *senhora* are used to address older people, or those in a higher class, or as a courtesy, even flattery, for someone you don't know. (One must take care in addressing women as *senhora,* which might age them more than they wish.) Another honorific at this level is *doutor,* which literally means doctor. It's a title of respect for people who look prosperous, have a college degree, or who appear as if they might have one. While he far outranks me in the family, Pai sometimes calls me Doutor Jimmy, an honorific of deference and esteem. Applied to me, however, it's pure irony. Sometimes he calls me Senhor Jing, or Seu Jing, translated as, Sir Jim. More irony. On second thought, he's striking the perfect comic tone, creating the appearance of respectability, while in fact placing me on a ludicrously high pedestal of undeserved status. Oddly, whenever he calls me Senhor or Doutor, I feel closer to him.

Finally, to address the cream of society—judges, governors, politicians, presidents—one must employ *Sua Excelência,* or Your Excellency, a towering compliment that Pai sometimes farcically bestows upon me.

There's one more wrinkle. Different regions have different rules. Gauchos, for instance, use only two forms: *tu* and *senhor*. They skip the middle one, *você*. People from other regions in Brazil are known to be offended if a gaucho addresses them with the familiar *tu*.

The point of all these various levels of "you," is to reinforce the notion that Brazilians live in a class and racial hierarchy. I yearn for the simpler and more egalitarian "you," applicable to paupers all the way up to presidents. But in Brazil, before I can even speak to people, I must know which rungs on the various social, economic, generational and educational ladders they occupy.

Here's a curiosity. I'm addressing him as Pai, or father. But he never calls me *Filho*, or son. He simply uses my name, Jim. Also, so far he rarely uses *tu*, for me, preferring the more neutral *você*. This is a crafty move. Avoiding *filho*, he deftly sidesteps dangerous familiarity that could lead to problems. Like asking to borrow his car.

Despite its complications, Portuguese is beautiful. Unlike spoken English, which bristles with hard corners and sharp edges, Portuguese is curvaceous, soft, graceful. Take the word *não* (no), or, *pão* (bread). These words, and others like them, have a muted, nasal, boom-like resonance, like a blow to a hollow tree deep in the Amazon. If Minnesota English sounds like a boot cracking ice, Portuguese sounds like a bare foot in soft sand.

There's also more softening at work. Brazilians are incapable of ending a word with a consonant. The language gods compel them to add an *ee* or an *ah* at the end of words that English hacks off with a cleaver. Take my name, for instance. Brazilians are incapable of calling me Jim. For them, the *m* at the end is too abrupt and ungracious. They soften it, creating *Zheeng*, with a soft *J*, or often, *Zheemmy*. This is soothing. My father used to call me Jimmy. When I hear Jimmy, or something close to it, I relax, let my guard down, feel at ease. I feel this even with people who address me formally, with the incongruous Senhor Jimmy, or Sir Jimmy.

Pai decides to assist me in the language department. His method is simple. Speak nothing but Portuguese at all times. I try mightily to follow his advice. But sometimes, desperate to be understood, I utter an English word.

"*Fala a lingua da gente!*" he roars. (Speak the language of the people!)

Stunned, I gamely try to obey and speak his "language of the people." The problem is, I simply don't have enough words in my toolbox to cobble together my meaning, prompting him to bark out the command again: "*Fala a lingua da gente!*" If Pai were a symphony, he'd be Tchaikovsky's *1812 Overture*, which features blasts from church bells, canons, and other weapons of mass destruction.

Besides, I resent his claim on Portuguese as the "language of the people." What people is he talking about? Okay, more people speak Portuguese than

French, German, or Italian, but I'm dying to remind him that millions more speak English than Portuguese. The problem is, those millions are far away.

It's worth noting that my father never shouted at me. When I was young, he was hands off, dealing with me from an emotional distance. I am, therefore, constitutionally unprepared for Pai's in-my-face education.

Worse, there's no letup. No slack for a gringo bungler. Maybe this is his revenge for having his daughter taken away. Maybe he loathes the sound of English. Whatever. His commandment galls me.

I call him Pai, but I'm finding that I could never be one of his children.

There is one shred of good news. Pai's primitive pedagogy, rooted in fear and humiliation, is highly motivating, like sitting on a cactus. The irksome thing is, it works.

Jim, get real. You live under his roof, sleep with his daughter, eat his food. If you need any business done, he's your sponsor, your godfather. You're totally under his thumb. You've got no leverage. No way to challenge him. Endure him.

At dinner I ask him to pass the potatoes. "Pai," I say, pointing to the bowl of mashed potatoes.

He looks at me, uncomprehendingly. Then he points to the bowl, a questioning look on his face, as if there may be a remote possibility that I want potatoes. Then he shouts, *"BATATAS? O Senhor Jimmy quer BATATAS?"* (POTATOES? Sir Jimmy wants POTATOES?)

I nod, forcing a sickly smile.

"Ah, então . . . " (Ah, in that case . . .) With great flourish, intended to etch forever in my memory the Portuguese word for this humble vegetable, he passes me the potatoes. He has me right where he wants me.

I read somewhere that an intelligent enemy is better than a stupid friend. Too bad he's not my stupid friend. If he were, I could fight back with zingers that would jerk his shorts, something like, "Today is yours, Old Man, but tomorrow belongs to another." That would burn his *batata*. But I never find the right moment to light the fire, because without the "language of the people" on my tongue, I don't even have a match.

If by chance I happen to get a Portuguese word right, I never hear about it from him. Truthfully, I wouldn't mind a crumb of encouragement once in a while. My mother used to praise me, which I thought was normal.

However, Pai believes praise enfeebles character. It must be avoided at every opportunity. Performing well is an unspoken family duty. Let's not wreck it with a pat on the back.

From this man, expect no love. Respect would be nice, but Jim, don't hold your breath. His respect is something hammered out on the iron anvil of his four simple principles:

> 1} Avoid praise.
> 2} Demand success.
> 3} Spurn failure.
> 4} Never embarrass the family.

With each passing day, it's increasingly clear that in marrying Daisi, I've also married her family. This was unexpected. Worse, I discover that my Gavioli family membership card has strings attached. They're tied to things that have nothing to do with Daisi. Like enduring his teaching. And enduring him.

The chasm between us—rooted in such trivialities as nationality, language, culture, personality, age, income, and body fat—is growing.

Fortunately, offsetting Pai's commandments is a gentle teaching from Sarah. For one thing, she knows grammar. After lunch, in the hot, drowsy time of day, she crawls on her hands and knees—a result of polio—up the concrete steps to her sweltering study, with me in tow. She limps toward the little couch in front of an open window, which at this hour is a hot-air blast furnace. We sit there together, sweating in one-hundred-degree heat and high humidity. Armed with a dreary Portuguese instruction book featuring small print and no cartoons, she attempts to illuminate the dark corners of her grammar-infested language, while I fight off sleep.

Grammar has always baffled me. It's like the motor of a car, a tangle of wires, tappets, valves, carburetors, and overhead cams. My method is simply to get in the car, slam the door, and start driving. In other words, just open my mouth and start talking, butchering the language as I go. This is not Sarah's way. She's rational, methodical. Sitting close to her on the tiny couch, it seems that my mother-in-law, seeking to build a language bridge between us, stone by stone, verb by verb, wants to be my friend. This is comforting.

Meanwhile, he remains my enemy. The two of them seem to be pulling a "good cop/bad cop" on me.

When I thank her, or anyone else in the family, the reply is always the same: *"Não por isso, Senhor Jimmy"* (Not for this, Sir Jimmy).

GAUCHOS

Pai is a gaucho. These are people descended from warriors. The classic gaucho retains traces of a warrior mentality. He's tough, stubborn, contentious, brave, loyal, and fiercely independent. Brazil is not considered to be a warlike nation. One of its states, however, is an exception: Rio Grande do Sul. Starting in the mid-1700s and for the next two hundred years, it was directly involved in twenty armed conflicts. They include:

> eight wars
> four revolutions
> three military campaigns
> one revolt
> one invasion
> one insurrection
> one cannon bombing, and
> a series of attacks by fanatics.

Most of these were early colonial territorial wars between the Portuguese and Spanish crowns over a shifting border involving Uruguay, Argentina, Paraguay, and Rio Grande do Sul. This area, like the frontier of our Wild West, far from colonial administrative centers, was hard to govern.

One conflict in particular shapes gaucho character: a bloody war of independence against the Brazilian monarchy. This war, which dragged on for ten years, from 1835 to 1845, is known as the *Guerra dos Farrapos* (the War of Men in Rags). Influential landowners in Rio Grande do Sul, angered by an excessive federal tax on their beef and grain, cobbled together several ragged militias. These men charged into raging hand-to-hand combat on horseback, wielding knives, swords, and spears—as well as the emerging technologies of pistols and muskets. After a decade of exhausting conflict, the gauchos, destitute and in rags, and outnumbered by the better-equipped forces of the monarchy, lost the war. But not their pride.

One day Daisi's sister, Lori, invites us to her house for a churrasco. There I meet a classic gaucho. His name is Julio, a neighbor, and he's in charge of barbecuing the meat, an enterprise of great prestige among gauchos. Julio is an imposing figure. A chunky man in his fifties, he has a red face, snow-white hair, one thick black eyebrow that has merged over both eyes, and a proud belly whose navel his shirt is unable to conceal. Working on a primitive wooden table in the backyard, Julio prepares for the feast by dismembering a great slab of beef.

OCTOBER 2, 1970
Three Years in Brazil

Next to the table is part of an oil drum containing hot glowing charcoal. Julio brandishes his churrasco knife, sharpens it with a flourish, tosses his head back, and downs a swig of *cachaça*. This is Brazil's national spirit, distilled from sugar cane, a transparent, lip-numbing gut bomb that sterilizes the cup and scorches the throat.

Hanging over the meat table are lovely branches of a fern, one of Lori's favorite plants. With one swift stroke of his blade, he lops off half a dozen branches, clearing his view of the meat. The men are impressed. Julio laughs with gusto and starts slicing the meat.

As he works, he proceeds to recount a particular day back when he was a boy, living on his father's *fazenda* (ranch) in the state of *Mato Grosso* (Thick Jungle), when a python crawled out of the forest onto their grazing land and crushed a cow. The massive reptile kept it in a stranglehold for two or three weeks until the cow rotted, then swallowed it.

Hearing this, I'm impressed with Brazil's wildness and savagery.

Rubbing handfuls of coarse salt on the beef, he launches into lavish praise of gaucha women of yore. These were voluptuous full-bosomed beauties, he says, cupping his hands in front of his breast, women with flowers in their hair and twinkles in their eyes, strong women, but submissive to warriors like himself, women who leap up close behind you on your horse, sink down into your soft sheepskin saddle, and wrap their arms tight around your waist.

All this seems pretty hard to believe because, obviously, we don't have pythons in Minnesota.

Just then Julio's wife appears from next door. She's a beefy, battle-ax of a woman, built like a bull. *"Julio! Vem para casa! Agora!"* (Julio! Come home! Right now!) Julio quietly places his knife on the table, turns, and with head bowed, obediently leaves the party.

Gauchos are disputatious and contrarian. They love the word *não* (no), for the sheer pleasure it gives them to disagree, which they do at every opportunity. For example, Gaviolis are so fond of disagreement that they even disagree when they agree.

For example, I might say, "Brazil has a big economy." In Minnesota, the reply might be, "Yes, it's big." But a Gavioli would look at me with a cocked eye, as if I had it wrong, and would say, "No, no, no, Jimmy, it's big." Okay, but didn't I just say that? Or, I might say: "Hollywood makes a lot of movies." The Gavioli would reply: "No, no, my son, what are you talking about? Hollywood makes tons of movies," returning my own words to me as baseless nonsense. Or, I might say, "This rose smells really sweet." The Gavioli would say, "No Jimmy, you haven't the slightest idea how sweet this rose smells."

To a Scandinavianized person like myself, "No!" has a stunning impact. Like an upward jerk on the shorts. A sudden, well-placed "No!" straightens the spine and opens a tiny crack in the conversation, into which the gaucho attacker rushes, bayonet drawn in full-blown discord.

This maneuver, a vestige of gaucho warrior days, is highly un-Minnesotan. When we Minnesotans disagree, we don't start with a "no." We begin with a "yes." Or, we might soften the yes with a "Yeah, but . . . ," or, "Uh huh." Our method is to soft-pedal disagreement with the initial impression that we actually agree. Example:

"Hey pal, I hate to say it, but you're getting kinda fat."
"Yeah, but I've actually lost weight."
"Okay, but your belly hangs over your belt."
"Yeah, but to tell the truth, it actually doesn't."
"Uh huh, could be, but then again I don't actually see your belt buckle."
"Yeah, but if you bend down you can see it."
"Okay, yeah, I'm bending down, but I still don't see it."
"Ya, okay, fine, but I know it's there. "

The reason behind our gentle dissent is simple: Minnesotans descend from the Vikings. These are the bloodthirsty barbarians who leaped from dugout canoes to kill, loot, plunder, rape, and set European villages ablaze. Smoldering deep in Minnesotans' reptilian brains are these violent Viking genes. This is why Minnesotans must handle even the least quibble with great care.

Unlike Minnesotans, gauchos possess a rough physicality and freedom in the male body department. They greet one another, for example, with embraces, insults, and manly whacks on the back. In public, they're free to adjust their genitals, known as their "documents," the all-important identification papers gaucho men carry in pouches. We Minnesotans adjust our genitals in closets with the door locked and lights turned off.

There is one area in which gauchos resemble Minnesotans: respect for authority. There's a saying that in Brazil, the law is made in Brasilia, the nation's capital, but not followed. It's published in São Paulo, the nation's economic engine, but not read. It's lampooned and disrespected in Rio de Janeiro, the cultural center. In Rio Grande do Sul, it is obeyed.

OCTOBER 2, 1970
Three Years in Brazil

THE CLOSET

Out of Pai's sight, I'm happy, even buoyant. Near him, I feel like bread dough under the heel of his hand. Living with him, under his roof, I'll either rise, like bread in the oven, or go flat, like lefse, a soft Norwegian flatbread inspired by the potato.

The truth is, at age thirty, I'm still lingering in adolescence, still rising in the oven, while he's been out of the kiln for years, hard as rock. If I can just stay out from under his heavy hand, I'll be okay.

I'm lucky to land a job teaching English literature at the Federal University of Rio Grande do Sul, which will get me out of the house a bit, but which doesn't start for another three months. It's only twelve hours a week, paying $160 a month. This, combined with Daisi's return to her former social work position, at a higher salary than mine, will be enough for us to live on.

Meanwhile, I need something else to do. Something mindless. Come to think of it, before we can move in, our apartment needs a closet. I might as well build one. The bedroom has a concrete enclosure that could be a perfect closet. Okay, Jim, let's get cracking.

I start by bolting wooden frames to the concrete enclosure, and manage to install the shelves. Now I have to attach wicker doors to the frames. I need long screws. I set out early one morning to buy some and finish the job.

At the bus stop, I ask people where I can find a hardware store. They don't understand my Portuguese. After several tries on my part, one guy catches my drift and tells me where to go. I don't understand him. The bus arrives. He tells me to get on, so I do.

I hold out my hand with some coins so the bus cashier can pick out what she needs, like the cab driver did a couple of weeks ago. Someone tells me where to get off. I manage to find the hardware store.

I don't know the word for screw, so I act it out. I make a hole with my thumb and index finger, screwing my other index finger through it several times. This draws a bunch of amused clerks who think I want something else.

By late afternoon, I'm back in the apartment. What would have taken a half hour in Saint Paul has taken nearly a day here.

I discover I don't know how to attach the doors to the frame.

Just then, without knocking, Pai barges into the apartment. This is understandable, since he owns it, but hey, hasn't the guy ever heard of privacy?

One of Pai's Rules for Living is: SOLVE PROBLEMS QUICKLY AND AGGRESSIVELY. He rapidly sizes up my carpentry problem, elbows me aside, and with his powerful, meaty hands, attaches the doors by driving screws into the frame without a drill, or any help from me, which he doesn't want. He's the uninvited guest who stays awhile and ends up rearranging your furniture.

I can't help but notice his big, working-class hands, with their thick muscular fingers, hard nails, and large veins running from the roots of his fingers to his wrists. Hands toughened by tools of wood and steel. Hands that now, late in his career, have moved up to pencil and paper, work orders, invoices, blueprints—hands that now direct other hands to get the job done. As his claws grip the pliers, they seem to grip me, an innocent bystander, hands in my pockets, observing him finish the job I can't.

Thanks to my Harvard degree in English, I have clean hands. But no skills in the hammer-and-nail department. This department is where Pai excels.

As he works, he talks, which by now I'm beginning to understand. Harvard, he says, is low on the world's educational ladder. It can't even touch the shoe of Oxford, the educational crown jewel of England, a nation he says sits at the pinnacle of civilization.

I know he's baiting me, but I lack the Portuguese to muster a comeback. Clearly, Pai is blessed with two outstanding characteristics. One is his passion for provocation, inherited from his Italian ancestors and gaucho warriors of yesteryear. The other is his relentless hammering, a gift from his German ancestors, who may have been blacksmiths.

In his mind, the English novels I've struggled through, the Romantic poetry, Greek philosophy, art appreciation, the many hours I misspent in the library—indeed my entire liberal arts education—is, at best, amusing. His library consists of a shed behind his house, containing not books, but hand tools. In his presence, my master's degree in English Literature feels like lemon frosting on a nail.

Moving quickly, he attaches one of the doors. He knows what to do. He's decisive, I'll give him that much. He's a man of action, absorbed in *living* life, not reading about it in books, as I did in college. I've never met anyone so earthbound, so nutsy-boltsy, so realistic, so completely and utterly "one-and-one-make-two." As an English major, I studied ways in which one and one might somehow imply three.

His hard-edged materialism cuts through my liberal education like a machete through chocolate mousse. My degree in English suddenly feels trivial, absurd, a butterfly sunbathing on a jackhammer. The higher life of the mind—books, film, music—these are not merely irrelevant, they're suspect. They're distractions to be avoided. His view is that when you boil education down to its bone, it's simply a

OCTOBER 2, 1970
Three Years in Brazil

tool—like a chisel or a crowbar—an instrument used to build a home, fix a toilet. Nor is it something one acquires by curling up on the sofa with Plato.

As he works on the second closet door, it occurs to me that despite my ivy-league education (heck, my high school education, piano lessons, Peace Corps, and graduate school—opportunities he never had), I'm not the man he is.

He's everything I'm not. Next to him, my soul feels like Silly Putty. His, on the other hand, is tempered steel, full of hard-headed realism hammered out in his knock-about past. He contains an earth force, as if made of elemental things, like rock and lightning.

As he works quickly on the final hinge, I wonder what he has that I lack? Let's count them. Ambition, drive, focus, cunning intelligence, physical strength, decisiveness, generosity, and—what I'm beginning to discover—the clear vision of an eagle. At least in finishing a closet. I wish I had his type of energy. I wonder whether one can acquire it without too much suffering.

He's not the Brazilian seen on travel posters—the bronzed, samba-dancing, soccer-crazed beach lizard wearing flowery shorts. No, he's a serious man, a child of the Great Depression, someone who has hoisted himself and his family up into the middle class. Without Pai and Sarah, and others of their generation, there would be no bronzed Brazilian beach lizards.

This brings to mind something I hate to admit: his generation has paved the way for my own. His is a strong generation, toughened by poverty and fearing it as earlier mortals feared Satan himself. I and my generation are playing in the earth they have plowed. Were it not for him and his generation worldwide, I and my generation would not exist.

It's hard not to admire the guy. But no way would I ever tell him.

He wraps up the job in about forty-five minutes. He's happy. He takes pleasure in bolting doors to frames, and delights in my mechanical incompetence and all the opportunities to remind me. I stand uselessly behind him, a fragile Minnesota strawberry repotted in his Brazilian earth. Despite his help, for which I should be grateful, my strongest feeling is something else: irritation that he's invaded my precious space. Again. And yes, while I admire his potent German work ethic, I wonder anew whether he's exacting revenge for my taking his daughter from him.

I force myself to thank him for finishing my closet. Maybe I should go further, and thank him for who he is. Nah. Does the bee thank the flower? Does the fish thank the water? Does the strawberry thank the earth? They don't appear to.

BORN IN MONTENEGRO

Pai rarely speaks of his childhood, but occasional tidbits emerge. He was born in Rio Grande do Sul in a little wooden house on the banks of the River Caí. The year is 1915, and the place is a little German colonial village named Montenegro. He is named José Gavioli Sobrinho (the last name means "nephew"), in honor of his father's brother. Unfortunately, his mother and father separate when she's pregnant with Pai. Pai and his older brother, Rui, stay with their mother, Amanda. His father, Augusto, returns to his hometown of Caxias, about fifty miles north of Montenegro.

The separation leaves Amanda and her two sons almost destitute, without even a toy, a detail that Pai recalls with some sadness. Amanda stays in Montenegro and moves in with her mother.

Amanda's mother was born in Germany, with the maiden name of Rosa Leibnitz. She was part of the first wave of German immigrants reaching Rio Grande do Sul in the mid-1800s, long after the Portuguese colonists had arrived. She married a German-Brazilian, named Finger, whose first name Pai doesn't remember. He owned a warehouse and a paddleboat that carried goods on the river linking Montenegro to the bustling state capital of Porto Alegre about fifty miles south.

Financial difficulties caused Senhor Finger's paddleboat business to run aground, along with his marriage. Amanda's father left Rosa, his wife, and children and moved away to become a salesman, just as Amanda's future husband would do years later. Rosa kept their house, and continued to operate the warehouse business.

Pai spends his first seven years of life in Montenegro, which at that time is a small village carved out of primeval woods with pickaxes, shovels, hatchets, and the sweat of German immigrants. It's an outpost reached only by horse, mule, ox, and cart. By the time Pai is born, it's already a riverboat stop, then subsequently a station on a small rail line. Montenegrins live close to the earth, a rugged existence sustained by muscle, stoicism, and humility. Men have tanned, unshaven faces, and wear loose-fitting gaucho shirts. Their pants have accordion pleats down the leg and their leather boots have accordion folds at the tops. Women wear kerchiefs and long dresses. On riverboat days, some sit on the riverbank with their baskets of produce, waiting for the boat to carry them to Porto Alegre. Over time, the village starts to grow, fueled by the industry of immigrants, which little Pai probably absorbs as a shirt soaks up sweat.

He absorbs something else, too. He learns how to live fatherless, never seeing Augusto, never knowing who he is or what he does.

As a child, likely wearing a tattered, but clean, cotton shirt and overalls, Pai runs barefoot on the red Brazilian earth. He probably carries water from a well. He likely pushes a wooden wheelbarrow on its squeaky wooden wheel. He perhaps climbs barefoot over fences made of crooked branches, lashed together by vines for rope.

If sent to buy vegetables for Amanda, he might traipse along a dirt path, feeling the grand responsibility of his errand. He passes the landing, where goods stored in his hard-working grandmother's warehouse are loaded onto paddleboats. He steps into a vegetable shack, stacked with wooden crates heavy with carrots, cucumbers and manioc tubers the size of forearms. There are apples, tomatoes, potatoes, peaches, pears, tiny sweet pineapples, deep purple grapes and curved gourds big as horse collars. In a corner sit wine jugs wrapped in straw casings, whose vinegary smell mingles with the fragrant cornucopia of fruits and vegetables.

Pai comes out of frontier Brazil, the New World, a blend of the virtues and defects of the venerable Old World cultures from which he springs—Italian from his father and German from his mother. Excellent cultures individually, they can be highly combustible when mixed, as they are in him.

A FOREIGN THREAD

There are days in which I crave solitude, a condition the Gaviolis regard as an illness. One Sunday, Daisi and I are invited, as always, to join Pai and Sarah in their regular family excursion into the countryside. Pai will be driving his Willys Aero sedan and its six-cylinder Hurricane engine. The purpose of this outing is to reinforce and intensify family closeness. For some reason today, I find this prospect to be particularly claustrophobic. I make a grave mistake. I decline his offer.

This hurts him.

Gaviolis are tightly communal. I'm not. I'm an odd thread in the snug fabric of this family. I want a buffer between me and others, some looseness, some leeway, some spaciousness in which to breathe. This roominess is hardwired into my genetic structure, stemming from the rambling, rural, ancestral Scandinavian countryside. Living with the Gaviolis, I realize how un-Brazilian I am. I'm more Scandinavian, something I hadn't fully understood until now.

The Gavioli family has rare power over its individual members. It's an organism unto itself, just as an army of Amazonian ants is a single organism, controlling each of its billion individual members. One day, about to leave the house to teach my English class, he refuses to let me out the door. The reason: I'm wearing sandals. Take them off and put on shoes, he says. I'm stunned. He won't allow me to stand in front of Brazilian university students while wearing sandals. Evidently, sandals are a scandal, like teaching while naked. They are an embarrassment, an emblem of poverty jeopardizing one's credibility, not to speak of one's membership in the middle class. I remove them and put on shoes.

Everything is under the family microscope. Nothing escapes judgment. Take cars, for example. Daisi's brother Davison loans Daisi and me his new Volkswagen bug to use on weekdays, while he has it on weekends. Cars in Brazil are hard to get. They're polished. They're pampered. They're middle class.

One day, backing out of a tight space, I accidentally scratch the fender.

Pai and Davison are shocked. I've done something foolish. Gaviolis have no patience with foolishness. They start calling me *"o barbeiro,"* meaning "the barber," someone who gives close shaves. Good. Rather funny. I guess I deserve it.

The family loves this nickname. After a couple of days, as it seems to me, the teasing grows stale, edging into mockery. The teasing becomes a sharp stick, poking and jabbing, attempting to maneuver me back into the bounds of acceptable behavior. Among Gaviolis, the bungler pays a price in humiliation, thinly disguised as humor. I'm the barbeiro for weeks. The reason: I've violated another of his Rules for Living: NEVER EMBARRASS THE FAMILY.

Jim, pay attention. You're carrying in your clumsy hands his hard-earned family name, which possesses extraordinary value, like the flag of a proud nation. A scratch on a fender is a blemish on family honor. A misstep by a Gavioli, or even a Gavioli proxy like myself, tarnishes Gaviolis everywhere.

Yes, I'm the strange thread in the family fabric. I wish he'd take me seriously. I want his respect. Without it, his teasing hurts more than it should. I am reminded of when I was a little boy, the age when I adored my father. I yearned to grow up to be just like him. I wanted him to look at me, pay attention to me, love me. But he was too busy.

My skin is too thin for Brazil.

OCTOBER 2, 1970
Three Years in Brazil

After four months of living with Daisi's parents, our apartment is finally ready. We now have our own space. Finally, some privacy!

One afternoon, Pai unlocks the door to our apartment, which of course he owns, walks in, and sees our bedroom door open. On impulse, he enters. It's an indelicate moment.

As I struggle into my trousers, he backs out and shuts the bedroom door. Daisi and I hastily dress to go to see why he came.

He stands in the living room silently staring into space. He's like the father described by author Bernard Cooper, who has the ashamed inward look of a man who's blundered, but doesn't know how to correct it. Pai doesn't apologize. He says nothing. Without looking at us, or saying goodbye, he abruptly walks out and closes the door behind him. We look at each other, hands over our mouths, suppressing laughter.

Among Gaviolis, there's little privacy. It's a foreign concept. While his home is my home, as he told me on my first day in Brazil, my home is also his home. It doesn't matter what we're doing; Pai can enter our apartment at any time.

His silence on the bedroom intrusion is so complete that I begin to wonder whether it even happened. And yet, for once, this misadventure is not mine. It's his. Evidently for this reason, it fails to qualify for family teasing. It should. Brazilians find sex a rich source of amusement. For instance, it's perfectly okay for someone at a Gavioli family gathering to explain that the Ford Pinto flopped in Brazil because *"pinto"* is slang for "tiny penis."

But this is not his type of joke. He's a hardworking, puritanical family man of ironclad chastity. For him, sex is like a welding torch. One does not look at it with the naked eye. Thus, all memory of bursting into our bedroom, like welding sparks, vanishes into thin air before hitting the ground.

ABSTINENCE

One sweltering evening, Daisi still at work, I arrive at Pai's house full of joy. I'm carrying a dozen bottles of beer, a carton of melting ice cream, and some news.

"Daisi's pregnant!" I shout. "I just came from the clinic. Her pregnancy test is *"positivo."* She's carrying our first child! Hey everyone, it's time to celebrate—with ice cream and beer!"

"Preciso ir na aula" (Gotta go to class), Davison says. He slips out. Sarah retreats to the bedroom and shuts the door. Pai is nowhere to be seen. One by one, everyone quietly vanishes. Abandoned, sitting at the heavy dark dinner

table, I slowly drag my spoon through melting ice cream.

I wander alone into the front room, all joy gone. Maybe Brazilians don't celebrate pregnancies. Maybe they're like Tanzanians, who don't make clothes for babies before they're born. This is smart. Don't count your chickens before they're hatched. This is folk wisdom. Jim, you fool, why don't you know this?

Then I notice something. In a corner of the living room, a bottle of whiskey and a bottle of wine sit on a small table in prominent display. The bottles sit there, like artifacts of historical interest, coated in a fine dust, where years of neglect seem to have quietly erased them from human consciousness. Apparently they're reserved for guests, whom I've noticed always depart from the Gavioli home as sober as they arrive.

Then—a Eureka Moment. Jim, you dimwit. *You're dwelling in the house of a teetotaler!* In this house, everything above root beer is Satan's brew! And when Pai teetotals, everyone teetotals. This is a Gavioli house law, one probably unwise to break. Maybe the smart thing to do, while living under his supervision, is to simply convert to teetotalism. This would be prudent.

Daisi arrives and I give her the good news. She's delighted, beaming, and relieved. She's been hoping to become pregnant for months. Then I tell her what happened when I announced it to the family.

"He doesn't drink."

"Yeah, good for him."

She took my hand in hers. "Jim, don't be like that. That's just the way he is."

"Okay. I know." I sigh. "More of his pristine moral goodness."

"Jim, it doesn't matter, okay?" She puts her arms around me.

I feel better. No big deal. People who drink in moderation, such as myself, are people I understand. Less understandable are those virtuous few who avoid the bottle with a praiseworthy shot of will power that lifts them above common souls. I suspect Pai's strict sobriety is something he's constructed in opposition to his brother, Rui, whom I hear is hitting the bottle fairly heavily.

A HIGHER VOLTAGE

Gaviolis operate at a higher and more dangerous voltage than my own. Sparks fly, casting momentary flashes of light on differences between Gaviolis and Martins. For example, in conversation, they often remind one another to calm down (*"calma, calma,"* they say), which isn't needed in Minnesota. We Martins discuss things, suppressing conflict with a blanket of pleasantries. Gaviolis argue, honing sharp verbal skills I now wish I had.

OCTOBER 2, 1970
Three Years in Brazil

Oh yes, Pai gives lip service to the exotic northern virtues of tranquility and serenity, which he acknowledges Gaviolis lack. For him, serenity is an alien concept, merely theoretical. It's something best left to Minnesotans, whose Scandinavian ancestors, imprisoned for long dark winters in narrow wooden farmhouses with no diversions, surrounded by snow fields as far as the eye can see, cultivated cool and protective distances among themselves. Hence, the notorious Scandinavian silence, which evolved in Darwinian fashion as an icy shield against insanity and mayhem. It's a survival tactic unknown to the Gaviolis.

I suspect that deep down, Pai believes those who live silently and serenely are insane.

The environment Gaviolis enjoy most, the one in which Pai prizes and feels most at home, is *"bagunça,"* translated in English as "uproar," or "pandemonium."

For example, one hot Sunday afternoon the entire family gathered at the home of Sidnei's wife's parents. We consumed a robust meal of shish kabob, fried potatoes, and *gnocchi* dumplings. After a heavy meal such as this, one might be ready for sedate discussion, reading, or simply staring at the four walls—something my Swedish grandmother used to do. Instead, the Gaviolis explode into an all-out water fight. It begins by tossing cups of water at one another, then quickly escalates into buckets of water hurled at family members, who are dashing deliriously around the outside of the house, and then bursting into the house itself, soaking everyone, along with the furniture and the lovely inlaid wooden living room floor.

The sole abstainer is Sarah, who, while refraining from the tumult because of her polio-weakened legs and somber nature, sits back and smiles on the bedlam.

In quieter moments, Gavioli men gratify themselves by chasing children about the house, jabbing them sharply in the ribs with their fingers. In response, the children take pleasure in stealing their uncles' sandals and tossing them into the woods at night so no one can find them. Then the uncles content themselves by chasing the little miscreants and innocently pulling down their pants, providing amusement for elder family members who relax in chairs and chuckle at the chaos and marvel at how much the children are learning.

It's my misfortune that these activities are occurring precisely at a time in my life when I seek to purify myself through the practice of Buddhist meditation.

Sadly, in this family, nirvana is unattainable.

A Brazilian humorist, Luis Fernando Veríssimo, once wrote that he wanted Brazil to be transformed into a Scandinavian country. He wanted

Brazil to be an orderly nation, without crime, without hunger, without injustice, without conflicts, magnificently dull. It would be okay for Brazil to be a boring nation. On second thought, he realized such a change would be difficult. Converting its money, language, temperatures, different customs . . . Besides, he knew it would be impossible to preserve everything that makes Brazil so charming, creative, and fun—in truth, Brazilians themselves—without retaining its disorder and bad character. Maybe it should be Scandinavian only during working hours and Brazilian after 6:00 p.m. Yes, he wanted Brazil to be Scandinavian immediately!

But then, alas, he decided to junk the whole idea, unable to live without *Carnaval*.

SHAMED

Even before Pai is born in 1915, his father, Augusto, leaves home. Augusto does well for himself. He becomes co-owner of a lumber company in Caxias, named Oliva, Gavioli & Co., selling curved barrel slats for the city's wine industry. Then he manages the Banco National do Commercio in Caxias. Meanwhile, he becomes a captain in the National Guard.

In 1922, he changes direction and moves to Porto Alegre. He becomes co-owner of a clothing store, Casa Monteiro. Located near Rua da Praia, the city's most fashionable street, the store sells stylish women's clothes, wedding dresses, perfume, cloth, and fancy articles for men and children.

After some years, he sells his share of the store to his partner, and invests in his younger brother José Gavioli's prosperous drugstore chain. Supported by earnings from his brother's pharmacy, Augusto begins a comfortable retirement on the upper rungs of life's ladder, far from its lower rungs where Amanda and her two sons are struggling.

The same year Augusto moved to Porto Alegre, Amanda decides there's no future for herself in tiny Montenegro. She takes seven-year-old Pai and his ten-year-old brother, Rui, to São Paulo, always a magnet for impoverished rural Brazilians. Pai attends a primary school for the indigent, where he likely receives skimpy meals and a skimpier education. Amanda cleans the pots, pans, floors and toilets of the wealthy, living with her sons in the back rooms of her employers' homes. Over the years, she continues to live on society's underside, cleaning other people's toilets, and becomes a harsh and crabby woman.

At age fifteen, Pai—like a young eagle—leaves his mother and flies into the world on his own youthful strength. Liberated from his restrictive family cage, he spreads his wings and soars toward independence, a high and powerful moment in his young life.

Traveling alone from São Paulo, he joins his older brother Rui in Porto Alegre, and immediately enters a world of deprivation. The brothers share a room in a boardinghouse while Pai looks for work. On Saturdays, they gorge on food to fool their hunger on Sundays when the kitchen is closed.

"Tive uma camisa só" (I had only one shirt), Pai tells me, "so after I washed it and hung it on the line, I went bare-chested until it was dry."

My life and Pai's life at age fifteen are in stark contrast. At his age, I'm attending a decent high school, doing my homework, playing basketball, and eating steaks my father cooks for me on the grill. While I attend the School of Meat and Gravy, Pai studies in the School of Bread and Water.

When Pai arrives in Porto Alegre in 1930, a political revolution that will change Brazil is happening all around him in Rio Grande do Sul. The revolt, which rapidly spreads nationwide, reverses a presidential election and installs Getúlio Vargas, a dynamic young gaucho politician, as Brazil's new president. Vargas will become Brazil's dominant political figure over the next quarter century. Meanwhile, as an adolescent on his own looking for work, Pai probably has little interest in these high political winds.

There is one man who could be tremendously helpful to him: his uncle. Seeking work, Pai pays a visit to the successful druggist José Gavioli, the man in whose honor he is named. A compulsive man of strict discipline, Uncle José takes his tiny cup of sweet coffee *(cafezinho)* at the same hour each morning, sipping it with such self-absorption that he's incapable of greeting or acknowledging anyone in his vicinity.

Uncle José Gavioli is a prominent businessman. His pharmaceutical chain, Gavioli & Co. Ltd., is known throughout Rio Grande do Sul. He represents the American pharmaceutical giant Lilly Labs, and is the statewide distributor of penicillin, and later insulin. He's the only one of his five siblings to visit Europe, where he studied the pharmacy business.

Pai knocks. His uncle opens his door. The two José Gaviolis eye one another. José the uncle, a man of wealth, education, and European travel, recognizes his nephew, the youngest son of his older brother, Augusto. Standing before him is his brother's rejected son, the boy who carries the worldly druggist's own name.

He slams the door in his nephew's face.

This slammed door, the one that might have opened the way back to his father's family, sends a powerful, unmistakable, cruel message—a message soaked in shame—*You Are Rejected.*

Young Pai will remember this message as long as he lives. This soaring-eagle boy, his wings cut, fatherless, shamed to his soul, falls down to earth.

A VOW OF PROSPERITY

One day, Pai—now forty years older—takes me grocery shopping. We start at a butcher shop. Without pausing, he marches behind the counter and puts his hand on a slab of beef. He pats it, lifts it, eyes it like a woman holding up a dress she might buy. The butchers step back in awe. Then he buys enough to feed an army, along with a thick tube of salami.

When Daisi was young, Pai one day brought home a giant, stainless-steel salami cutter. Evidently, his love of salami is matched only by the size of the machine that cuts it. This monster had a slicing arm that shot out so far they couldn't use it in the kitchen without jackhammering the wall. They repositioned the arm so it thrust through the doorway. This proved dangerous, so they moved Colossus to a corner of their tiny dining room. Eventually, Toco, their mongrel dog, used it as a bed.

In those days, he'd buy two hundred pounds of sugar at a crack, plus enough powdered coffee to serve a restaurant, and enough disinfectant to clean a hospital. With one eye always fixed on approaching doom, Sarah encouraged him. *"Gavioli, vem revolução, compra muito"* (Gavioli, the revolution is coming, buy a lot). The feared rioting and looting of grocery stores never came. But these veterans of Brazil's temperamental economy were ready.

Our next stop is the supermarket. For me, shopping is a task I like to dispatch as efficiently as possible. I want to move quickly down the aisles and get out before buying things I don't need. Not him. He creeps along, touches everything, smells everything, weighs everything, turns everything over in his big hands, absorbing produce and products into his bloodstream, into his very soul. For him, grocery shopping, like cleanliness, is close to godliness. Besides, it's recreational. It's foreplay, second only to consuming food itself.

Pai loves excess. More is better than less. Bountiful is beautiful. He's a human cornucopia, the goat's horn out of which magically and endlessly pours abundance from the earth—fruit, vegetables, grain, pasta, and choice cuts of meat.

My mother has an opinion about excess. "You have to experience it before you know what it is," she says. Raised on a farm in Isanti, Minnesota, Mom became a nurse and supported her parents during the Great Depression. She married Dad, and, in the prosperous fifties, she experienced enough excess to recognize it, and sometimes to control it.

While she and Pai have both known excess, he feels little need to control it.

Excess and money are close cousins. I notice a one-liner about money on a bus a couple of days later. It says: *"Tenho dinheiro, ergo existo."* Translated: "I have money, therefore I am." The converse would be, without money, I don't exist. Mother Teresa speaks to this. She says the tragic thing about poverty isn't lack of bread or a roof, but the feeling of being no one. This is something that members of the Brazilian service class may feel. They are sometimes called *João Ninguem*, or John Nobody.

For Pai, shopping is a reminder that he exists.

In his opinion, the greatest economic system in the Milky Way is capitalism. In my opinion, godless capitalism and its barren fruit—big cars, big burgers, and big plastic pouring out of the industrial cornucopia—appeal to humanity's lowest instincts and threaten to suffocate the earth. Capitalism, originating in the cravings of the stomach—his favorite organ—reaches like a cancer into the brain. It's a phase of human evolution gone berserk. We'd best outgrow it soon before it overwhelms us. I happen to know this because I'm a child of the affluent sixties. So I confront him.

"Pai," I tell him one day, "did you know that one of the byproducts of your favorite economic system is poverty? Poverty is an institution created so the not-poor can feel superior."

"Sim, eu sei" (Yes, I know), he replies, which surprises me. Then he adds: "The way out of poverty is for people to work hard, like Sarah and I have."

Okay, valid point. They work hard. He's keeping his kids, Davison and Lori, afloat, paying for his night classes and her university tuition. Oh ya, I forgot. They're also keeping Daisi and me afloat, largely paying off our apartment. But I press forward. "Pai, did you know that poverty actually contains elements of goodness? Some people even choose poverty, like Buddhist monks."

He says nothing. This is a point for me. Obviously, he's no Buddhist monk. For him, there's no nirvana in austerity, much less in fasting. He's taken the vow of prosperity.

Emboldened by his silence, I say: "Pai, a little more simplicity might be good for your body, your soul, and even our planet!"

Ha, ha, ha. He erupts in a monster belly laugh.

"Jim, austeridade é para os pobres. Só intelectual gosta de pobreza." (Jim, austerity is for the poor. Only intellectuals love poverty.)

"Pai, I'm no intellectual. I don't love poverty. Or hunger, or disease. But a good life consists of wanting less, not more. One's duty is to leave a small footprint on the earth, not a big one."

I'm scoring more points here, using the rhetoric of the voluntary simplicity movement I read about somewhere.

"Jim, quando era criança, fiquei na porta da miséria e na rua da amargura." (Jim, when I was a child, I stood at the door of misery and on the street of bitterness.)

Apparently, these are real places for him. He scores.

Neither of us wins. He adores abundance. I admire simplicity. He loves shopping. I prefer the woods. We travel different paths. Mine, obviously higher and more virtuous than his.

GLASS SKULLS

Pai has one remarkable virtue: his uncanny ability to see into the brains of other Gaviolis. Actually, all Gaviolis have this baffling capacity. For example, a Gavioli knows in advance what others are thinking before they say it. It's as if their skulls are made of glass.

This means a Gavioli has no need to finish uttering a thought, because the other Gavioli has already spotted and replied to it. Here, for instance, is an astonishing exchange between Daisi and Pai that took place when she was a teenager. This verbal ping-pong occurred at a sleepover at a girlfriend's house. Suspecting boys were there, Pai drove to the sleepover, woke Daisi from a sound and boyless sleep at midnight, and took her home.

To get the full effect, one should read this translation aloud quickly:

> *Daisi:* "Why are you . . . ?"
> *Pai:* "You have no business . . ."
> *Daisi:* "No, what have I . . ."
> *Pai:* "No young lady, you come . . ."
> *Daisi:* "No, this isn't fair, I . . ."
> *Pai:* "Stop! Don't even start to . . ."
> *Daisi:* "No, why don't you ask . . ."
> *Pai:* "Absolutely not. I know what I . . ."
> *Daisi:* "No, you've got no . . ."
> *Pai:* (Sighs) "My daughter, just get in the car."

These shortcuts and blinding speed are a stunning refinement of communication, exceeded perhaps only by dolphins. It's something totally foreign to the plodding conversation in Minnesota. The great benefit of Gavioli

OCTOBER 2, 1970
Three Years in Brazil

communication is its economy. It saves them astounding amounts of time. For Pai, saving time and plunging to the heart of the matter is what makes him who he is. The rest of the family must either learn this quick communication, or be lost. (This does not apply to Sarah, who slowly and deliberately waits for dust to settle before voicing her often-decisive opinions.)

Gaviolis, and maybe Brazilians generally, don't mind being cut off in mid-sentence. They expect it. Interruptions are not rude, as they are among Minnesota Scandinavian types, who are accustomed to speaking in paragraphs while the next Scandinavian patiently waits in line to take his or her turn. The two styles differ because the essence of Brazilian conversation is heat; everything is personal and conversation can quickly become overcharged. They're forever revealing their anxieties, depressions, obsessions, joys, and loathings. Minnesotans, on the other hand, prefer topics such as stock market trends, or the future of soybeans.

One would think lopping off another's thought would provoke short tempers. Gaviolis solve this problem elegantly by requesting calm. For example, a Gavioli whose thought is hacked off by an interruption may hold up a hand like a policeman directing traffic, and say, *"calma, calma."* These words are like cool water running through a hot engine. The use of *"calma"* gives space for two, possibly three, additional words to extend one's thought fragment—not the whole thought, but merely the gist—all a Gavioli really needs.

But these extra words are rarely granted, due to high Gavioli voltage levels and low tolerance for detail. The general rule is more interrupting, dovetailing, overlapping, slicing, dicing, and slashing back and forth, which in practice produces communication closely resembling Morse code. If Gavioli conversation were basketball, it would be constant fast-break versus continuous full-court press.

Bad news arrived today. Aunt Cecilia, Sarah's youngest sister, who lives in São Paulo, had a stroke and is paralyzed on her right side. Sarah and Davison will take a twenty-hour bus ride to the hospital in São Paulo to bring her to Porto Alegre. Cecilia's unlucky. Years earlier, after separating from her husband, she met a big, wonderful Brazilian guy of German ancestry, and just as they were about to live together, he suffered a diabetic coma and died.

ROOTS

German and Italian blood, like two merged rivers, mingle freely in Pai's veins. These two venerable cultures, distinguishing Rio Grande do Sul from the rest of Brazil, arrive in the nineteenth century. They are not the first to arrive. The first wave of immigration to Rio Grande do Sul—not Pai's ancestors—are Portuguese fishermen and small farmers from the Azores Islands, an archipelago in the Atlantic Ocean nine hundred miles off the coast of Portugal. These humble Portuguese families establish Porto Alegre in 1752, part of Portugal's effort to control territory claimed by Spain.

About seventy years later, the Germans begin to arrive. Between 1824 and 1914, approximately fifty thousand Germans reach southern Brazil. Among them is Pai's maternal grandmother, Rosa Leibnitz. They move inland, away from the Portuguese-populated coast, occupying rich lowland farming areas.

The third wave of immigration, mostly from northern Italy, begins in 1875. They settle on remaining farmland not occupied by the Germans, the sides of hills and mountains in the state's interior, the hardest places to scratch out a living. An Italian colonial town, Caxias do Sul, becomes their focal point, displacing Indians who had lived there for centuries.

Among the Italians is Felix, the first known Gavioli to set foot on the shores of the New World. Felix comes from Modena in northern Italy. Then in his twenties, he and his young wife, Marietta Serafini Gavioli, land in Brazil in 1881. They soon join other Italian immigrants in Caxias, which will come to be known as the Pearl of the Colonies.

According to family lore (there is no documentation, no passport, no evidence at all that he ever reached the New World), Felix begins his new, intense, and productive Brazilian life. Skillful and enterprising, he becomes a land surveyor, drawing the lines upon which Caxias will grow. He establishes a branch of the Masons, a semi-secretive fraternal organization whose members communicate with mysterious gestures, grips, and handshakes. Masons seek moral rectitude, believe in a supreme being, and do charitable community work. Felix rises in masonic hierarchy to the thirty-third level, the loftiest attainable at the time.

Fertile in his spare moments, he fathers five children. The eldest is Augusto, who, as we know, marries Amanda Finger. Next is José, for whom Pai's is named. He eventually creates the pharmacy chain, and who, after Felix dies, becomes the economic head of the family. The other three children, Pai's aunt Adelina, and uncles Hugo and Clodoveu, play little or no role in Pai's life.

OCTOBER 2, 1970
Three Years in Brazil

The dynamic Felix, then only in his thirties, is felled by a mosquito. He dies of malaria and is buried in Caxias, not by the church, but by the Masons, at a date and place unknown to history.

On official paper documents, Felix doesn't exist. But he does in bronze. Or at least he did. His name was carved on a large plaque, along with those of other Italian immigrants, bolted to a heroic statue of an immigrant in Caxias.

Years later the plaque was stolen. Rumored to be stored in the small gaucho town of Nova Milano, it's probably been melted down for cash. A thief's gain is history's loss.

Thus, the birth and death of the Gavioli family progenitor are equally lost in the mists of time. He appears suddenly on the shores of Rio Grande do Sul, undocumented, officially a non-person, a spontaneous combustion, a creature sprung whole, like Adam, from Brazil's ochre-colored earth. A short decade later, he vanishes in the mountains, leaving behind five children and a genome packed with energy, enterprise, and productivity, qualities destined to resurface once again—in his grandson.

I have watched today's Gaviolis eat like Italians, argue like Italians, and embrace like Italians—but they are not pure, unalloyed Italians. They contain other ingredients—chunks of German, Portuguese, Lebanese, and native Brazilian—forming a salad tossed and mixed in a Brazilian bowl. To my taste, they're mostly a Caesar salad, thanks to the potent primal ingredient—Felix the First.

A FAMILY MEETING

Like a toggle switch, Pai clicks back and forth between his two ancestries—sometimes German, sometimes Italian. As an Italian, he craves pasta. As a German, he craves sausage. As an Italian, he lies on his recliner and listens to opera, the mournful howlings over broken love, betrayals, and roads not taken. In his Germanic mode, he absorbs the achingly beautiful strains of *"Edelweiss,"* the ode to the little Alpine flower that grows and blooms and blesses its homeland forever. However, on Sunday mornings, he and Sarah turn gaucho, dialing their radio to the interior of Rio Grande do Sul and its herky-jerky accordion folk music.

On the day he decides to assemble all his children for a family meeting, he's the volatile Italian. This will be no ordinary family gathering. He's also an impatient man. Not waiting for life's final moments, when he or Sarah departs for the next world, he will disclose the contents of his will—now! He will reveal who gets what of their worldly goods—the car, the big dark table, their bed, his tools, and above all, the family home as well as three apartment units—one property for each child.

He will conduct this ceremony. Everyone will sit around the big, dark, heavy dining room table. It will be a grand display of his power in the family. It occurs to me that his bold candor and transparency in facing final things take courage. My Minnesota family doesn't face final things openly and head on like this.

This ritual has two purposes. First, he will consign his and Sarah's worldly possessions to his children. Here he will be playing with fire, determining winners and losers. Second—and here's the all-important subtext—he'll dredge up the story of his life. He'll remind his children of the hard road he and Sarah have traveled, not omitting one drop of blood, sweat, or tears shed along the way. This is his opportunity to grieve, to lament, to exorcise pain. All men his age should have this opportunity.

His children have heard pieces of this saga many times. Now they are being summoned to hear the unabridged version. Make no mistake: he will make it crystal clear that the final fruit of this grand struggle is the comfortable life his children now enjoy—and for which they should be grateful.

The ceremony appears charged with drama. I'm really looking forward to it, and watching Pai—by nature an impulsive and eruptive individual—control his emotions in a ceremonial framework. My first exposure to his ceremonial character occurred during my very first hour in his home, at my impromptu family membership ceremony. This ceremony will be different. It will remind his children of life's brevity, of the day their parents will be gone, and likely resurrect old family wounds—hurtful things said and done, helpful things not said and not done. Because these are Gaviolis, and not Martins, this will be a ceremony soaked in memory, sadness, weeping, wailing, possibly ripping of hair and gnashing of teeth.

But alas, it's children who best know their own fathers.

"I will not attend such a meeting," declares Sidnei, the first son, the good son, who inherited composure and deliberation from his mother—certainly not from his father—who, when it comes to family matters, can be a raging bull with pepper under his tail.

"It's laughable," says Davison. He will not attend, either. Also boycotting will be Lori.

No one is eager to hear the sad strains of the violin, the lonely playing of taps.

Daisi, the family peacemaker, also dreads entering this minefield. "He's way too emotional, the meeting would be a disaster." She's right. It will probably produce heartache, spiced with inheritance jealousy.

OCTOBER 2, 1970
Three Years in Brazil

Clearly, the problem with this summit meeting is the one planning it, the master of ceremonies himself. He's known to possess a trick Gavioli heart, which goes haywire under too much emotion. He's too volatile, too nostalgic, too close to Sarah to imagine her gone, too tightly attached to a family he never had as a child.

This is a perfect moment for Buddhist detachment. Buddha could handle this meeting. But Pai is not Buddha. He's more like Shakespeare, he creates theater. Like Shakespeare, he's both director and actor and needs others to join him on stage—his stage—to play out roles he has written for them. But his children refuse to join him onstage. They deny him the opportunity he wants, the permission he needs, to grieve the past and guide the future.

In short, he's way too Italian to pull this off. A better choice would be someone like Abraham Lincoln, or Mother Teresa, or King Solomon. In their absence, the meeting never takes place.

A BIRTH

A ferocious downpour howls outside our apartment window at midnight. I'm propped up in bed, ready to prepare for my university classes tomorrow. We're entering our second year in Brazil and Daisi, seven months pregnant, is resting next to me. She gets up and goes to the bathroom.

She returns. Water is trickling down her thighs onto the floor. What the . . . ? She grabs the book on babies by Doctor Spock, which says something about water bags.

Water bags . . . what are water bags? Where are they? Why are they? The point is, it's past midnight, the wind is howling, the gutters are overflowing, and I have classes to teach tomorrow morning. This seems like an inconvenient time for whatever is happening.

I point to the puddle on the floor. "I think it's pee."

"No, it's not."

I drop to the floor on my hands and knees. Right. It doesn't smell like pee.

"I still think it's pee."

Minutes later, I knock at the door of a couple we know who live directly above us. Maria, a mother of four, opens the door. She's wearing a bathrobe and looks sleepy.

"Water is running down Daisi's legs, but it's probably nothing to worry about, right?"

She observes me for a few seconds in silence, one eye growing larger than the other. *"Por via das dúvidas"* (Just to be on the safe side), she says calmly, "we'll

Pai grows fond of our son Marcus, age one.

drive you both to the hospital."

Her use of the word "hospital" reinforces in me the distinct possibility that this is not happening.

Because we don't have our car today, Maria's husband, Petri, pulls up to the curb in his Volkswagen bug. Holding hands, Daisi and I plunge into the downpour, splashing through puddles to his car.

I'm calm.

The hospital, named *Moinhos de Vento,* or windmill, is located near the top of one of Porto Alegre's biggest hills. I go directly to the reception desk to register Daisi and discover I've forgotten her name. Evidently, there's a little person inside me refusing to check her in, which in this person's twisted logic, will prevent her from having a baby at this inconvenient time when my classes are not yet prepared.

Petri steps forward and provides the receptionist with my wife's name.

I thank him.

Rarely does a neighbor know a husband's wife's name better than the husband himself. But apparently this does happen.

Taken into a room to wait for Daisi, I fall asleep in a chair.

A nurse wakes me at 3:00 a.m. "Do you want to see your child?" In a stupor, I follow her down a long, dim, utterly silent corridor. I stand in front of a dark pane of glass, staring into a pitch-black maternity ward. A tiny blue light shines far back in the inky depths of the ward, like a single star in the night sky. Then, behind the glass and out of the gloom, a ghostly white embodiment

OCTOBER 2, 1970
Three Years in Brazil

gathers shape, as if in a dream. The embodiment turns into a large nurse wearing a white mask, holding something wrapped in a white cloth. She lifts it and places it close to the window, as if offering me something to purchase. His tiny face is red. His eyes are shut.

Maybe this is happening after all.

At 4:00 a.m., Daisi is wheeled into the room and tucked into bed. I approach her bedside. Words fail me. We've never had a child before.

"Congratulations, good job," I say, taking her hand, shaking it. One would think this is the proper form with people whose name you don't know.

Groggy, she nods and says, "Okay."

A half hour later, I call the Gaviolis to announce the blessed news. After many rings at this sleepy hour, the phone is answered by Pai. In my halting Portuguese, I tell him we're at the hospital, and his daughter has given birth to a baby boy, seven weeks early.

After a long silence, he asks me who I am.

Great. Things are going smoothly. First, I forget my wife's name. Now my father-in-law has forgotten who I am.

I repeat the news. Then he says—in perfect English—"Mister Martin, will you repeat that?" This is the first time he has ever spoken to me in English, or called me Mister Martin. He knows more than I thought.

A couple of hours later, at 7:00 a.m. sharp when the hospital opens for visitors, Pai and Sarah enter our room. He positions himself at the foot of Daisi's bed, looking down at her. Sarah sits in a chair.

"*Quando é que ele nasceu?*" (When was he born?) he wants to know. He seems excited.

"Two-thirty this morning," I say.

"*Tem certeza que foi hoje?*" (Are you certain it was today?)

He's getting emotional. His eyes are glistening. Why does he ask this? Of course we're certain. "Yes, we're certain."

"*Já decidiu o nome dele?*" (Have you decided on his name?)

"*Sim,*" I say proudly. "It's Marcus Jeffrey Martin. His middle name is in honor of my only brother."

He draws a deep breath, growing in height and volume.

"*Não, não pode ser!*" (No, this cannot be!) "His name must be Marcus *Gavioli* Martin—because he was born today, May 25, my birthday."

I'm speechless. Did this actually happen? Then I start feeling irritated. Now I'm angry. Listen here Mister, I'm thinking, your birthday is one thing. You've had many. But right now, the birth of our son—a first for us—seems infinitely more important. Okay, Jim, calma, calma. Let's think this through. But then again, I think, how come you're butting in? Can't we name our own kid?

I struggle to prevent these thoughts from reaching my tongue.

He stands at the foot of Daisi's bed like a statue, feet spread, apparently bolted to the floor. His face resolute, jaw clenched, eyes wet with emotion, he waits for our response.

Like me, Daisi's flustered. The moment passes with no decision.

Then there's a flurry of Portuguese. They kiss Daisi on both cheeks, they congratulate me, and leave.

Daisi," I say angrily, "doesn't it seem outrageous for him to name our son after himself? This is what kings did in the Dark Ages."

"Yes, I know, but if we refuse, he'd never forget it. It would be a wound that would never heal."

Whew, Jim, Jim my boy . . . take a deep breath . . . okay, it's not the end of the world. The only thing you've lost is the right to name your own son. This honor belongs to your father-in-law.

Next day we learn it's actually Brazilian custom for a child to have the wife's family name, as well as the husband's. Turns out he's right. He's right again. He's always right. And I'm always wrong.

Later that morning, after faking my way through classes at the university, I rush back to the hospital to see Daisi and our new baby.

It's closed. The door is locked. They won't let me in. They tell me to return at visiting hours.

Outraged, I run around the building, scoop up stones and throw them at Daisi's second-floor window. I shout pathetically, "Daisi! Daisi! They won't let me in!" She comes to the window, looks down at her wreck of a husband, and says there's nothing she can do.

This isn't Brazil. This is Nazi Germany.

As months go by, Pai grows very attached to Marcus. After supper one evening at Pai's house, I see him holding in front of my infant son's open mouth a heaping spoonful of white sugar. This is his version of love and affection.

"*Pai, não faz isso!*" (Pai, don't do that!) I blurt out.

Holding the spoon in midair, he turns to me.

"The sugar will ruin his teeth," I say, even though Marcus has no teeth. My sharp protest to Pai surprises even myself.

Fixing me in an icy stare, his reply comes slowly and coldly: "*Quando está na sua casa"* (When he's in your house), "feed him what you wish. When he's in mine, I will do the same."

The load of sugar goes in.

Wonderful. Another reminder that I'm in his castle, where he's lord and I'm the vassal. The gap between us opens even wider than before—a chasm in age, profession, wealth, home ownership, social rank, family status, will power . . . He's superior in every important category. Sidnei calls him *"O Cacique,"* meaning Indian chief, also referring to ruthless political bosses in the Amazon.

He's the man. I'm still a mere boy. This is hard to bear.

Hey Jim, just jump up, slam the door and walk the couple miles back to your apartment! This will sting him and give me great pleasure. Oh yeah, that's right, now I remember. It's not really my apartment after all. He owns it. It's part of his castle, part of the realm.

Open your eyes, Jimmy Boy. You're part of the family now, and the price of admission is a bunch of strings tied to you at one end and tied to him at the other. You're a puppet and he's the puppet master.

I yearn for the day I can cut these strings.

But hey, for the first time you spoke up to him! You challenged him, yanked one of the strings!

For the three seconds it lasted, it felt good.

WITCHCRAFT

In addition to his will power, Brazil contains other forces, magical forces. One morning on my walk down the hill to the university, in the dead-center middle of a quiet intersection, I come upon scattered feathers and the bloody remains of a chicken. Next to it is a puddle of wax, once a candle, surrounded by red and white tissue paper sprinkled with kernels of corn.

What the heck is this? It feels scary. I've heard about these sacrifices. They're either a curse, or possibly a blessing, invoking good or evil powers to bend fate in someone's favor. Cars and pedestrians avoid this ritual slaughter, which eventually is scattered by birds, dogs, and mice into the spirit world.

It's a *"despacho,"* Pai tells me, a word apparently related to the English "dispatch." He says they're often located in "power spots," like crossroads or waterfalls, and are gifts to a personal deity offering thanks, or protection, or requesting a favor.

"É comum, não te preocupes" (Don't worry, they're normal). Okay, fine, but Pai comes from Europeans. He seems out of touch with Brazil's widespread

African influence, and may not know what inscrutable things are going on here.

Even though the witchcraft from these mystical little piles—which sometimes contain liquor, flowers, fruit, and cigars—are intended for people I don't know, I find them unsettling.

Some days later, a woman in the apartment next to ours screams in horror. I rush into the hall. She's shrieking and pointing down at the threshold to her apartment. Nestled there, in the crack between her door sill and the hallway, are little bubbles of mercury. This is a curse. The woman, who's from Piaui, a small, poor, and desolate state in northern Brazil, whimpers and trembles at this wickedness someone has laid at her doorstep.

The silvery bubbles, like evil eyes, are impossible to pick up by hand. With the edge of a sheet of paper, I carefully guide the droplets, which are breaking into smaller ones, onto another sheet of paper. I slowly carry them into our apartment toward a wastebasket. The sinister little beads roll angrily about on the paper, trying to fall off and curse us, too.

A FINANCIAL SYSTEM

Witchcraft is actually a prominent feature of the Gavioli family. It's called money. One day I ask Daisi's brother Davison to loan me twenty dollars. Davison has a slender face, a sharp nose, and, like his father, a cunning eye that sees things I don't.

"No problem," he says.

"Great, I'll repay you as soon as I can."

"No, don't pay me. Pay Aunt Cecilia."

"Why Aunt Cecilia?"

"Jim, isso é simples" (Jim, this is simple). He tells me to sit down. He explains that I should pay Aunt Cecilia to help him pay for his VW bug that Daisi and I use during the week, which isn't actually his. It's Aunt Cecilia's. She pays the monthly installments and loans it to him permanently, as long as he drives her wherever she needs to go, which, because of her stroke, is virtually nowhere.

Daisi and I use the car Monday through Friday and pay the gas and insurance. He has it on weekends. Okay, it's tricky, but I get it.

Evidently, for a Gavioli, repaying the one you owe is a backward, slow-witted practice lacking style and sophistication. Repayment always goes to someone else, someone completely unrelated to the original loan. I pay twenty dollars to Aunt Cecilia, because I'm borrowing the car he borrows from her on a forever basis. Fortunately, the loan involves only Davison, Aunt Cecilia and me.

Wrong. The next day, Pai tells me that *Sidnei,* not Davison, will loan me the twenty dollars.

"How do you know I need twenty dollars?"

"Todo mundo sabe" (Everyone knows), he says, surprised I don't.

Apparently, all Gaviolis know the financial condition of all other Gaviolis. This is because money doesn't belong to anyone in particular, it moves around within the family like minnows in a pond. The Gaviolis have developed a tight-knit financial system, bound by a complicated web of mutual debt. It's like the International Monetary Fund, only more complex.

The system begins and ends with one simple fact: all Gaviolis are indebted to all other Gaviolis. Their system, like a Swiss clock, has hundreds of moving parts, possibly thousands. For example, I will borrow twenty dollars ostensibly from Davison, who owes money on a car owned by Aunt Cecilia, who owes grocery money to Pai, who, in a cash-flow pinch, has borrowed from Sidnei. Repayment follows the same path. I'll pay Cecilia, who will repay Pai, who in turn will repay Sidnei, who will have loaned me the money for Davison, who now owes Sidnei.

It's stunningly simple.

Like a fly caught in a spider web, my loan jiggles the entire netting. It attracts attention from all linked to the family ledger. Which is everyone.

This ledger, by the way, is invisible. You can't see it, touch it, hear it, smell it, or taste it. It exists solely in the labyrinthian monetary mind of the Gaviolis. It's a glue that bonds the whole family, a form of dark matter, which science believes holds the universe together.

Because my loan request touches everyone, it's subject to extensive family review and opinion, including whether I really need the twenty dollars in the first place.

Eventually, I do manage to obtain the twenty bucks, apparently from Sidnei, but I'm not completely certain. No one mentioned any of this when I received my family membership.

SEPARATION

The day I arrived almost three years ago, I was fairly emptied out. I was married, but had no job, no house, no car, no children. Now some of that emptiness has filled in. I'm a part-time teacher and a father. I possess two keys: one for a borrowed car and the other for a borrowed apartment for which we pay Pai a hundred dollars almost every month. I've also picked up a working knowledge of his "language of the people." I'm no longer completely lost, but I'm not fully found, either. I'm giving Brazil my best shot. Sometimes I even think Pai silently acknowledges this, but maybe not. He's silent on issues of achievement.

Pai also is giving his best shot—to keep us here. He and Sarah provide us with an apartment, child care, meals anytime, and help navigating Brazilian bureaucracy. He and his family are always there for us, a subsidy impossible to repay, and which cannot last.

Daisi and I decide Minnesota offers a better financial future. The combined income of a teacher and social worker don't sustain a Brazilian middle-class life, which, by the way, I now accept and desire, no longer keen on toying with poverty as we did traveling to Brazil.

"You're a momma's boy," a friend tells me one evening at a party. "You have to return to momma."

This stings, but in some ways he's right. I miss Minnesota. I'm unskilled in juggling two or three jobs at once to survive, as Brazilian teachers are forced to do. Plus, I'm sure I'll do better where I no longer squirm under Pai's thick thumb.

As our departure draws near, Daisi is already feeling *saudade,* a mix of sentiments peculiar to Brazilians, an aching blend of nostalgia, fondness, homesickness and loss. Portugal's sixteenth-century poet, Camões, described the past as *"tempos idos e vividos"* (times lived and gone). If this were music, it would be a weeping violin. Unlike Americans, who believe the past is past and would rather move on, Brazilians don't let go of the past easily. They recall it, savor it, relive it.

I fear dissolving in the juices of *saudade,* something Pai and other Brazilians don't fear and somehow seem stronger for. I avoid its depths, preferring shallower emotional waters. But despite my best efforts, even before we're gone, I'm starting to miss the Gaviolis.

For Daisi, cutting lifelong ties to her family, friends, city, country, and language is a sea change. It's a decision that contains surrender, abandonment, and, to be effective, a touch of renunciation. When she gets to Minnesota, she'll probably need to practice resignation.

For her, it's more painful than I imagined. For several nights in a row, leading up to our departure, she has a series of frightening dreams. She describes them to me each morning, and they're always the same. Night after night, a friend, holding a knife, pursues her from room to room through a large house, trying to kill her.

Each night it's a different friend. One night it's Ozomar. The next night it's

OCTOBER 2, 1970
Three Years in Brazil

Ozomar's sister Benita. Then it's Dionema. Then Fanny. Then Liana.

In terror, she flees from these attackers, her best friends, running from one room to the next, lost and disoriented in the immense house, which may resemble the one I lived in when we first met. The dreams appear with such regularity that she dreads going to sleep at night.

Maybe leaving Brazil is the wrong decision.

Then one night she's chased by Jaci, an Afro-Brazilian kid from the slums of Porto Alegre, whom Daisi has provided with social work counseling. Of all the youngsters she counsels, Jaci is her favorite, an adolescent who is showing early signs of becoming a gifted wood sculptor. But this dream is different. As he chases her, she summons her courage, turns to face him, then shoots him with a revolver. He's wounded, but he doesn't die.

The nightmares end.

I suspect she feels guilty abandoning her friends, who may view her departure as a betrayal. But in the end, she turns to face her fears. I begin to wonder what sort of wound our departure may be opening.

Meanwhile, I've come up short. I've failed to sink deep roots in Brazil, failed to establish permanent life with the Gaviolis despite all they've done for me. I'm sure this is what he thinks. He probably questions my work ethic and, by extension, our marriage, and by further extension, me as a decent human being. But he's silent on these matters.

I dread our leave-taking for these reasons, and for yet another reason: Pai is a man of considerable stagecraft. He creates ceremony. He magnifies the drama and poignancy of beginnings and endings, and is capable of lifting them to scary heights. It's precisely this power that spooks me.

The day of farewell takes place after lunch under a blue January sky beneath the gnarled scrub tree in front of his house. My plan is simple. I'll bestow upon him a grand and gracious thank-you for all his help over the past three years, and assure him that we'll return soon. When that will be, I have no idea. Probably not so soon. But I won't say this. What words should I use? Obviously, in bidding farewell to a father-in-law, the precise words are important. And because of their importance, they'll surely come to me. I'll rise to the occasion.

However, if parting words fail me, my consolation is that over the past three years, I've done my best. At least I think so. Okay, maybe I've not done enough. But it's what I could do.

I wonder which of his two natures, the Italian or the German, will show up? My hope is for a cool, German, businesslike emotional temperature, the one we use in Minnesota. This will help me leave him in smooth Scandinavian style.

My fear is he'll go Italian on me.

We face each other in the shade of his old tree on his broken sidewalk. I'm tongue-tied. We glance around the neighborhood, averting eyes. Suddenly, his eyes mist up and he slams me into a powerful embrace.

In swift Portuguese, he says, "Jim, I'm very happy Daisi is with you, and I know you'll do well, and that you'll do well for her in Minnesota."

I wrap my arms around his broad shoulders. His big stomach presses against me. The familiar chasm between us is gone. Everything I planned to say is caught deep in my throat.

"Obrigado" (Thank you), I whisper.

The embrace lasts an eternity, and as it goes on and on, I begin to feel its fullness, and its emptiness. I can feel him releasing his daughter, releasing his cherished grandson Marcus, approving our marriage, and, incredibly, even approving a son-in-law who's taking all this from him.

Almost lost within the jumble of these feelings, I sense deep inside me the faint existence of a man who wasn't there when I arrived three years ago.

He continues, at a lower temperature. "Jim, you probably wouldn't make a good living in Brazil anyway. Our economy is unpredictable. This country requires *jeitinho*, something you don't have—improvising, living by your wits. You'll do better in a stable economy."

This is generous. He blames our departure not entirely on me but partially on Brazil itself, particularly its unpredictable economy. I manage to choke out an assurance that we will meet again, as soon as events allow. *"Se Deus quiser,"* (God willing) I say, which is how Brazilians always cast the future, even though, as a Unitarian, I lack a personal god looking down upon me. But it feels right to say this to him now, holding a higher power responsible for meeting again. Besides, I need all the higher powers that might be available in dealing with Pai.

Our embrace finally unlocks. I force myself to look directly into his face, which, to my dismay, I can barely see. It's veiled by my own tears, as if looking through a windshield in a downpour. Actually, my windshield is cracked and the rain is coming in. His grief has broken through my defenses.

How idiotic to think I could coolly and rationally bid him farewell. This is what happens when one gets too close to Pai Gavioli.

OCTOBER 2, 1970
Three Years in Brazil

He drives us to the airport, which, when we arrive, feels like a funeral parlor. Something has died. Our faces turn away, eyes don't meet, hands hide themselves in pockets, shoes kick nothing in particular on the airport floor.

At last, a voice on a loudspeaker summons us to our gate. Pai's cup of emotion overflows again. His Italian tears sweep like a deluge over my Scandinavian seawalls. It's a law of nature that when Pai breaks down, everyone breaks down. With him, there's no holding back.

We show our tickets and move toward a doorway. Before going through it, I turn and wave. He turns away. A door closes behind us.

In Miami, we're greeted by my brother, Jeff. In the cab on our way to the hotel, I notice how Miami's highways are broad, smooth, and quiet, with king-sized automobiles moving like great fish drifting toward unknown appointments. This is not the darting, honking, helter-skelter, aggressive Brazilian traffic.

The next day, a cold January Minnesota rushes back at me, almost obliterating Brazil, already breaking apart in memory, just as three years ago Minnesota melted in the hot, all-consuming immediacy of Brazil.

Brazil and Minnesota are different planets. And Brazil has many advantages. It has the Atlantic Ocean; we have Lake Nokomis. Brazil has curvaceous Latinate Portuguese; we have plainspoken English. Brazil has a blinding noonday sun; we have a pale disc over a cold horizon. Brazil has the ubiquitous hibiscus; soon we'll have the ubiquitous dandelion. Brazil has mammoth butterflies; we have the ladybug. Brazil has the corner bakery and its chatty owner, his arm around my shoulder, sharing with me his despair of government and his out-of-control children; we have the donut vending machine.

Clearly, our marriage is again at a crossroads. Here in Minnesota, the balance of responsibility in making everything work well tips toward me. I promise myself I'll do all within my power to help transplant my tropical wife into my frozen earth.

1973-1977

Transplanted

When we arrive in January, Daisi points out some defects in Minnesota I'd not noticed before. Like winter is really cold. And really dark. And that it lasts almost forever. And neighbors don't speak to us. Well, yeah, it's winter. Neighbors don't speak until spring. I thought everyone knew that.

Just as her parents housed and helped us in Porto Alegre, mine do the same for us in Saint Paul. They buy a triplex and rent the first floor to us. As in Brazil, it takes us about six months to start paying rent.

I get a job teaching English at a private school in Minneapolis. When spring arrives, Daisi gets her first-ever driver's license. Then she gets a job recruiting volunteers to tutor disadvantaged kids.

Eighteen months pass. Daisi's pregnant again. One day, carrying a large platter of food from the kitchen to the dining room, her oversized belly blocks her vision and she trips over a board I had placed in the doorway to keep our new puppy in the kitchen. She hits the floor and breaks her water bag. That darn water bag again! Always breaking.

When Daisi and our second son, André, arrive from the hospital, my back goes out. I go to bed. Still weak from childbirth, Daisi takes care of André (four-days old), Marcus (three-years old), our new puppy (three-weeks old), and me (thirty-four-years old).

Four months later, we take another step toward adulthood: we buy a house. Now we have two jobs, two sons, one car, one house, and one dog. We're firmly middle class, a position in life that only six years ago, traveling to Brazil and admiring the virtues of poverty, seemed crushingly tedious. Now however, considering Pai—his struggle to buy a house, his respect for education, his hard-work ethic, his saving for the future, his relentless climb up the ladder—the middle class doesn't seem that bad. Another chip of my boyish naiveté falls off.

Except for an occasional, expensive long-distance phone call, our only contact with Brazil is through letters. Sarah writes once a month. Pai never writes; it's too emotional for him, Daisi says.

At school, I'm in conflict with the headmaster over the school newspaper. One day he calls me into his office and chews me out for allowing a front-page story about student smoking and drinking. We have different goals. He wants to sell the school to parents. I want freedom of student expression.

Teaching grows oppressive, uncreative. Some days I hate going to school.

I feel sorry for myself. Then I remember him, a working-class guy who throws himself into his labors, who attacks the job and works swiftly. If he can't finish it quickly, he just grinds it out. Grind and grind and grind until it's done. Pretty simple. He gives me courage to face the day.

But I can't take it any longer. After three years at this school, I quit. I want to be a writer.

We haven't seen the Gaviolis in four years. We save enough to buy four expensive plane tickets, but the day before we're about to leave, a job offer Daisi had just accepted is retracted. We board the aircraft carrying two children, a mortgage, and no jobs.

As I gaze down at clouds below me, I feel more ready for Brazil than I was seven years ago. At thirty-seven, I'm no longer a boy. Daisi and I have each passed the five milestones to adulthood: leave home, finish school, start work, get married, and start a family.

I'm eager to get a job writing. All I need are qualifications, experience, direction, confidence, and authenticity.

JANUARY 1977
A Torrid Welcome

Stepping off the aircraft, my shoes sink into a soft, hot tarmac. Brazil is stunningly hot, brilliant, and humid after a cold, dark, and snowy Minnesota, the memory of which is already curling and fading like an old photo on fire.

Walking across the tarmac to the terminal, I see people on a balcony waiting to greet arrivals. Suddenly, among them, there he is, arms raised like Richard Nixon's when he boarded an aircraft to leave the presidency in disgrace. But unlike Nixon's, Pai's arms are raised in triumph. He's welcoming us back.

I begin to feel a tingle of excitement in my belly, the old promise, still unfulfilled, that Brazil, like a big-hearted sun, will ripen my apple.

The whole Gavioli family is here, a wild blur of laughing, shouting, teasing, hugs, and backslaps, spiced with insults at our heavy Minnesota clothes and snow-white skin. The loudest and craziest is Daisi's younger brother, Davison, who has driven twenty hours on dangerous roads from São Paulo to be here.

Daisi embraces her father, whose cheeks are wet. *"Não chora pai, não chora"* (Don't cry, Dad, don't cry). *"Lágrimas de alegria minha filha, lágrimas de alegria"* (They're tears of happiness, my daughter, tears of happiness). His hair is whiter and his belly's still portly. Despite the heat, he's wearing a white shirt, dark tie, slacks, and suit coat.

Then he sweeps our sons up in his arms. André, age two, has never seen Pai, and Marcus, now five, hasn't seen him for four years. He holds them, one at a time, high in the air, like trophies. Suspended up above the airport crowd in his big hands, their faces have a wide-eyed, startled look, not aware that for him, children are life's most precious gift.

Then he grabs me in a sweaty bear hug, tighter and longer than a Minnesotan can handle. I feel his energy pulsing through his shirt and suit coat, almost more than my small Scandinavian-made transformer can handle, an energy that seems to have been building for four years.

Soon we're in his car, moving swiftly through blast-furnace heat shimmering off the asphalt. We arrive at his modest, wooden house, now painted green, topped with its ochre tile roof.

At the front door, he turns to me and says, in Spanish: *"La casa es suya,"* which means, "The house is yours." But in Portuguese, suya means "filthy," as in, "Our house is filthy." It's one of his favorite puns.

Once inside, I say, "Pai, it's hot. Relax. Take off your suit, be informal."

A frown darkens his face. He's suddenly serious. *"Não, esta é uma ocasião séria"* (No, this is a serious occasion). For him, our return, after an absence of four long years, requires formality. The suit stays on.

But not for long. Shirt off, thick white hair on his tan chest, he chases Marcus and André between tables and chairs, inflicting himself upon them.

As usual, he's on the offensive. He pokes, he tickles, he teases without mercy. He's a boisterous, provocative, pudgy giant bent on squeezing a reaction out of our little people. Any reaction will do—frustration, anger, tears—he doesn't seem to care. He's testing their tiny souls. Like he tests mine. Like he tests everybody's.

"Isto é o Brazil!" (This is Brazil!) he roars into their astonished little faces. *"Isto não é a neve pálida de Minnesota!"* (This isn't the pale snow of Minnesota!) Then he stabs me with a piercing glance, a sharp reminder of how we've abandoned him for four years.

For a fleeting moment, with his exuberance, joy, embraces, and tears of welcome—like the big-hearted sun that could ripen my apple—he *is* Brazil. The boys have no idea how to respond to their fireball of a grandfather. Nor do I.

I thought this was going to be a vacation.

His teasing goes on too long. He's overdoing it. I'm getting annoyed. I'm on the verge of asking him to tone down the exhilaration, which is like asking the sun, please don't rise in the east today. But alas, this is his house, his turf, and his appalling way of welcoming his grandchildren to Brazil. With Pai, you have to accept the whole package. He doesn't come in parts. So I hold my tongue and the teasing goes on.

The next day he gives us three hundred dollars in Brazilian currency to spend as we wish. *"Seu dinheiro não vale no Brasil"* (Your money is worthless in Brazil). By this, I am reminded that we're family, and therefore subject to his generosity.

Great. Right off the bat I'm in debt to him again. Why do I feel his generosity is paternalism in disguise? As usual, I accept his magnanimity, but not him. At least not completely. Yes, I'm aware of my low, mean feelings toward him and find them distasteful, especially because he maintains a remarkable forbearance toward me, which, when I think about it, is extraordinary for a father-in-law. Especially this one. When he was a boy, the door to his family was slammed in his face. And yet he opens the door to me. Furthermore, none of this seems to matter. I can't help feeling ticked off at him, and too ashamed to tell Daisi.

THE PINNACLE

Last year, after nearly fifty years of hard work, Pai retired. He bought a cottage in Santa Terezinha, a tiny seaside village two hours north by car from Porto Alegre. It's one of maybe a hundred such bungalows sprinkled throughout the little resort town. His one-level, two-bedroom, cinder-block cottage is capped with a carrot-colored tile roof, as are all the others. The roof flattens out on two sides, like the brim of a hat, shading a wide L-shaped veranda that has a shiny dark red-tile floor, and two hammocks hung from the concrete pillars that support the roof. A small indoor garage with a ceramic floor doubles as a dining room for family feasts.

Like the unpretentious little town itself, this simple cottage, perched comfortably on its sandy soil, isn't going anywhere. It sits at the corner of two unassuming roads, grass sprouting between their cobblestones. There are no signposts, possibly because the roads have no names.

Surrounding the cottage on all sides is tough, thick grass that absorbs the sun's heat and helps cool the house. Facing the two roads is an L-shaped brick wall, about knee high, whose sole purpose in life is to define the humble property. Beyond the wall at the streets are curbs made of granite slabs that will outlast mortals for centuries.

Across one road is an empty plot where a neighbor's brown horse, tied to a rope, has its head down munching grass. At night, the horse beds down in the cool grass, which springs to life with hundreds of frogs. These are like the philosophical creatures I heard in Porto Alegre seven years ago, who sing out in unison life's deepest question—in English, for me—"Why? Why? Why?" Probably this time they want to know why jobless refugees from Minnesota are here. Marcus calls back to them with a child's simple answer: "Because! Because! Because!" He's right. It's because four years have been too many away from Daisi's family.

The beach is an easy two-block stroll away. It's a broad, featureless expanse of honey-colored sand stretching virtually the entire length of the state's Atlantic shoreline. This beach, as are all in Brazil, is public land, held in trust for all Brazilians. Long, wide, and straight, the beach is raked endlessly by waves from the open sea. The sea changes daily. Sometimes it's like coffee and cream, stirring up sand. Other times it's transparent, the tips of its waves like light-green lime juice. Wealthy Brazilians don't come to Santa Terezinha. For them, its flat sand,

These paintings by Sarah, a somber person who never had lessons, portray harmony and balance, and express a joy of movement denied to her by polio.

JANUARY 1977
A Torrid Welcome

stretching beyond where the eye can see, offers the tedium of a midwestern prairie without the grass. The elite go to Santa Catarina, the next state north, whose lovely coves, giant black boulders, and gentle surf are as far from humble Santa Terezinha as heaven is from earth.

But for me, this is paradise, fifty times better than Lake Nokomis.

Sarah never goes to the beach, whose sand doesn't support her bent ankles. She stays in the cottage, moving slowly among its five rooms, supported by the *andador* (walker), her four-legged aluminum companion, corroded by sea salt and spotted with kitchen grease. On the living room wall are three oil paintings she did years ago. They feature happy children in brightly colored clothing, leaping and suspended in the air, each bent backward almost in a half circle—evoking a physical joy that childhood polio denied to her.

Sarah resigns herself to five months of confinement in these five unhurried rooms as a change of scene, but mostly as a duty to her husband.

Santa Terezinha is where Pai feels on the top of the world. Here, he reports to no one. He does simple things: watching children play in the sand, chatting with neighbors, touching up the paint of his cottage. His only hobby is cooking. With time and ingredients on his hands, he produces pizzas, churrasco, and *pastéis*, little pastries filled with ground beef, garlic, onions, and olives. Feeding his own stomach, and the stomachs of visiting family members, is his joy, his reason to exist.

I awake one morning feeling a need for privacy. I find it at a table in a quiet space in Pai's cottage garage. I settle down and begin penning intimate thoughts into my journal—how my life is an untidy thing, full of unfinished business, and unreached goals—when he discovers me.

"Aqui que tu estás!" (Here you are!) he exclaims, as if he's been looking all over for me, delighted to rescue me from my solitude. He flops down loudly on a yellow plastic couch and releases a tremendous sigh. *"Ahh,"* he says, *"não tenho certeza se isso é a vida que pedi a Deus"* (I'm not quite sure this is the life I requested from God).

Clad only in swim trunks and flip-flops, he sprawls on the couch as if he owned it. Which he does. His skin, thanks to months in the sun, is a surprisingly deep, rich ochre, the color of his tile roof. Daintily held between his large thumb and thick index finger, is a tiny cup of *cafezinho,* strong, sweet, and black. He sips it with visible pleasure.

I drop my pen with a clatter on the table, annoyed at the interruption. He ignores this and expansively surveys his garage, sighs once more and begins his familiar what-a-hard-life routine.

"I'm really not quite sure this is the life I asked for," he says again. I close my eyes, plunk my elbows down on the table, and drop my jaw into my hands, resigning myself to another installment in his endless series of lessons on the good life.

"For instance, tomorrow at nine sharp I gotta go to the beach." He shakes his head, as if depressed at this chore. "And then I gotta barbecue chicken . . . and then I gotta eat the chicken." He grows silent, looking at his white ceiling, his mind-numbing flowered wall tiles. I wait for him to continue. He no longer seems to notice I'm here.

He shifts into a deeper gear. He pronounces three words slowly and distinctly: *"Trabalhei quarenta e oito anos"* (I worked for forty-eight years). His eyes dart this way and that, memories apparently flashing through his brain. *"Quarenta e oito anos,"* he repeats, curling his lips defiantly, as if he's survived, and prevailed, in a long guerilla war, a war that's shaped him into the hungry, crafty, and oppressive individual he is.

I know that it wasn't until he reached the fruitful years of his late fifties that he started winning this war. That's when he finally became entrenched in Brazil's hard-to-enter, but easy-to-exit, middle class. The middle class, plus the tiny number of elite who enjoy spectacular wealth and privilege, sit upon a vast mass below, people living in often-appalling poverty. That multitude below is where his journey began. I'm probably going to get an earful of this now.

I also know, because he's told me many times, that it wasn't until near the end of his long economic war that he was able to furnish his war chest: three small condominium units (one in which Daisi and I lived for three years) that provided him modest rental income. This was shrewd; in Brazil, real estate is safer than money saved, since the military government raises salaries to keep up with rising prices, riddling the economy with inflation.

Here he sits, on his plastic couch, victorious, living in a manner he says he never dared imagine. He's healthy. He's strong. He's nestled here in his little brick castle by the sea, freely sharing with me his personal fulfillment at reaching this pinnacle on his journey. I must admit his flower is blossoming.

But why that snarl on his lips? For him, living well almost seems to be a form of revenge. Yes, that's it. Revenge on those who shamed him and rejected him.

Then his face softens. *"Gosto deste lugar"* (I like this place). He glances about his garage, taking in his tools neatly tucked into boxes cunningly suspended over the door, his boxy orange Ford that fits with barely inches to spare on all sides. "I like what's mine. I don't know why, but I like it. I never thought I'd be able to own a little place like this."

More silence. His eyes grow moist. Uh-oh, here comes the sentimental Italian again.

I, too, remain silent, caught off guard by his intimacy and depth of feeling. Brazilians will do this. They open their personal doors and windows, while we Scandinavianized Minnesotans shut them to conserve heat.

Stretched out on his plastic couch, the proud owner of a bang-up belly, he basks in his memories. I try to picture him, this sturdy oak of a man, as he must have once been, sixty years ago, a fragile green shoot sprouting from an acorn, struggling to grow in stony ground. Imagination fails me. The toddler he once was is lost forever.

As for me, I will never be a rugged oak.

Now he sits erect on the couch, lost in reverie, hands folded in his lap, like a worshipper in a church pew, his head steady, eyes looking inward deep into memory's well. Whatever he sees down there seems to satisfy him. Brazil, like the United States, is a country where the most humble, with effort, can move up the ladder. However, in Brazil, the effort must be great.

As I look at him, surrounded by his fulfillment, his seaside retirement bungalow, I consider myself to be the perfect Not Him. If I were candid I would say to him, "Pardon me. Unlike you, I'm still preparing, not yet fully a man." I might add that I'm derived from different stock. I've inherited only trace amounts of your character—the ambition, exuberance, shrewdness, and determination that form the genetic jumble shaping your destiny. Moreover, you have something else I don't—a deep wound. Poet Robert Bly has said, "No one gets to adulthood without a wound that goes to the core."

I'm quite free of wounds. I'm a floater, a surface person, a mere scribbler in journals. I may never be as grounded as he is. May never reach true adulthood.

Then, a consoling thought. Whatever my seed, whatever grain I've come from—certainly not the acorn, but possibly a seed of grass, pea in a pod, tulip bulb—I wish to be it fully. I wish to be as authentic as the sturdy oak firmly planted here on the plastic couch he's bought and paid for. At the very least, time is on my side.

On occasion, a short, distinguished-looking man wearing glasses walks by Pai's cottage and waves. Pai smiles politely, but doesn't wave back.

One day, following a town meeting concerning Santa Terezinha's vague municipal boundaries, Pai is holding forth before a small group of listeners. The distinguished-looking man approaches him and asks whether he might have a word. *"Claro"* (Certainly), Pai says. Then the man says he prefers to speak with him in his, the distinguished man's, house. Pai is a gregarious individual. He speaks with everyone in this little town—street cleaners, butchers, priests, and even young men he suspects are thieves. Pai eyes the distinguished man carefully, turns his back on him and resumes his former conversation. The distinguished man walks away.

STREET SCHOOL

One day, I ask Pai about his earlier life. *"Não tem nada para dizer"* (There's nothing to say), is his stock reply. But sometimes, without my asking, pieces of his youth fall from him, like ice off a glacier. Some things I already know. He was rejected by his father. Shunned by his uncle and the other Gaviolis. No financial support from his impoverished mother. At fifteen, he left her for a risky independence. He received no education in higher things, such as music, art, literature. His education was down close to the ground, focused on life's fundamentals. His classroom was the street, where he was schooled in alertness, cunning, avoidance, opportunism, perceptiveness. The street taught self-reliance of the hard and sharp variety, along with a sense of existential danger.

When I was that age, my high school offered nothing in these subjects. My greatest challenges were homework and jump shots.

Remarkably, Pai doesn't succumb to rejection. Instead, he takes hold of it. With fierce energy, he avoids taking a path toward delinquency, choosing hard work instead, wanting to make something of his life.

At age fifteen, he says, he finds work as an office boy. He's entrusted with carrying documents, messages, and money among various office buildings in Porto Alegre's downtown financial district. I've seen these buildings, lovely, ornate colonial-style structures, including banks, the post office, the customs office at the edge of the Guaíba River, the revenue building, and others. His job as a courier, done mostly online today, allows him to send small sums to Amanda in São Paulo, supplementing her thin earnings as a housekeeper.

Carrying a cash payment to an office one day, he encounters a crowd at the

JANUARY 1977
A Torrid Welcome

cashier's window. Because forming lines and waiting one's turn is not instinctual for Brazilians, the young Pai fights his way to the front and manages to submit the payment. Later that day, he discovers he received more change from the cashier than he should have. He returns, but the cashier's window is closed for the day. "I need to see the cashier," he tells the guard. The guard refuses to let him in the building. "It's personal business." Because Brazilians tend to respect the personal over the institutional, the guard lets him in. Pai returns the money. The cashier is so impressed with this extraordinary honesty, that from that time forward, Pai is told to come only after closing time, when the cashier will open the window for him, and him only.

Pai shares this instructive nugget with me as a lesson in virtue, a tale he's polished over the years and hammered into his children. When I was a boy, my father told me how young Honest Abe Lincoln had trudged miles through snow to return pennies to a customer who had been overcharged. I was impressed.

But perhaps not enough. One day, I filch three ten-cent comic books from a corner drugstore. Months later, at the dinner table, I mention this peccadillo, and glance at my father, expecting him to approve my cleverness. Unexpectedly, his spine stiffens. His face grows dark and angry. He orders me to leave dinner and return the thirty cents to Harold the druggist. NOW!

With head hung low, I drag myself to the drugstore. Harold is working the soda fountain. I sit on a stool and confess the crime I committed several months earlier. I put thirty cents on the counter. Harold looks at me, then at the quarter and the nickel. He turns away to make a malted milk for a customer. For a couple of minutes, he says nothing to me. Then, without saying anything, he turns to me and puts his finger on the quarter and slides it toward himself. Then he puts his finger on the nickel and slides it toward me—my reward for honesty.

The point is, three of us boys—Abraham Lincoln, Pai, and me—all virtuously return money that isn't ours. The only difference is that my money was stolen and I hated to return it.

Pai had no such family dinner table to guide him. With no parents and no other family support, except for boarding with his older brother, Rui, in Porto Alegre, Pai has to grow up quickly. Rejection from the Gaviolis settles into his soul as an irritant, a grain of sand in an oyster. He spends his days coating it over and over, until it becomes the pearl of his ambition to legitimize himself in the eyes of the world. It's the spur to his self-creation. He becomes, more than anyone I know, a self-made man.

After some years, Amanda moves to Porto Alegre, still confined to her station in life as a domestic servant, living in the back rooms of those whom she serves. Ironically, it's during this time that all four members of what once was the Gavioli family—Augusto, Amanda, Rui, and Pai—are living in Porto Alegre at the same time. Except for the brothers, they live there in separate locations.

Over time, Pai loses contact with Rui, who gets married, fathers children, and buys a small amusement park, which has a merry-go-round, roller coaster and small Ferris Wheel. Later, Rui sells the park, buys a bar, and descends into drink.

FEBRUARY 1981

A Painful Chat

In Minnesota, Daisi and I each find work, Daisi as a social worker, and I as an editor at a regional government agency. After four years, we save up enough to be able to visit Porto Alegre.

We arrive to find good political news. The military dictatorship is allowing more openness, making room for the formation of a new political party, the Workers' Party. It's headed by a young labor organizer, Luiz Inácio Lula Da Silva, known as Lula, along with liberation theology advocates and others.

Because he has a collection of hats, I bring Pai a multicolored beanie. It sports a battery-powered propeller on top that spins in a whimsical attempt to lift him off the ground. Wherever he finds children, he turns on the propeller. He has a weakness for battery-powered gadgets, which he sees as symptoms of technological progress.

His collection includes a cowboy hat from Minneapolis, a Russian fur cap my father gave him, a wool cap from northern Minnesota with ear flaps against cold unimaginable to Brazilians, a cone-shaped Chinese straw hat used by rice harvesters given by our son André, plus lots of baseball-style caps. He pays particular attention to where each cap is made, connecting him with a world that's mushrooming from local to global in his lifetime.

He collects others things, too, like his pins for perfect attendance at Lions Club meetings. He also has a shelf of German-style beer mugs, each decorated with well-fed Teutonic revelers in lederhosen. I read somewhere that people who collect things are intelligent. I don't collect anything.

One afternoon at his cottage in Santa Terezinha, he flops into one of his two hammocks.

"Jim, deite na rede. Fica a vontade." (Jim, lie down in the hammock. Make yourself comfortable.) He wants to chat. I feel something ominous coming.

Wearing only shorts and a pair of worn rubber flip-flops, he stretches out in his hammock, arms crossed behind his head. One leg hangs to the tile floor, a flip-flop dangling on a big toe, whose toenail is disfigured, the only genetic flaw in an otherwise perfectly workmanlike body.

I drop into the other hammock, which is unexpectedly low, notably lower than his.

"Jim," he intones lazily, *"a Segunda Guerra foi ótima para o mundo"* (Jim, the Second World War was great for the world). This is the way he often starts, laying out an opening gambit to bait me. "Jim," he says, gazing into the distance, evidently seeing in his imagination marvelous stainless steel factories rising from the ashes of war, "you have no idea how much technological progress the war generated—jet planes, satellites, atomic energy." His voice rises. "All developed during war, and because of war!"

The terrific benefits war has bestowed upon humanity is one of his favorite opinions. Other topics—world politics, international relations, world economy—topics I know surprisingly little about, are all at the service of the most important thing: his opinion.

Feeling provoked, I remind him that millions died in that war.

"Progresso tecnológico não vem sem sacrifício" (Technological progress doesn't come without sacrifice), he counters, apparently having anticipated my point.

"Pai, you're forgetting the six million Jews who died in concentration camps."

Incredibly, the Holocaust is merely the price the world must pay for marvelous technological advances.

As I'd feared, our cozy little confab in hammocks is sliding in an unpleasant direction. Why can't we simply *discuss* things? Why not a gentle musing on a benign topic? Why not a tranquil sharing of ideas? Why can't we be more like English gentlemen, nibbling serenely on intellectual tidbits in the club library?

This is unthinkable. He springs forward, expounding on the creativity of German war machines, matched by equally creative Allied counterattacks. He puts forward a mind-spinning mix of assertion, logic, fact, and warped opinion.

However, the Holocaust and even technological progress are trivial compared with the overriding, primary thing: pummeling his son-in-law into a stupor. The emotional subtext of this chat, and others like it, is simply to throw me off balance, staggering, hanging on the ropes, powerless to change his mind. This obeys another of his Absolutely Essential Rules for Living: ARGUE AGGRESSIVELY.

I dig into my tiny drawer of knowledge about World War II, which frankly I've never found all that fascinating, searching for a weapon to attack his misguided love of technology. My best argument is the Holocaust, which he somehow shrugs off, discharging like a bazooka one conviction after another, inflicting damaging hits. I discover I'm out of new ideas. Whatever other argument I dredge up, he shoots down with his oratorical anti-aircraft weaponry.

Triumphant, he's still not satisfied. He comes up with something new. Raising his index finger, he announces: "Richard Nixon *era um grande presidente!*" (Richard Nixon was a great president!), trolling for another quarrel to pass the time.

I take the bait. "No, he was not a great president! He was a pathetic paranoid who approved a secret break-in to the headquarters of the Democratic Party, then lied about it, betraying the American people."

He pauses to absorb my counterattack. I've nailed him!

"That doesn't hold a candle to Nixon's great step in opening the door to China!" he shouts, eyes blazing, finger wagging furiously above his head like a senator delivering deathless oratory to a full house of rapt lawmakers. Catching fire, he lurches out of his hammock to his feet, waving both arms and fingers in grand sweeping gestures, spittle flying from his lips, like tiny pearls of wisdom falling from his golden tongue into a thousand ears of transfixed spectators in the Senate gallery.

"Nixon was a president with vision and a sense of history!" he roars. "He was great for your country and great for the world—even though you fail to recognize it!" He accompanies this bombardment with a bewildering flourish of waving limbs, which he whips about violently like Italians arguing over the price of fish. I avoid his wild eyes as one avoids gazing at the sun.

He pauses in his verbal pyrotechnics, waiting for my rebuttal.

I hate this. I hate the conflict. I find absolutely no comfort in it at all. In my Scandinavianized family, we were expected to agree on things. If not possible, we were to keep our mouths shut. This was absolutely the worst possible training I could have had in dealing with this volatile firebrand.

"You're wrong," I say, in a flat and empty rebuke, all my ammunition gone.

Then, a new thought. Why lock horns with him? I depend on him for everything. He provides me with his seaside vacation cottage, access to shade, cool water, a bed, a car, and abundant food. Why bite the hand that feeds me? That would be uncivil and just plain stupid.

Wrong. The cold truth is he intimidates me. My candy-assed lack of pluck must look cowardly to this warrior gaucho.

And frankly, by now, at forty-one, I should be a man. But around him, I'm a man in theory. In his presence, I regress. I'm an adolescent aching to rebel against his father, but without tools. My own father is Pai's opposite: gentle, patient, passive, studious, and emotionally distant. These are precisely the qualities a warrior distrusts. Pai is everything my father isn't—sweaty, bear-hugging, intimate, domineering, a rawhide teaser. Conflict is his meat, his sport, his style of companionship, his measure of himself against the world.

Today, I have not measured up. I'm not a worthy companion. What I am today is a lump of burning shame.

The great gaucho orator eventually cools down, losing interest in history's high points—World War II, Richard Nixon, China—and in me. He wanders off to seek entertainment elsewhere, probably to torment my two little boys.

I take a deep breath. I count to ten. I remind myself that as a middle-aged

Married during the Great Depression, Pai and Sarah, pictured here in 1937, are about to start a family, and, with courage and determination, claw their way up into the middle class.

PAI GAVIOLI
Thirty-six Years of War and Finally Peace with My Impossible Brazilian Father-in-Law

man, I'm capable of tolerance. This, too, shall pass.

And yet, for the hundredth time, I feel violated. He's broken my window, entered my room, and knocked me around. And for the hundredth time, I yearn for revenge.

A SIMPLE WEDDING

*If one advances confidently in the direction of his dreams,
and endeavors to live the life which he has imagined,
he will meet with a success unexpected in common hours.*
–Henry David Thoreau

In 1935, at age twenty, not knowing it at the time, Pai makes a fateful decision. He goes back to school. Because he never attended high school, he enrolls in general education classes at night, focused on business and accounting. His Portuguese teacher, five years his senior, has an oval face, soft, dark, almond-shaped Portuguese eyes, and a graceful, melancholic manner. She walks with a limp.

One year later, Sarah Medeiros becomes his wife.

Their wedding invitation, no bigger than a business card, is a flower of simplicity:

> **Sarah e Gavioli**
> *Convidam a V.S. para assistir ao seu enlace na Igreja Esperança
> à rua Mariante, 807, às 19:30 horas do dia 2 de Outubro.*

Translated:

> **Sarah and Gavioli**
> *Invite you to attend their wedding at the Church of Hope,
> 807 Mariante Street, at 7:30 p.m., on October 2.*

The invitation contains several curiosities, starting with their names. Each has only one name, unusually informal for a wedding invitation, suggesting the invitees know them well. Also, it's Sarah's first name and Pai's last name. This probably means Sarah wrote the invitation, because even today she calls him Gavioli, his family name, and never José. Third, the old-fashioned word for wedding, *enlace,* is notably lovely, signaling a weaving of two strands into one, twice as strong as either strand alone.

The invitation also omits the city (Porto Alegre) and the year (1936). The invitees obviously already know these details, which, if included, might seem slightly grandiose on the part of the newlyweds, who are not, by any stretch, pretentious people. Finally, they are married in Igreja Esperança, or Church of Hope. All marriages need hope, and theirs, occurring deep in the Great Depression, perhaps more than most.

They have almost no family support, little money, no house, no car, "not even a knife," Pai once told me. A gaucho without his knife is like a stomach without food. By comparison, our marriage starts out several rungs higher on the economic ladder, with a parental safety net spread out below us.

When Pai's mother, Amanda, visits the newlyweds' apartment, she announces that its sparse furniture and other effects belong to her son. Nothing belongs to Sarah. Pai immediately defends his offended wife, who at this moment begins a lifelong aversion to her mother-in-law.

Pai and Sarah team up at a time when the Depression hits Brazil in its solar plexus—coffee exports—causing as much, if not more, economic devastation than in the United States. As a result, Brazil's landed elites, who control coffee production and the government, are weakened, paving the way for a new

Sarah, pictured here not long after her marriage to Pai in 1936.

populist president, Getúlio Vargas.

Pai admires Vargas, who's also from Rio Grande do Sul. With similarities to Franklin Roosevelt's New Deal, Vargas's *Estado Novo* (New State) helps modernize Brazil. When Pai is twenty-two, Vargas institutes a progressive labor law that guarantees a minimum wage and other worker benefits. Nicknamed the Father of the Poor, Vargas becomes the favorite of the peasantry and the urban working class, like Pai and Sarah.

Pai wears a Vargas lapel pin shaped like a lunch bucket. *A lunch bucket! Signifying work and food, two of Pai's favorite things.* This tiny pin probably resonates like a liberty bell for the young couple and for millions more in their generation.

HIS BELOVED BANKS

Apart from food, Pai has no hobbies. He doesn't read books. Like author Bernard Cooper's father, he's a man who "manages perfectly well without literature." He doesn't attend movies, concerts, or theater. He doesn't practice woodworking or pottery. He spends no time gardening. Beautiful Brazilian soccer holds no interest for him. Neither do highly popular Brazilian *tele-novelas* (TV soap operas). He doesn't even drink. He skims the newspaper with detachment because for him news isn't new. He's seen it all before.

Instead, he entertains himself with visits to his neighborhood banks. He's diversified his savings into four separate banks. This strategy is designed to minimize fraud, corruption, and computer meltdown in any single bank, which would jeopardize his membership in the middle class.

His financial security system rivals Switzerland's in complexity. In each of his four banks, he has a checking account and a savings account—a total of eight accounts. In addition, he's established eight similar accounts for Sarah, for a total of sixteen. Furthermore, he controls a checking and savings account for Aunt Cecilia, who's housebound and lives across the street. To help manage her apartment, he's created two additional accounts. And let's not forget single accounts for each of his three condo units. All told, he controls twenty-three separate accounts, accessed by twenty-three different passwords.

With a system like this, who needs hobbies?

No less important, banks are also his social clubs. This is consistent with one of his Rules for the Good Life: MAKE FRIENDS WITH BANKERS, BUTCHERS, SHOPKEEPERS, DOCTORS, AND LAWYERS. Nowhere on the street does he feel more welcome and comfortable than in his banks,

FEBRUARY 1981
A Painful Chat

except maybe the butcher shop. He'll walk a couple of blocks to one of his banks, sit down with a friendly young employee, and accept a leisurely *cafezinho*. He'll crack jokes, greet other employees with friendly insults, and before leaving, educate rookie clerks with well-worn nuggets of wisdom, instructive gems like, "Wear clean clothes." Or, "Keep your nose clean."

However, banks have a dark side. One day some years ago, while he was

Augusto Gavioli, Pai's father, pictured in the center of this photo, was a traveling salesman in the rugged interior of Rio Grande do Sul.

The arrival of a traveling salesman on horseback in an isolated village in the interior of Rio Grande do Sul can be a major event. He provides stylish merchandise, news from the world beyond, and an excuse to celebrate.

chewing the fat at the desk of an employee he'd befriended, an armed man burst through the door. Pai rose from his chair, white with fear, perhaps less for himself and more for his savings, his lifeline to the middle class. Seeing him in this state, and worried about his heart, the employee rushed around her desk and gently lowered him, face down, to the floor, holding him there until the assault was over. I've heard him tell this story several times, always praising the employee.

DRIVING WITH GOD

Pai came to the art of driving an automobile at the ripe age of fifty-two. He never grew comfortable with it. On his first day as a car owner, he seized the wheel before buying insurance and instantly rear-ended the car ahead of him. He worked out a damage payment on the spot.

In Brazil, the car ahead of you is your enemy. You must defeat it by passing it. If you fail to show sufficient valor, your manhood is diminished.

Sitting in the back seat one day, I observe Pai's method for passing a car on the highway. He begins by clutching the steering wheel in a white-knuckled death grip. Next, he lurches into the lane of oncoming traffic, pulling himself forward off the back of his seat, neck veins pulsing, jaw muscles bulging, eyes big as headlights.

Next, he rams the gas pedal to the floor, choking the engine. It coughs and gasps for oxygen, temporarily slowing us down. When the engine regains consciousness, he continues aiming our vehicle directly at oncoming traffic, charging full speed ahead toward the enemies.

My heart is pounding and I wish I were Catholic so I could pray to one of their many protective saints. The combatants approaching us are taken by surprise, and, like spineless cowards, are forced onto the shoulder, opening his path to conquest. Now he's in position to creep past his adversary, which he does, ducking back into his lane, ready for a new round of hostilities.

Minutes later, a truck passes us. It has a hand-painted sign on its bumper: *Dirijo, mas Deus guia* (I drive, but God guides). A comforting message, even for an atheist like myself.

LIKE FATHER, LIKE SON

Before separating from his wife, Amanda, in 1915, Pai's father, Augusto Gavioli, was a traveling salesman. He journeyed on horseback through Rio Grande do Sul's rugged interior to tiny German and Italian colonial villages, selling European cloth and sewing materials.

Back then, salesmen on horseback needed skill, stamina, and smarts. Augusto had these, plus salesman flair and charisma. Yet to manage the perils, fatigue, and monotony of journeys that can last for months, one also needs to be self-starting, independent, enterprising, and self-confident. Augusto, in the bloom of life, was all of the above.

Leading a mule caravan over streams and rivers, sometimes hacking through underbrush, Augusto cuts a dashing profile. He wears spurs and knee-length boots against thorns and snakes. He carries a horsewhip and a revolver, with a belt of bullets wrapped around his waist against jaguars and thieves eager to separate him from his wares and cash. A floppy hat protects him from the sun. A thick poncho shields him from the cold. He brings with him the all-important cook, together with peons to do the heavy lifting. The crew camps in tents, roasts meat on spits over a fire, and drinks *chimarrão*, a strong mate tea adored by gauchos throughout southern South America.

Augusto's arrival in tiny isolated towns can cause a minor sensation. Villagers gather about him for news from surrounding towns and beyond, much of which he's gleaned from other salesmen along the way. He's a link to the outside world, a supplier of news, and a source of new and fashionable things—from Europe!

The following day, Augusto sponsors a lively party for shopkeepers, which features dancing, speechifying, and frivolity. Armed with only a primary school education, he delivers newsy speeches dressed in flowery Portuguese. His glib oratory, embellishing his adventures beyond the small world of the village, entertains and astonishes the townsfolk whose lives are otherwise weighed down with hard work and tedium.

Augusto loves this part of his job. He's dashing, charming, witty and well liked. Women find him romantic, if not astoundingly handsome. He is, however, good-looking enough, with abundant amounts of Italian testosterone flowing through his veins. He's the classic traveling salesman.

The following day he gets down to business, showing samples of his wares and taking orders from shopkeepers, promising to bring the merchandise on his return trip.

A generation later, his son José Gavioli is a crew captain leading men deep into the same rugged interior of Rio Grande do Sul that his father had traveled. In the late 1930s, Pai begins a thirty-year career working for the Brazilian branch of American Telephone & Telegraph. He leads crews of sometimes two dozen rawboned gauchos, some black, some white, some speaking only German, some only Italian. They hack their way through jungles and trek across treeless pampas, erecting poles and stringing telephone lines, methodically linking towns and villages to the greater world beyond, an eerie echo of the traveling salesman father he never knew.

Like his father, Pai is gone sometimes months at a time. He and his crew sleep in tents, confronting heat, cold, wind, rain, insects, snakes, jaguars, and thieves. He buys provisions from nearby farms and villages, hiding the cash from his own men. He entrusts the money to a man named Policarpo, the poorest-looking worker in the crew. Policarpo wears battered sandals, ragged pants, and tattered shirts within whose folds and crevices he conceals the cash. A man of unshakeable honesty and frugality, Policarpo works to save every penny he earns, and eventually, like Pai, buys a house.

The penalty for drinking or fighting is instant dismissal. A consummate teetotaler, Pai loathes drunkenness. In matters of alcohol he's iron-fisted, a virtue that doubtless contributes greatly to his future parenting skills.

Arriving in town with his never-before-seen telephone technology, Pai and his crew are met with open arms. It's hard to overestimate the importance—and status—of a telephone connection to the outside world. The town fathers are likely to treat this young foreman of humble origin with deference. He's in the enviable position of determining precisely where phone lines should go. Instructions from the head office in Porto Alegre would certainly require a line to the mayor's office, but in addition, a local priest or merchant also might request a line, installed at cost, for which the young foreman could obtain permission.

In 1938, Sarah becomes pregnant with their first child, Sidnei. Meanwhile, she continues to teach high school math, Portuguese, and English, supervising up to eighty pupils in her classroom. *"As aulas da Sarah eram absolutamente quietas"* (Sarah kept an absolutely silent classroom), Pai has told me. Two hundred miles away in Santa Maria, Pai writes Sarah a letter nearly every day, insisting that she rest and eat lots of fruit. Despite lack of money, he insists she stay off her weak and sometimes swollen ankles by hiring a housekeeper to cook, clean,

FEBRUARY 1981
A Painful Chat

and wash. Her modest salary helped put food on the table, he said, a sacrifice he never forgot.

Over the next dozen years they have four children. Eager to build a house for his young family, he volunteers for longer and more far-flung assignments. Sarah continues to teach, raise the children, and manage the household. Despite her heavy limp, she walks seven blocks to school, teaches on her feet much of the day, and returns home to find them sometimes swollen and blistered. Over the years she becomes the stable, patient force in the family—frugal, practical, rational, and no-nonsense. Her children address her as *Dona Sarah,* or Lady Sarah, out of affectionate respect.

RELENTLESS RECTITUDE

Sitting on his couch one evening, Pai gazes at the ceiling, where he stores his memories. He recalls a time years ago when he worked for "Mister" at the phone company.

"Mister" is an American AT&T executive, whose name Pai has forgotten. One day this big shot arrives to review operations in Brazil's southernmost branch of the company.

"Senhor Gavioli," Pai says, mimicking Mister's thick accent and mangled syntax, *"como estão as coisas trabalhando?"* (how are things working?)

Pai describes how he promptly responds to Mister's many questions, taking him to operating sites, and staying late to review technical details. Meanwhile, the local Brazilian AT&T directors view this guy as a meddlesome busybody. After several months studying the operation in Porto Alegre, Mister returns to US headquarters.

Some months later, Mister is made director of AT&T's Brazil operations. Soon he shows up in Porto Alegre. He demands to see "Senhor Gavioli."

"Eu estava tremendo" (I was trembling). "What did I do wrong? Will I be fired? I arrive at his office and see several directors also waiting to see him. Now I'm trembling even more. I tell the secretary I'm here to see Mister. She tells him I'm here.

"Suddenly, Mister's door swings open and he roars, 'Senhor Gavioli is not to wait! He is always to enter my office immediately without knocking! Those men, however,' pointing at the directors, shaking in their chairs, 'they're to wait until I'm good and ready!'"

Pai has a weakness for stories of good versus evil in which he's featured among the good. I've heard this one before. The industrious Pai—a lowly technician—is rewarded, while arrogant, thumb-twiddling directors are punished. His repeated tellings have polished the story to nearly fairy-tale quality—like "The Three Little Pigs," in which Pai is the diligent pig. In this story, as in all his others, the hero Pai, always mindful of danger and evil, uses his toolbox of moral hammers and nails to build his blue-ribbon life. These tools are:

> Work relentlessly
> Make sacrifices
> Earn the trust of supervisors
> Educate your children
> Don't smoke or drink
> Never quit

These tools keep him on the straight and narrow. Slackening leads directly to the slippery slope.

These are among the rules immigrants live by. Pai and Sarah are immigrants in their own county. They've climbed the steep mountain from Brazil's Lower Kingdom of Want all the way to its Upper Kingdom of Stability. They've spent twenty years on this journey, carrying their children along with them. It's a journey that shapes the traveler, one I've never had to take. This is the great difference between us.

Meanwhile, life under his relentless rectitude goes on.

SWEET REVENGE

Pai has no interest in Brazil's four great passions—soccer, samba, carnival, and song. He considers them hedonistic, morally corrupting distractions. They are precisely why Brazil lags behind the rest of the world. While the world may view them as the heart of Brazil, Pai shuns them as emblems of poverty from which he has spent a lifetime struggling mightily to escape.

Raised in the shadow of this sober man, his children grow up to be curiously unBrazilian. It's true that the teenage Daisi celebrated carnival with her friends four nights in a row, but unlike most of them, she's dutifully back in school the following day. And it's true that when Brazil wins the World Cup in *futebol*—triggering a nationwide roar that shakes the foundations of social order—the Gaviolis are pleased, but not exultant. They're all business the next day.

As a child, he played no sports, unless one counts survival as a sport. Sports are all about victory, which his childhood lacked. To compensate, Pai enrolls his two eldest children, Sidnei and Daisi, in competitive swimming at Grêmio Náutico

At left, Pai with Daisi and Sidnei in downtown
Porto Alegre in the 1940s.
At right, Sarah with Davison and an older Daisi.

União, a middle-class sports and social club to which he's belonged for years, a key stratagem in his upward mobility. Maybe his children will give him the triumphs he never had. Any victories would be partly his, welcome revenge on those other Gaviolis who figuratively held his head under water when he was a child.

By age six, Sidnei is already competing. When Sidnei reaches fourteen, Pai decides his coach is incompetent, so every morning at dawn Pai secretly takes his son to the pool when no one else is there. He grimly drives Sidnei to plow through the frigid early morning waters, shrewdly instructing him to "hold his fire" for the final kick.

After months of secret training, Pai enters the adolescent in the men's 1500-meter race. For most of the race, Sidnei is far behind. However, nearing the end, he comes to life and mounts the relentless final push taught by his father.

With grit, talent, and pressure from Pai, Sidnei becomes a South American champion and Daisi a state champion.

Nearly eclipsing two adult leaders at the finish, the youngster comes in a close third. Pai is ecstatic.

Sidnei goes on to become South American champion and record holder in the 400-, 800-, and 1500-meter races. He is the athletic star of his family, city, state, and nation. His lofty position in Brazil's swimming pantheon is due to his talent, his grit—and his father.

Bursting with pride, Pai doesn't stop with Sidnei. He pushes Daisi to become state champion in the 100-, 200-, and 400-meter races. He's on the verge of producing a Gavioli swimming dynasty! For Pai, his children's victories are sweet revenge, a reproach to those in his youth who slammed the door on him.

Then he pushes his luck. He wants his third child, Davison, to produce even more family triumphs. But with no stomach for the discipline, and perhaps to avoid the shadow of his brother and sister, Davison rebels. Instead, he has the audacity to choose a sport his father associates with Brazilian poverty—*futebol*. The impudent Davison becomes the ringleader of a motley gang of street urchins, yelling and kicking the ball around in the street right in front of Pai's house. It borders on insubordination.

FEBRUARY 1981
A Painful Chat

Lori, the baby of the family, is free to go her own way. He doesn't even try to make her a swimmer.

After fourteen years of swimming competitively under Pai's pressure, Sidnei abandons the sport at age twenty and never returns.

One day years later, I watch Sidnei swim. The former record holder glides effortlessly through water evidently much thinner than the thick liquid through which I drag myself. Because I'm a bad swimmer, I ask him for advice. He tells me how to insert my arms in the water, and how to pull through the stroke. I try it. Then he says: "I'll show you one more time—AND I'M NOT GOING TO SHOW YOU AGAIN!"

In his fierce tone, I hear his father. But his advice works. I've never forgotten it.

Gavioli children survive their paternal blast furnace in one of two ways: absorbing him or rejecting him. Sidnei—the first born, the obedient "good child"—is an absorber. He survives by adopting many of Pai's excellent qualities: integrity, realism, diligence, caution, wit, and determination.

Daisi is another absorber, soaking up his work ethic, strong family loyalty, and aversion to poverty so complete that she refuses to drink from a cup flawed by even the smallest chip.

Third in family order comes Davison. He's a rejecter, openly challenging Pai, producing violent clashes between them. He survives Pai by fighting him, emerging from their battles as an unwavering contrarian, thus involuntarily becoming yet another version of his father.

Lori is another absorber, incorporating several Pai-like qualities. She's gregarious, feisty, an exuberant storyteller, scrupulously moral, willful, tempestuous, quick to give advice, and a doting parent to her three daughters. She believes all problems are, at their root, materialistic. The good life rests upon a three-legged stool of money, food, and a car. Art and culture are irrelevant legs that unbalance the stool. In Lori, presto! We have Pai all over again.

Pai survives, alive and kicking in his children. What a relief that they're the ones who survived childhood under him, which means I did not have to.

CLIMBING THE LADDER

Even though Pai is promoted at AT&T when he's in his thirties, his lack of education keeps him from rising further in the company. This doesn't prevent him, however, from advancing in two other areas: the local Lions Club, and his beloved sports club.

When he turns forty in the mid-1950s, he takes on substantial duties as treasurer at the sports club, a position he holds for several years. A decade later, he volunteers to be vice president. A couple of years after that, the board "volunteers" him to be president, the club's highest position.

As president, despite internal controversy, he spearheads the purchase of a large tract of city land to develop a completely new site, the club's largest expansion ever. The decision pays off. Soon the new site's pools, tennis courts, and social areas attract new members and spur upscale development on one of the city's hills, altering the face of the city.

Meanwhile, he attends Lions Club meetings with religious regularity, rubbing elbows with civic leaders and other professionals. At Lions, he hones his public-speaking skills, becoming the cream of courtesy, the flower of ceremony. Year after year, the Lions elect him club president.

Pai has arrived. He belongs to Porto Alegre's small middle class.

In the early 1960s, AT&T provides him time and flexibility to pursue his volunteer work. This is because the company decides it's in their interest to have one of their employees in a leadership position at the popular sports club, whose ranks include other civic and professional leaders. Pai takes scrupulous care that on his watch absolutely no special favors are granted between the club and the company.

Then he gets a new opportunity. In the late sixties, the sports club, Grêmio Náutico União, offers him a full-time position as club manager. By now, the club is operating three separate facilities. One is a mile from home, where Daisi and

Pai spearheads the development of a large, new, additional facility for the club, which paves the way to upscale housing growth in the area.

FEBRUARY 1981
A Painful Chat

Sidnei trained in swimming. Another is a large island in the middle of the wide Guaíba River close to downtown. The third is the big new facility on a hill in Petropolis, now emerging as a new, upscale part of town. This is a big job, but Pai loves to manage people, a fact well known at home. He accepts the position, and, after thirty years at the telephone company, he retires.

For a man of limited education, the equivalent of high school accounting and night school, Pai's ascent up the administrative ladder at this growing sports and social club is remarkable. Nor is it without envy from snobs. One day after swim practice, Daisi overhears condescending remarks by certain club officials who sneer at what they say is his unrefined elocution and unpolished writing.

Achievement is the best revenge. I have seen Pai's austere, unsmiling photo hanging on the club's wall of honor alongside other past presidents—doctors, lawyers, businessmen, and other professionals. Did they, as children, run barefoot on dirt paths in a small town? Did they, like Pai in São Paulo, attend school for the indigent? Did they find themselves rejected by their fathers at birth?

I doubt it.

Compared with my own father, Pai is a world away. In many outer respects, my father also led a good professional life. He graduated from the University of Minnesota Medical School. He worked diligently and took his turn as chief of staff at a major Saint Paul hospital. He was president of my high school parent-teacher association, and was the team doctor for our football team. Furthermore, he paid for my schooling at Harvard, for which, to my chagrin, I have been insufficiently grateful.

Yet, while Pai is a "hard male," Dad is a "soft male." In his book *Iron John*, Robert Bly describes soft males as having a gentle attitude toward life, not interested in harming the earth or starting wars. "But many of these men are not happy," he writes. "You quickly notice the lack of energy in them. They are life-preserving but not exactly life-giving. Ironically, you often see these men with strong women who positively radiate energy."

Bingo. This is Mom all right. More on her later.

PESSIMISM

Brazilians are pessimistic these days. One day I ask my nephew Beto how things are going. "A little better than tomorrow," he says. No wonder. People are engulfed by a fragile, fickle economy, a heavy class system suppressing upward mobility, and a suffocating bureaucracy. Add to this mix high levels of corruption, violence in the streets, and a military dictatorship. Given all this, it's not surprising to find, underlying everything, a streak of fatalism, reinforced by the hierarchical and paternalistic nature of society.

"Everything will be all right in the end," goes a popular saying, "and if everything is not yet all right, that's only because we haven't reached the end."

While the middle class complains that tomorrow will be worse than today; that the economy is stagnant; that burglary, assaults, and corruption are on the rise; that marriage is on the decline; that too much wealth is held by too few; that the soccer coach is an idiot and the team is a bunch of Barbie dolls in high heels—Pai is an optimist.

Like bread yeast, optimism is needed to rise in society. I see it in his energy and quick decisiveness. I feel it in the pride he has in his car. I smell it in his clean white shirts. I taste it in his profusion of barbecued chicken and beef. I even sense it in his goading me to learn the language of his people, or his dismay at my weak grasp of World War II, always implying that if I work hard, like he has, I, too, can rise in life.

That said, there's little quite so irksome as unbending optimism.

MENSTRUATION CEREMONY

"Eu fiquei menstruada. Agora sou uma mocinha!" (I've menstruated. Now I'm a young woman!) These are the words that one of Daisi's nieces, Pati, then twelve, delivers to her parents one day. For Pati, a modern girl, menstruation is not shameful, not a female curse as it has been for centuries.

Sidnei and Maria Eunice take her to her grandparents' house, and, standing in Pai's small living room, Pati proudly breaks the news. Sarah wraps her arms around her granddaughter in a long, loving embrace.

Pai tells her to sit on the sofa. He sits next to her. He leans in close, tears streaming down his face. *"Pati, isto é um momento maravilhoso na tua vida, e na vida da nossa família"* (Pati, this is a marvelous moment in your life, and in the life of our family).

His emotions rising, he places his arm over her shoulders. "You are no longer the little girl I have loved so much." He leans in even closer and raises his index finger, like a priest delivering a sermon: "You have passed from childhood into womanhood," he declares, "and you will always have a place in my heart," placing his hand over that very organ, "and I will love you as I always have from the moment you were born into this family!"

Embracing her, accepting her, words in this vein pour from him for several more minutes, like blood flowing from a wound he suffered many years

FEBRUARY 1981
A Painful Chat

ago, as a boy about her age.

Pati is in tears. Maria Eunice is weeping. Sidnei can't handle it and leaves the room. Sarah, who knows him, keeps her silence.

Once again, Pai becomes a ceremonial man, rising to the occasion, grasping it, defining it, molding it. He has the genius of honoring family milestones, shaping them into impromptu ceremonies, makeshift as they may be.

At such moments, his over-spilling passions are even more unendurable than usual.

JANUARY 1986
Penetrating Granite

The streets of Porto Alegre are filling with more small cars, which emit a fragrance of burnt sugarcane from ethanol, cheaper and less polluting than gasoline. More than three-quarters of the nearly million cars produced annually in Brazil now run on ethanol. And, as of last year, political power has been transferred to civilians. Twenty-one years of military rule are now history. Democracy is restored. This is the good news Daisi and I find as we return after five years away.

With Sarah beside him, Pai drives us to his bungalow in Santa Terezinha. The brown horse, still tied to a rope on the grassy plot across the cobblestone road, is still munching grass.

Pai has grass here at his cottage, too, a tiny plot whose purpose in life is to remind the world of his membership in the middle class. One day I help him mow it. I spend an hour in the hot sun after lunch dragging around his cast-iron, Soviet-style weed whacker, loud as a chain saw and about as efficient. Exhausted, I collapse into a deep nap in one of his two hammocks. Meanwhile, the seventy-one-year-old dynamo is still sparking, hauling things and fixing things, reminding me how little is changed between us. He's still a giant, and I'm a dwarf napping in his shadow.

When I awake, he's finally relaxing in the other hammock a few feet away. In a chatty mood, he shares with me one of his Cardinal Rules for an Excellent Life: WORK RELENTLESSLY.

"Quando trabalho, não paro, não. Continuo—vai! vai! vai!—até que fico cansado." (When I work, I don't stop. I keep at it—Go! Go! Go!—until I get tired.) He offers this lesson in hopes that something might sink in. Work, he

believes, is not punishment for our sins in the Garden long ago, as I have always assumed. Far from it. Work is a joyous gift, something we mortals should throw ourselves into at every opportunity.

Many affluent, upper-class Brazilians hold manual labor in contempt, viewing it as inherently demeaning and beneath their dignity. Their exalted position in life has not required them to perform it. They fail to appreciate the skills and endurance it demands. For Pai, however, manual labor is an opportunity, a challenge to accept. I grow weak just thinking about it.

A couple of days later I notice two workers in the hot sun in front of the cottage. They're using hoes to scrape weeds growing between cobblestones in the street next to the curb.

I ask him why they're doing this. This prompts another instructive yarn from the spool of his memory, this one illustrating the long-standing war between Brazilians and their oppressive bureaucracy. Resembling one of Aesop's fables, this tale features another tool in Pai's work belt—skill in waking sleeping bureaucrats from their stupor.

"Aqueles trabalhadores" (Those workers), he says, "are in front of my house because of my visit yesterday to Santa Terezinha's secretary of public works."

The secretary's office is housed in a tiny, nondescript municipal building. Pai says that when he walks in, the secretary is sitting behind his desk fiddling with papers, neglecting to provide a chair for his elderly visitor. An attendant notices Pai standing patiently while the secretary, head down, diddles at his desk. The attendant kindly brings Pai a chair.

Facing the secretary, Pai loudly clears his throat and begins to describe Santa Terezinha's three persistent problems—*"muito capim, pouca limpeza e muita falta de luz"* (too many weeds, too little garbage collection, and too many interruptions of electricity).

The secretary keeps shuffling papers and doesn't look up. *"Fiquei brabo"* (I grew angry), Pai tells me, his face darkening. "And yet, I remain patient by using a mental trick of counting to three," his face brightening, as though he's the one who has invented this never-before-used stratagem. "Mr. Secretary, I'll stop talking so you can finish your paperwork."

The secretary replies, *"Não. Pode falar. Estou escutando."* (No. Keep talking, I'm listening.)

"Não," Pai says. "I can return another day when Your Excellency has time to hear to what I have to say."

Feeling the sting, the secretary straightens up, moves his papers aside and gives Pai his full attention. Then Pai inserts one more needle. "The previous mayor of Santa Terezinha was the only one in twenty years to attend to our problems, because," he goes on, "that mayor listened to what people had to say—and because he was a *gentleman!*" Pai lands hard on this word—in English—suggesting that the secretary is facing, in the person of Pai, someone of consequence, someone who knows words in a foreign language. The following day, workers are hacking away at the weeds in front of Pai's bungalow. The squeaky wheel gets the grease.

I must give him this—he owns a streak of fearlessness. Speaking up in public, as he's able to do, is a quality I lack, placing me deeper in his shadow.

One of his favorite weapons is what he calls *"política chinesa"* (Chinese politics), which Daisi has told me he deploys at public meetings. He arrives early, ready for combat, and stays late—as long as it takes—outlasting and wearing down the opposition. When others go home exhausted, he emerges as triumphant as water, which, dripping for a thousand years, bores a hole through granite.

HOW TO EAT CHICKEN

As a boy, I had enough of everything. At age ten I entered the charmed decade of the fifties, amid its materialism, abundance, and comfort. But in the sixties, after spending two Peace Corps years in Africa witnessing scarcity, I grew impatient

A radiant Pai greets Marcus, pictured at left, and André when our family arrives in Porto Alegre in 1990.

PAI GAVIOLI
Thirty-six Years of War and Finally Peace with My Impossible Brazilian Father-in-Law

with US affluence. I was drawn to simplicity, and now, to life without meat. Since my last visit, I have become a vegetarian.

For gauchos, meat is sacred. It is to be worshipped and consumed communally. Gauchos believe vegetarians are not merely thin and anemic, they're infidels. To rescue my body, and my soul, Pai finds it his mission to thrust meat upon me.

I respectfully decline, preferring Brazil's traditional staple, black beans and rice.

"Jim, podes comer essa carne" (you can eat this beef).

"No, I can't. I'm a vegetarian."

"Yes you can, because this cow ate only grass."

He never quits.

One day Pai decides to educate Marcus, our hungry fifteen-year-old, in the mysteries of eating chicken.

His face shining with chicken grease, Marcus devours piece after piece of Pai's crisp barbecued chicken, then gnaws on the bones. Speaking in hushed tones, as if in church, the wise old gaucho instructs him: *"Come devagar"* (Eat slowly). Marcus obeys, slowing his torrid pace. Pai's pleasure is obvious.

Suddenly Pai erupts. *"Come!"* (Eat!), he shouts. "Don't embarrass the family name! Eat! Eat!" Shaking his finger high in the air, as if rallying troops for battle, he thunders, "Show your respect for the colors of the Brazilian flag!" At which point he shoots a withering, anti-vegetarian glance at me.

Little gives more pleasure to an adolescent son than seeing his father under attack. Seizing the moment, Marcus aligns himself with his grandfather. The two of them, like goose-stepping soldiers, patriotically fall into synchronized chicken eating, bite for bite.

This goes on for several silent, highly charged minutes. Then, momentously, Pai declares, "A good barbecuer always leaves best for last," ceremoniously placing the last piece on Marcus's plate. Then he slowly rises from his chair and, in a grave voice, proclaims, "Today, Marcus has become a true Gavioli—and a true Brazilian!"

Thus Marcus is awarded an honored place at his grandfather's table.

It's another triumph for Pai. Achieved through another of his makeshift ceremonies, this one is akin to baptism, or perhaps a bar mitzvah, the Jewish rite that marks the transition from boyhood to manhood. The mundane act of eating chicken becomes transformative, magically carrying Marcus across a broad divide, the chasm between one generation and another, between a Minnesotan and a gaucho, and between a Martin and a Gavioli. These are precisely the chasms I have been unable to cross. To Pai's huge satisfaction, Marcus has bridged them, becoming all I am not.

For some mysterious unwritten law, I find myself compelled to resist my father-in-law. My son, on the other hand, accepts this man who is not his father-in-law, but his grandfather. Today he prefers his grandfather to his father. Today the two are in perfect harmony, and share, for the moment, a common enemy. Me.

Meanwhile, my devotion to vegetables threatens to undermine my connection to Pai, the Gavioli family, gauchos, and Brazilians everywhere.

Today Pai has baked a giant plateful of *pastéis,* about thirty of them. These are little meat pies shaped like half-moons, the size of croissants. A thin pastry is wrapped around hamburger, chopped egg, parsley, and garlic.

He carries a magnificent platterful to the table, lays it before us with a flourish, and offers his standard blessing, his favorite pun: *"Come sem vergonha."* If one says this quickly without a pause, it means, "eat without shame," suggesting there's enough food for everyone. However, spoken with a pause after *"come,"* it becomes, "eat, you shameless person," suggesting there's not enough for all. Pai adores this pun, which resonates to his twin obsessions—food and poverty.

Accustomed to grains and veggies, my stomach doesn't like these greasy, beefy pies. If I were a man of principle, I'd declare that eating meat is immoral, environmentally damaging, and unhealthy, and I'm not gonna do it. Period. However, in a gaucho meat culture, this would be like lobbing a grenade into a church. I'd be excommunicated.

The pastries are directly before me. How can I avoid them? Just then, Daisi shoots me a dark look that says; "Don't embarrass me by not eating again!" Oh, for a hungry dog under the table.

Pai has strategically placed one telltale green olive in each pastry, so he can count the pits on each plate and thereby determine how many we eat. Luckily, André, our eleven-year-old, who doesn't like olives, sneaks his to me under the table. I eat these "tracer olives" and spread the pits prominently on my plate. I also break open a pastry and spread it around, producing the illusion of heavy eating.

Pai senses something is amiss. "Jim, you're not eating my pastries. You don't like them. You're weakening. You're dishonoring Gaviolis, gauchos, and all Brazilians!"

At that very moment, miraculously, I manage to display two additional olive pits, deftly falsifying my allegiance to his flag.

The olive pits quiet him. Even though the main platter is piled suspiciously high with uneaten pastries, I've escaped. My family membership is intact.

Upon our return to Minnesota, André's teacher asks him to describe his trip to Brazil. "My grandfather is very rich," he writes. "He has a shed in the back of his house and its shelves are full of bottles of soda pop. My grandfather said I could drink as much as I want."

Wealth comes in many disguises.

DECEMBER 1990-JANUARY 1991
A Soaring Hero

Another five years pass and we arrive in Porto Alegre's cozy little airport, *Salgado Filho*, whose open-air windows, palm trees, and hibiscus flowers seem straight out of a Humphrey Bogart film.

The small terminal contains on one wall a large and remarkable mural, *A Conquista do Espaço* (The Conquest of Space). The artist is an Italian-born Brazilian, Aldo Locatelli, born in 1915, the same year as Pai. He portrays large heroic figures depicting the epic pursuit of human flight. The central character is a well-muscled figure in overalls striking a bold posture: legs apart, standing between the past, on the left side of the painting, and the future, on the right. With his rolled-up sleeves, and flight goggles around his neck, he has the look of a dauntless, fearless common man.

It's a forceful portrayal of Brazilian progress, whose central character reminds me of someone I know.

The central figure is actually Alberto Santos-Dumont, whom Brazilians claim made the first public heavier-than-air flight in 1906, thus inventing the airplane. The Wright Brothers' flight at Kitty Hawk in 1903, Brazilians contend, is a fraud, having taken place in secret and aided by a catapult, instead of wheels, which Santos-Dumont used.

In Daisi's view, my naive belief in the Wright Brothers, drilled into me in grade school, is brainwashing perpetrated by a US conspiracy to undermine Brazil's greatness. I've never heard of this Santos-Dumont guy, which annoys Daisi. Dispute over who is the first human to fly is one disagreement in our marriage that may never be resolved.

Three days later, I take a tumble. Falling backward, I hit the corner of a chair, and scrape skin off my spine. Aunt Cecilia gives me an ointment used for animal tumors and cow udders. I ask Pai whether it works for people, too.

"*O Teirceiro Mundo*" (The Third World), he declares, "doesn't bother with all the needless drugs and ointments of the First World. We use one medicine for everything."

I find no comfort in this broad-brush approach to medicine, but, in my case, it works.

It's been twenty years since Sarah's youngest sister, Cecilia, suffered a stroke. She walks with a cane, slowly and awkwardly, swinging her lifeless leg forward with a twist of her hip. Cecilia has a slender, innocent face and large ears that peek out modestly from her plain, straight gray hair. Except for women she hires as housekeepers to live with her, she lives alone in an apartment she owns across the street. Before her stroke, Cecilia was a competent professional auditor, cheerful and humorous. But afterward, losing her profession, her mobility, and her independence, she grew nervous and lonely. She harbors irrational fears, like getting an electric shock by walking past an air conditioner she's had for twenty years. She hangs cloves next to her light bulbs to keep mosquitos from entering her open windows.

COMBATTING THE GOVERNMENT

Pai defends his family and property with locks, chains, fences, and steel bars on his windows, as do others in the nation's small middle class. These precautions, however, have little effect against the government.

Brazil has a new president, Fernando Collor de Mello, the first to be democratically elected in twenty-nine years. He defeats Lula, leader of the Workers' Party, in a controversial election marred by a sensational political kidnapping. Media censorship prevents Lula from defending himself from accusations that his party was involved in the kidnapping.

On his first day in office, a few months before we arrive, Collor appropriates the savings accounts of the nation's middle class. His goal is to shrink the money supply as part of a plan to kill hyperinflation, a huge and chronic problem. Before he took office in early 1990, prices had been rising 80 percent *in a single month*, and still growing. People were getting their paychecks and rushing to buy things immediately to avoid the next day's higher prices.

Collor freezes individual bank accounts and turns them into government bonds to be repaid eighteen months later. At the end of his first year in office, inflation has fallen to a still staggering 400 percent a year.

"Jim, o ano passado quase fiquei louco" (I almost went mad last year), says Pai. That's when the middle-class floor he had spent a lifetime building threatened to collapse under him, thanks to Collor. Pai feared losing money he'd been saving for when he or Sarah might fall ill.

Pai's shrewd safety plan, distributing his savings among four different neighborhood banks, nearly failed him.

Events moved quickly. A friendly bank employee Pai had cultivated over the years tipped him off. "You didn't hear this from me, but withdraw your savings as fast as you can, because a government freeze is imminent." For two weeks, the desperate seventy-five-year-old literally jogged from one of his neighborhood banks to the next, to the next, and to the next, pounding his fist on marble counters, demanding in plain Portuguese: *"Quero meu dinheiro!"* (I want my money!)

He narrowly managed to rescue his savings before the freeze hit. The rest of the middle class, with no advance warning, was not so fortunate. Pai's chummy relationships with his banks paid off big time, helping him sidestep this radical attack on inflation. Even at seventy-five he proved himself nimble, key to survival in perilous Brazil.

The crisis inflicts collateral damage; the younger Gavioli men go temporarily impotent. For gauchos to peter out, men who rank themselves among the most virile primates on the planet, one can only assume this to be a crisis of biblical proportions. Were I in their shorts, I suspect my apparatus also would drop like a rock.

Collor holds people's savings in the form of bonds for eighteen months. By the time it's returned, its value has shrunk. They're never repaid in full.

Collor has more trouble. Four months after we leave, he's accused of corruption, leading to his impeachment and resignation. When he leaves office at the end of 1992, less than two years into his term, virulent inflation roars back to 1,000 percent per year, and still growing out of control.

JUNE 1993

An Eating War

Two years later, I'm now fifty-three and Pai is seventy-eight. I discover we've mellowed. At least I have.

In a happy turn of events, my perennial eating war with Pai mercifully shifts to my cousin David Kienitz, who with his wife, Elaine, is visiting us in Porto Alegre. We all sit down to a large meal, and Pai proceeds to pile heaps of food on Dave's plate.

"The food is very good," Dave says politely, "but no more, thank you." Instantly, more beef falls onto Dave's plate. Dave politely says no thank you again. This has no effect. To avoid offense, Dave bravely girds his loins and keeps eating. This silent war goes on for a while. I remain quiet, glad I'm not Dave.

Finally, Pai asks me, *"Ele se rendeu?"* (Does he surrender?) I ask Dave whether he's had enough. "Totally. I give up." I translate the news of his surrender to the generalíssimo, who receives it with a triumphant smile.

Old habits die hard. Some never get around to dying at all. As children of the Great Depression, he and Sarah continue to practice one of their most durable Rules: BE FRUGAL. Curiously, this sturdy standard is practiced by purchasing colossal amounts of bulk food, even though they're eating less these days. For example, he buys a three-month supply of shelf-stable milk, which needs no refrigeration, at a bargain for fifty-four dollars. He hoards this, along with dozens of jars of instant coffee, dozens of boxes of cookies and crackers, dozens of boxes of chocolates, scores of soft drink bottles, and several tubs of ice cream. He's prepared for famine.

KEYS

One evening he spreads seventy-five keys onto the dining room table, organizing them into several sets. I ask what they're for. *"Estas chaves"* (These keys), he says, his face steeped in innocence, "are for all the locks Daisi will have to open to get into the apartment she'll inherit when I die."

It takes me some moments to catch his drift. He seems to be ridiculing Brazil's extraordinary need for locks and keys. He also seems to imply he won't be dying anytime soon.

I smile. He smiles back.

INTIMACY

Winter turns cold in June. Daisi and I return after a movie one evening, and, as usual, their bedroom door is open. They're in bed, tucked under the covers, their white hair spread out like fleecy halos on their pillows. They invite us to sit on their bed and chat.

From beneath his warm covers, Sarah at his side, Pai makes a solemn declaration: *"Talvez vou me divorciar"* (Maybe I'll get a divorce). He pauses, looks around the room, "Then again, maybe I'll wait until next spring, after the weather warms up." Sarah rolls her eyes, a faint smile on her lips. She's heard it before.

Intimacy in marriage is a gift at any age and is especially welcome in old age. Their venerable marriage seems to be the gold standard, one by which to measure all others. Seeing them tucked in together, sharing an old joke, I hope that someday ours could approach it.

Their marriage endured for 70 years.

JUNE 1993
An Eating War

Pai with his imperfect son-in-law.

Wear Clean Clothes. Be Frugal. Drive Hard Bargains. Solve Problems Quickly and Aggressively. Never Quit, Never Quit. These are the tools he uses to confront life in Brazil, which is full of resistance. He offers these gems to his imperfect son-in-law free of charge, a reminder that life is a moral journey.

JUNE 1993
An Eating War

FEBRUARY-MARCH 1995
Driving Lessons

Surprisingly, when we arrive this summer, our seventh visit, Pai hands me the keys to his car. At the age of fifty-five I'm finally awarded a tiny measure of control in my relationship with this eighty-year-old. It's about time.
Wrong.

Before the car moves an inch, he instructs me where to go and how to get there. Okay, fine. I don't know the streets very well. But his instruction doesn't stop there. It includes the manner in which I am to drive.

Before I even turn the key in the ignition, he tells me how to buckle up. Then he tells me how to start the car moving forward by pressing on the gas pedal. Then he tells me how to stop, which involves pressing on the brake. Then he lectures me on the clutch, a pedal I have been using for forty years. Then he tells me to keep both hands on the wheel at all times. Okay, okay, okay. I don't have a great IQ, but whatever its number, it feels insulted.

Finally, we start. It's our first journey together with me behind the wheel.

"Fica no meio" (Get in the center lane). Then, only two seconds later, much louder—*"NO MEIO!"* (THE CENTER!) Pause . . .

"Stay in the center." Pause . . .

"Don't let him pass you." To obey, I speed up. "Slow down!" Pause . . .

"There's water on the road—stay in the middle—STAY IN THE MIDDLE! Don't go off to the side. You never know about the sides."

Pause . . . "Get in the left lane. We're going to turn." Pause . . .

"Get behind the bus. Do what the bus does! GO WHERE THE BUS GOES!"

I'm getting tense. I pull myself forward off the back of the seat. I lock onto the steering wheel in a white-knuckled death grip.

"Olha a sinaleira! (There's a stoplight!) Look, it turned red." Pause, as we slow down . . .

"Stop at the red light!" I stop at the red light, as I have been doing ever since Eisenhower was president forty years ago when I learned to drive.

"Okay, it changed to green. You can go." Great. Thanks for telling me green means go.

"We're coming to a police station. Slow down . . . slower . . . Okay, you can take off." Pause . . .

"There's a brick in the road—don't run over it." Oh, really? I think. Can't I hit the brick and pop a tire? Darn.

Then a car whizzes past us from behind. "My Lord," he says, "looks like he wants to get there yesterday. My way to get there sooner is to start earlier."

I grind my teeth, enduring yet another of his endless moral lessons. I have a fair amount of gray hair. I should know this stuff already. But he ignores my age, my experience, my common sense. In his eyes, I'm a schoolboy in desperate need of instruction.

We come to a shallow stream of water flowing across the intersection, so superficial it wouldn't cover a kernel of corn. "Go at it crossways." Pause . . .

"Now go crossways the other way." Pause . . .

As I follow orders, driving harmlessly through this trivial wet patch, he smiles broadly. *"Agora o senhor está aprendendo!"* ("Now the gentleman is learning!")

Okay, this is true. I'm learning to endure the unendurable.

He's always looking out the window, watching, anticipating. If life were to hinge on the two seconds that you never see coming, he's the type that actually would see them coming, and therefore will probably live a long time.

I stew in silence, loathing his countless directions. But the truth is I can't relax. I can't get complacent. Brazilian roads are war zones.

Almost before I notice them, from the opposite direction, two cars come charging directly at me, side by side, one struggling to pass and the other resisting defeat. The car attempting to pass is bearing down on me in my lane. Startled, I swing onto the shoulder, avoiding a head-on collision.

Pai says nothing. Apparently everything is normal out there.

Another car rushes up behind me, impatiently flashing its headlights. Again, I move onto the shoulder, a gesture Pai says is called *gentileza,* or "courtesy," which is allowing homicidal maniacs to pass. In this case, the madman passes me by coming so close that he nearly grazes my outside mirror. Again, no editorial comment from Pai, because this, too, is normal. It's part of the culture. Brazilians love closeness, intimacy, coziness—even with their automobiles, like women kissing one another on the cheek.

At the end of the two-hour drive, my hands ache from gripping the wheel.

But it's not the driving. It's him. He's constantly controlling, supervising, commanding, and—here's the galling part—he's constantly right. There's no disputing him. His logic, like gold in Fort Knox, is impregnable. Of course I must keep my hands on the wheel at all times! Any idiot knows that! But when he gives me this order, I seethe. I fume. I rebel—I lift one hand off the wheel just to provoke him. I'm dying to disobey him, defy him, free myself from him.

Jim, just forget it. Let it go. He always wins. The reason he wins is because the true warrior carefully picks his positions, advancing only those that guarantee victory, and then, like a pit bull, he never lets go.

Another of his terrific Rules: ALWAYS BE RIGHT IN ADVANCE.

Acquiring an automobile late in life, Commander Gavioli never became comfortable at the art of driving. He was always tense and awkward at it. But there's one thing at which he is absolutely magnificent: turning a fifty-five-year-old man with forty years of experience behind the wheel into a sniveling, smoldering, resentful juvenile.

ATTACKING THE DRAGON

"How does Brazil manage inflation?" This is the question I asked Pai the first day we met twenty-five years ago. The answer is—which he didn't give me then—it doesn't. Since that day, inflation has exploded. The government has fought it valiantly, even changing its currency six separate times. When I arrived in 1970, the currency changed from the cruzeiro novo to the cruzeiro. In 1986 it changed to the cruzado. In 1989 it changed to the cruzado novo. In 1990 it changed back to the cruzeiro. In 1993 it changed to the cruzeiro real. In 1994, it changed to the real.

During these twenty-five years, inflation ratcheted up into hyperinflation, skyrocketing an unimaginable 2.8 *trillion* percent. People manage to stay afloat, Pai tells me, because salaries keep rising, indexed to inflation—but always a little behind.

Now, some good news. This year, Brazil's new president, Fernando Henrique Cardoso, is the first to get a stranglehold on hyperinflation, which Brazilians nickname "the dragon." It's only 26 percent this year, 1995. Cardoso is attacking the dragon from four different angles simultaneously with his *Plano Real*, which he started last year as finance minister. First, he's pegging Brazilian currency to the US dollar, making trade and investment more predictable. Next, he's offering higher interest rates for the outside world to invest in Brazil. The arrival of cheaper foreign goods is forcing Brazilian companies to lower their prices. Next, he's slowing the rate at which the government spends more than it takes in. Finally, he's piling up reserves in foreign currency.

Brazilians are crossing their fingers in hopes this all works.

FURTHER WITCHCRAFT

One evening, I stay up late to see Brazilians worship Iemanjá, a Brazilian sea goddess. I go to the beach in Santa Terezinha and stand about fifty yards back from the water, watching waves roll in, rising, cresting, then collapsing in a thud, reborn as long, foam necklaces sliding gracefully toward the shore, dying in the sand with a hiss.

Wading into the night's black water are a couple dozen white-robed worshippers, embraced by the slow-moving necklaces. The worshippers release homemade wooden boats one or two feet long, painted sky blue and containing offerings to the goddess: lighted candles, flowers, fruit—along with prayers. Some are carried out to sea, accepted by Iemanjá. Others are rejected, washed back onto the beach.

Actually, I never see Iemanjá, unless she's in the waves, which are magical.

At dawn the next morning, my commonsensical father-in-law combs the beach, collecting candles rejected by the goddess the night before. He takes them to the Catholic priest in the village, with whom he is friendly, offering the candles for use in his little church. As Pai knew he would, the priest considers them unholy and politely declines. Then Pai takes them to his cottage for practical uses, thus exercising another fundamental Rule: WASTE NOT—a nugget of wisdom he picked up in the Great Depression.

Pai is a practical, no-nonsense guy. Not a superstitious bone in his body. But he's also Brazilian, which means that, regarding pagan beliefs, Pai leans agnostic. *"Não acredito, mas respeito"* (I don't believe them, but I respect them), is his stock opinion. On the day he is to leave his beloved little cottage for the season, I witness him invoke witchcraft against evildoers.

LOVE MADE VISIBLE

But first he has to close the cottage for the winter. I'm up at 6:00 a.m. to help.

Pai has his own home-grown security system. It begins by sealing shut his five windows with heavy plywood panels. Perhaps not by accident, they're painted the same hopeful sky blue as the tiny boats of the sea-goddess worshippers. He attaches the panels, which are slightly larger than the windows, with screws. But that's not enough. Then he anchors them at each corner with ten-inch bolts that penetrate all the way through the wall.

Pai needs no help sealing up his cottage. He's been doing it alone for years using tricks based on self-reliance. For example, to manage the heavy plywood panels, he's installed beneath each window a narrow supporting shelf to hold the panel in position while he bolts it.

The patron saint of self-reliance, Henry David Thoreau, could take lessons from Pai.

Perhaps as a courtesy to me, he accepts my help. As well he should. His legs are thinning, his muscles are sagging, his skin is loosening and bunching up at the elbows.

He holds a panel in place while I drive a screw into the window frame as far as I can, a half inch shy of flush. *"Me dá isso"* (Here, gimme that). He grabs the screwdriver from me, and with a few quick twists of his mighty eighty-year-old arm, he sinks the screw into the wood as if it were a bar of soap. He shoots me a disdainful glance.

By now, Daisi and Sarah have finished loading the car. They sit on the plastic couch in the living room, ready to go. Daisi asks her mother whether she wants to pee beforehand. *"Não, faço xixi só às quatro"* (No, I pee only at four o'clock), says her mother, whose entire life is built upon self-control.

He screws two nuts plus a washer onto a bolt. *"Senhor Jim,* this is a Third World country," he says, highlighting his skill as a survivor. He's clearly proud of his indigenous security system.

Oops. A setback. The panels aren't fitting the windows, screens and shutters properly. We have to unscrew the screws, unbolt the bolts, realign everything and then re-screw and re-bolt them all back together again.

"Ai, meu Deus, por que tanto trabalho?" (Oh my God, why so much work?) he whispers to himself, while unscrewing and unbolting and re-screwing and re-bolting. It's getting hot. He's sweating and losing patience.

This is an opportunity to get philosophical and remind him that work is punishment for our ancestors' disobedience in the Garden. In our time, it's a punishment measured out in drops of sweat wrung from our mortal brows. But I notice he's not in the mood, so I skip it.

The last two windows take a full hour to undo and redo.

Finally, except for the front door, the house is boarded up. Daisi and Sarah are still sitting in the living room, now completely shuttered and dark, impatiently twiddling their thumbs.

But before attacking the front door, Pai goes to secure the front gate, a barrier so low that any burglar can step over it with ease. He lashes the gate to its moorings with thick insulated copper wire, twisting the ends tight and clipping them off at the nubbins.

Clearly, this is overkill. Wiring shut this low gate, only slightly taller than my knee, is like repulsing mosquitos with a picket fence. I'm tired and irritated. Let's finish this.

At last, the front door. He barricades it shut with another large, heavy panel of thick plywood. He secures it with two massive padlocks, wrapped in plastic bags to prevent the ocean air from turning hardened steel into dust. From dust they come, to dust these padlocks shall return.

"If he wants to break in, he can, but this will make it harder," he says, imagining an intruder. The cottage is now sealed so tight that mosquitos trapped inside will die of suffocation.

By now, Daisi and Sarah have moved and have been sitting in the car for more than an hour, their patience at the snapping point, when Pai discovers he left his identification documents inside the cottage.

We step over the wired-shut gate with depressing ease and lay siege to the front door, unwrapping the wires that seal the bags that contain the padlocks that secure the bolts that hold the plywood that barricades the door. We unlock the door and he collects his documents. Then we back our way out, locking the door, mounting the barricade, bolting the barricade, padlocking the bolts, bagging the padlocks, and sealing the bags with wires.

This all borders on insanity. We started at 7:00 a.m. and now it's 3:00 p.m. The cottage is secured with five padlocks, six plywood panels, ten built-in locks, seventeen bolts, and fifty-nine screws. What's missing is a moat filled with alligators. The indefatigable German has worked me to exhaustion. Why I chose him for a father-in-law is beyond me.

Maybe now's a good time to remind him where work comes from—punishment for our sins. Actually, as a Unitarian, I don't believe this. I don't believe he does, either. He worked hard today. Perhaps one day I will consider it a privilege to have witnessed his Herculean efforts to protect his humble cottage by the sea, his jewel, the crown of his retirement. Regarding work, I suspect he's close to the Quakers, who believe work is love made visible.

At long last—the cottage locked, bolted and boarded—he's ready to leave. But not quite. Let's not forget the sorcery. He assembles a dozen empty tomato cans that he's saved to complete the final step in delivering his bungalow from evil. He fills them with gravel. He sticks a candle in each one and arranges the cans in the form of a cross at the threshold of his front door.

Daisi and Sarah, at their wits' end, call for him to stop the madness and get in the car.

Ignoring them, he chants a magical word, with force, *"Saravá! Saravá! Saravá!"* At each chant, he shakes his right hand once, which flops loosely at the end of his wrist, causing his meaty index finger to snap loudly against his middle finger. Like a maestro wielding the baton, he waves his arm this way and that to get the utmost out of this witchcraft. Then, gradually slowing the rhythm of his snapping finger, like a priest, he sprinkles holy water on the cryptic tomato cans.

By summoning the pagan spirits of house insurance, he doesn't need State

Farm, which we have in Minnesota. His cottage is now protected against thieves, he says.

I chuckle in disbelief.

"Jim, não mexe com isso" (Jim, don't mess with this). "If you do, you'll develop a tic, or walk with a limp, or something will false inside you."

I smile, searching his face for irony. I find none.

In the car on our way to Porto Alegre, he tells me that fully one-third of Santa Terezinha's cottages have been burglarized. *"Muitos dos ladrões são adolescentes"* (Lots of the thieves are adolescents), "who steal for alcohol or maybe a bicycle. But there are some professionals. I greet and talk to all of them, regardless of color. In twenty-two years, our cottage has never been broken into."

Okay, maybe his absurd fortifications aren't so ridiculous. Maybe his enchanted tomato cans actually work. Maybe he's a magical realist, like the great South American novelist Gabriel Garcia Marquez, whom Pai wouldn't be caught dead reading.

DEAD GIRL

Driving him home one day we see a dead girl sprawled on the hot asphalt. Her legs lie in an awkward position and she's partially covered with a cloth. Slowly, we pass the body, the police, and a silent crowd of people. She'll be going to Pedestrian Heaven, I hope, while the driver who hit her will be sent to Motorist Hell.

"Vai, Jim, vai" (Keep going, Jim, keep going).

He's quiet for a long time. Then he begins talking about his fatherless childhood. I don't know why. Maybe it has something to do with seeing the dead girl. This is the first time he's said anything about his father to me, even though Daisi and I have enquired several times. "There's little to say," he'd respond. One time he bluntly said, "Put a stone on this subject."

Burial with a heavy stone is one way to dispose of an unfortunate childhood. No air, no water, no sunlight is allowed to fertilize these memories. Everything is silent down there. A silence that poet Robert Bly says exists in the "grief-knowing man." The burial is so deep that when his father died, and people came to the house to offer condolences, Daisi was astonished to learn she even had a grandfather. She didn't know he was alive until he was dead.

After another long silence, still looking out the car window, he matter-of-factly states, in his rational German mood, that when he was born his father rejected the family, and his mother became "unraveled." I'm not sure what this means. He doesn't go into detail. She eventually recovered, he says, and took him and his older brother, Rui, with her to São Paulo, where she found work as a domestic in homes of wealthy people. Years later, at fifteen, he moved to Porto Alegre, where he began sending her small sums of money by working as a messenger boy.

When I was fifteen, I believe I was still reading comic books.

If he were to tell the story of his life, the first sentence would have to be the departure of his father. And yet, over the years I've known him, this is a sentence he almost never utters, much less explains. Despite our attempts to know more, he always glosses over this first sentence. Indeed, the first fifteen years of his life, the foundation of everything to come—like the submerged part of an iceberg beneath the sea, a huge chunk of his personality—remain dark to his children, and me. Perhaps even to himself. His autobiography, were he to write it, wouldn't start at birth. It would always begin at fifteen, when he "became independent."

Of course, he would never consider his life to be a story, as in a book, for example. This is because books drift toward art, and art drifts toward fairy tale. For him, life is no fairy tale. It's hard as stone. It hurts like a stick in the eye. He wastes no time on books.

But from age fifteen on, the story would be called—and these are his words—*"A Luta"* (The Struggle).

Bits and pieces of his story actually do crop up over time, like springtime stones in a farmer's field. They might appear at lunch, or in a car, or on the couch after supper, or at bedtime. It's never a full story. It's always an incident here and there, separated by gaps in time and space in the natural way that lives of old people are revealed to their families. Author Wendell Berry says stories told by old people contain a music so subtle and vast that no ear can hear it all, except in fragments. Over the years I've heard fragments of his story, parts of a long chant perhaps resembling the prolonged, intermittent song of the humpback whale.

Still driving after seeing the dead girl, I ask whether he resents his father.

"No. He never existed for me."

Then, in a fragment floating up from the bottom of the iceberg, he recalls his mother, Amanda.

"She never really understood me, but Sarah did."

Sarah, I knew, lost both her parents, her father to the influenza pandemic of 1918, and her mother to typhoid fever.

"Sarah and I had something in common" he said, "we were both used to survival living."

Survival living. I know it from movies and books, meaning I don't know it at all. As children, neither one had much of a family. What they did have was each other.

Still driving, feeling him lift the heavy stone—even just a crack—from his buried childhood, so alien to my own happy childhood, and, still driving on these perilous streets, recalling the dead girl in the street, the weight of his losses overcomes me. My mind darkens. A heavy hand plucks a string in my chest, a low resonating string I've not heard before. My eyes blur. I'd better pull over and stop the car.

Then the weight lifts.

Thoreau wondered whether there could be a greater miracle than to look, even for an instant, through another's eyes. Maybe this just happened.

"O sinal mudou para ti—para!" (The signal changed for you—stop!) His anxious driving advice starts up again.

"Get into the right lane." Pause . . .

"Go straight . . . STRAIGHT!" Pause . . .

"Watch out for that speed bump." I slow down over the bump.

"Okay, you can go ahead now."

Oddly, the sting of his commands is gone. My resistance vanishes. I simply do what he tells me. I become his tool, an extension of his will. His orders are still tinged with his usual anxiety, but now I see they express something deeper—his caution, his alertness, his habit of looking ahead, his intimacy with the Brazilian street and the hazardous Brazilian world.

They all spring from another of his Cardinal Rules: BE WATCHFUL.

Why has it taken me so many years to notice his frailty? I guess it's because connections between people sometimes grow slowly, mostly underground, unseen.

On another day, I'm driving him somewhere again. It happens to be Father's Day. I congratulate him on being a father and wish him a happy Father's Day. *"Não tenho pai"* (I have no father). Then, these slow, sad words: "I have no family." This catches me off guard. After a silence, I say he should be proud to be the father of a great family. But he's thinking of a different father, one he never had, and a different family, one that was broken. He touches the wound.

No one can be whole who hasn't been broken.

SUMMER 1997
Dona Sarah and the Two Josés

Brazil has made positive reforms in the past two years. The state-owned telephone company where Pai used to work, for example, had become an inefficient drag on the economy. President Fernando Henrique Cardoso broke it up into regional chunks and sold them off to other companies, increasing competition, improving service, and expanding telephone availability, including cell phones. The President is taking charge.

Today is hot in Santa Terezinha. Pai and Sarah have just finished their noon meal of black beans, rice, sausage, and fried potatoes. They're spending the summer at his beloved bungalow at the sea. Visiting them is their youngest son, Davison, from São Paulo, now fifty, along with his wife, Laura, and teenage daughter, Fernanda. Pai is eighty-two, Sarah is eighty-seven. They are happy.

The news of what happens next reaches me in Minnesota by phone and letter.

Sarah sits in the tiny living room, in front of the dusty little fireplace, as useless in today's heat as a snow shovel in the desert. Above the fireplace hang two large blue oars, crossed like an X. They are gifts from the sports club where Pai used to be president, Grêmio Náutico União, originally a rowing club in the Guaíba River. Covered with years of dust, the oars still appear seaworthy, and, crossed as they are, they seem to protect the household against misfortune.

The day is humid, smack in the middle of Carnaval, Brazil's annual four-day pandemonium, the four most unScandinavian days in the Brazilian calendar. This is when work stops, night and day exchange identities, and revelry reshapes reality.

In the little kitchen, dabbing perspiration from her forehead with a handkerchief, Sarah prepares *cafezinho*, a daily ceremony that helps anchor their marriage, now sixty years old.

They share it punctually at 3:00 p.m. This is the moment in the day when she takes charge, presiding over a narrow kitchen table below an open window where a dish towel hangs to dry. As always, she controls precisely how much sugar her husband's cup will get.

"*Mais açúcar, Sarah*" (More sugar, Sarah).

"*Chega, filhinho*" (That's enough, son). Because it's the wife who knows her own husband, that's all he gets.

Cafezinho finished, Sarah is seated once more beneath the benevolent crossed oars. Davison is on the couch reading the paper.

Without warning, Sarah moves her mouth, but no sounds emerge. Her voice is gone. Then her right arm and leg go soft.

"*Mãe, o que que tens?*" (Mother, what's wrong?) Davison asks. "Is your tongue caught in your throat?" She doesn't reply.

Fernanda rushes into the room, then flies out the screen door, which bangs shut, in search of a doctor.

Davison and Laura, too distressed to remain in the house, sit on the curb, hugging each other. She is weeping. Within minutes, a man in his early sixties, out of breath and dripping wet from a shower, comes jogging toward the house. The face of the man, who's wearing glasses, is white with anxiety.

"Who are you?" Laura asks.

"José Gavioli," he says, panting. Now it's Laura's turn to go soft. This man says he is José Gavioli, but doesn't look like José Gavioli, doesn't quite sound like José Gavioli and obviously isn't José Gavioli.

He's an impostor, when what they really need is a doctor, not some oddball posing as Pai.

Meanwhile, the "real" José Gavioli stands like a statue beside his wife, frozen in fear, helpless as an infant, his formidable stomach churning in pain.

In the confusion, this seeming impostor, carrying a stethoscope and blood pressure wrap, enters the tiny living room and strides swiftly past the green plastic sofa and paintings on the walls toward Sarah, still seated in the center of the room.

"*Sou um médico*" (I'm a doctor), he announces, and immediately sets to work taking her pulse, just as a real doctor might do.

An hour later, the indomitable family matriarch is taking baby steps toward Davison's car, supported by her venerable aluminum walker, the *andador*. Everyone watches as she inches forward, barely moving, like the proverbial African moon, which moves slowly, but it crosses the town. After a tiny eternity, powered by her own determination, or a life force not of her own making, Sarah reaches the car.

Soon they arrive in the nearby town of Tramandaí. Helped from the car, Sarah propels herself forward, her body rising and sinking with each step on her crippled feet like a boat tossed on a rough sea. She moves slowly toward the doors of the institution she has never entered or trusted, except to have babies—the hospital.

She suffers another attack, losing control of her urine. But she keeps surging forward. Davison holds onto her, tries to guide her, tries to support the woman who bore him, a woman who, despite—or maybe because of— her childhood polio, the loss by age ten of both parents, her upbringing and schooling by American Baptists, has built a life out of refusing help from almost everyone.

The Gavioli matriarch enters the hospital doors largely under her own power. *"Ela tem fibra,"* (She's got fiber) says an exhausted Davison. Once inside, still mute, she suffers two more strokes.

She might not leave the hospital alive, he thinks. He tells his wife to call his sister Lori and brother, Sidnei, to come immediately. Daisi, in the United States, is too far away.

Meanwhile, the impostor, the supposed doctor, who seems more like a real doctor with every passing hour, and who accompanies the family to the hospital, calls a neurologist he knows to examine Sarah. The call is made at the height of Carnaval, and the neurologist, fresh from a half bottle of wine, comes immediately.

At this point, Pai turns to his impersonator and declares, *"Doutor, quero que o senhor cuide da Sarah"* (Doctor, I want you to take care of Sarah).

Sarah stays two days in the hospital, which she later describes as "limpo, limpo, limpo" (clean, clean, clean), having expected the opposite.

She returns to the cottage improved, but still weak in her right leg, arm, eye, and right side of her mouth. Pai decides they will continue to stay at the beach. The family goes into an uproar over this decision. After a family conference—marked by shouts, accusations, recriminations, pounding on the table, and finally forgiveness—Pai agrees that their season in Santa Terezinha is finished. Sarah must return to Porto Alegre for medical observation.

But what about this puzzling newcomer with the same name as Pai—José Gavioli—who comes out of thin air to Sarah's aid?

Turns out he's no impostor after all. He's José Augusto Gavioli, a psychiatrist.

He also is—incredible to astonished younger family members—Pai's half brother. This is the man Pai has been avoiding for six decades. This is a shock rivaling Sarah's stroke, marking a stunning reversal in family history.

No one on Pai's side of the family has ever tried to scale the wall separating Gaviolis from other Gaviolis. Pai's children, raised in the shadow of this wall, know as much about the half brother as they do about the Man in the Moon. At times, they inquired about their father's family. "I have no family," he'd say darkly, in a tone leaving nothing more to say. Pai buried his past in the Tomb of the Unknown Ancestors so deeply that even he seemed to forget he had a brother.

This tomb is so dark, so deep, that his children feared approaching it. It was best to steer clear of this mysterious Other Gavioli, who suddenly has entered their lives, as a psychiatrist, with almost the same name as their father, a man who lives only two blocks from Pai's beach cottage, and only two miles from Pai's home in Porto Alegre. He's the man with glasses who would wave to Pai in friendly greeting, a man whom Pai knew, but wouldn't speak to—an educated and cultured man, a living, breathing painful reminder of a family and privilege he never had.

What bittersweet pleasure it has been for Pai to ignore his half brother, slamming a door shut on any relationship, revenge against that old, never-forgotten door slammed in Pai's face sixty-seven years earlier when he asked his uncle the druggist for a job in the family business.

Family secrets are like buried rivers. They run through us, and shape us in ways in which we're not always aware. Such a river runs through Pai, shaping him, his marriage, his children, and even a peripheral innocent who marries one of his children, like me.

Sarah's stroke, a blow from destiny's hammer, opens a crack in the Gavioli family landscape, allowing the buried river to flood the surface.

Davison is the first to explore this newly opened crack. Two days after his mother returns from the hospital, he walks the two short blocks to the cottage owned by the uncle he has never known, a cottage the uncle purchased five years before Pai had arrived in Santa Terezinha. Davison wants to thank him for rescuing his mother, for arranging medical care, and especially for revealing who he is.

To those who know him, José the psychiatrist is an ebullient, talkative man, full of stories and clever observations, never at a loss for words. But now, in front of Davison, a scout on a reconnaissance mission from the other side of the wall, he chokes on words.

"Não consigo falar" (I can't speak), the uncle says in a trembling voice. "My heart is full. I am overcome."

The buried river surges to the surface in tears.

Davison knows immediately that this man is a true Gavioli.

In the next few days, the dry terrain of Pai's heart is moistened. Its heaviness grows lighter. Its airless part, after so many years in a vacuum, is breathing oxygen again. He and his rediscovered half brother arrange to meet.

Like Italians, they laugh and shout. Like gauchos, they embrace and slap one other on the back, five times in perfect unison. And, like the wall that separated Germany, the barrier between the two Josés begins to crumble. Family members stare at each other across the rubble in astonishment.

The two brothers knew of each other, but never really knew each other. This is because the Gavioli heart, the one that beats in the breast of all true

Gaviolis, is a volatile, mercurial organ capable of dividing and separating family members. Like the confluence of Brazil's two great rivers—the clear Amazon and the dark Rio Negro, merging but flowing separately side by side for many miles until downstream they finally blend into one river—the two brothers and their families are now becoming one.

And maybe, just maybe, in the churning and mixing of the separate waters, Pai is starting to forgive someone far upstream, his father.

Whether this is true or not, the brothers are happy men. Perhaps a genetic hand is at work here. Their grandfather—the root of all Brazilian Gaviolis—is, after all, *Felix*. His name is *Feliz* in Portuguese, *Felice* in Italian, and "Happy" in English. The brothers share the happiness gene their grandfather brought with him across the Atlantic in his voyage from Italy to Brazil.

With ceremonial flourish, a jubilant Pai announces to his family: *Estou reconciliado com meu irmão!* (I am reconciled with my brother!)

"Reconciliation? What reconciliation?" Sidnei dares ask when Pai is out of sight. "How can there be reconciliation when they were never together to begin with?"

Never mind. Pai is uncontainable. "Sarah," he proclaims to his wife, as if addressing the Lions Club, *"Descobri meu irmão!"* (I've discovered my brother!)

Let history take note that Pai did not make this discovery alone. It was destiny's lightning bolt that struck Sarah Madeiros Gavioli voiceless, a mute silence loud enough to shatter the ancient wall between the brothers.

Mindful of this, Sarah lowers her head and, over the tops of her glasses, eyes her husband with a reproachful glance. *"Bem, estou casada com um Gavioli por sessenta e um anos"* (Okay, I've been married to a Gavioli for sixty-one years, and I have to suffer a seizure to get him to speak to his own brother!).

The two Josés;
Dr. José Augusto Gavioli,
left, with Pai

Like Italians, they laugh and shout. Like gauchos, they embrace and slap one other on the back, five times in perfect unison. And, like the wall that separated Germany, the barrier between the two Josés begins to crumble. Family members stare at each other across the rubble in astonishment.

MARCH 1998:
A Slice of Salami

Leaving snow and ice and arriving in ninety-seven-degree air is disorienting. I become a dishrag with no energy, direction, or inspiration. In my fatigue, the Gaviolis seem to become moving mannequins, lifeless imitations of their actual selves.

Over the last three years, Pai has grown thinner. His hair is whiter. His skin is sagging. His wit, however, remains indestructible.

At lunch one day at his heavy, dark table, he announces: *"Ah, Senhor Jim, nossa situação econômica da casa está catastrófica"* (Mister Jim, our home economic situation is catastrophic.) "It's definitely not good. Not one bit." He points to the last slice of salami, offering it to me.

As I reach out to accept it, a worried look spreads across his face. He wrings his hands in despair. In a shaky voice, watching my hand reach for the slice of salami, he says ominously, "Oh, what a shame. This is very bad for me."

My hand hovers over the salami. Should I take it? No, better not. Then, why not? I take it.

He looks at the empty plate for several moments, shaking his head, accepting this last straw, which apparently is breaking the camel's back.

All this theater for a slice of salami.

Sarah is also thinner. She may never walk again. She's fought against the wheelchair for years, but now must succumb. She says her memory is slipping, which Daisi thinks is caused by tiny strokes. Her false teeth, which no longer fit her shrunken gums, move in her mouth when she talks. Despite everything, she's in good spirits.

Daisi and I sleep on the second floor, across from Sarah's room, which has her books, paintings, dolls, and phonograph records. It's a room she used to reach by crawling up the stairs on her hands and knees to teach me Portuguese. It's a room she'll never enter again.

ONE MAN, TWO FATHERS

Pai's half brother invites Daisi and me to dinner at his exclusive club in Porto Alegre. José Augusto Godoy Gavioli is twenty years younger than Pai, shorter than Pai, but with the same stout build. His black hair receding at the temples, fleshy face, large nose, and wire-rim glasses give him an uncanny resemblance to the German-American psychiatrist Erich Fromm. A jovial raconteur, José

Augusto holds forth nonstop on a multiplicity of topics that blend seamlessly into one another without any help whatsoever from listeners. On one of his rambles that evening, he rejects psychotherapy as expensive and worse than useless, "... *causando depressão nas pessoas que não tinha antes*" (... causing depression in people who didn't have it before). I guess he prefers paralyzing the soul with drugs, rather than curing it through meditation and therapeutic dialogue. Which is odd, because his love of dialogue is surpassed only by his love of monologue.

Pai and José Augusto have the same mannerisms, same bearing, same roly-poly physique, same timbre of voice, and same exuberance, wit, verbosity, and love of churrasco. Not to mention the same father.

José Augusto recounts his family history, starting in 1932, during the Great Depression. That's when his then-future father, Augusto, age forty-seven, finally ends his seventeen-year separation from Amanda, and marries for a second time.

Augusto's new wife is Aracy Godoy Gomes, who's already forty and comes from a strong Catholic family in Porto Alegre's thin upper crust. She's a strong-minded, energetic music teacher, who once directed a high-school girls' choir singing "God Bless America" for visiting World War II General Mark Clark, allegedly bringing tears to the general's eyes.

Initially, the Gomes family disapproves of Augusto owing to his previous marriage. A devout Catholic, Aracy insists on a church wedding. Because divorce and remarriage are illegal in Brazil at the time, the couple crosses the border to Rivera, Uruguay, where Augusto obtains an annulment from Amanda, opening the way to a church ceremony.

Three years later, Aracy gives birth to a son. This fortunate infant acquires no less than four names, following a Brazilian fondness for not leaving anyone out. His first name, José, comes from Saint Joseph, his mother's favorite saint. His second name, Augusto, is his father's first name. His third name, Godoy, is his mother's middle name. His last name, Gavioli, links him to the chain of Gaviolis stretching all the way back to Felix and his murky origins in Modena, Italy. The infant, bearing on his tiny shoulders the weight of history imbedded in these four names, becomes known as José Augusto for short.

The elder Gavioli's two sons travel widely different roads. One is the rocky back road traveled by Pai and his impoverished mother. The other is the smooth highway traveled two decades later by José Augusto, a distinguished professional, supported by his esteemed father and wealthy mother.

José Augusto, who will be raised receiving copious amounts of food and education, develops into a prominent Porto Alegre psychiatrist. He inherits his father's handsome stone-block, colonial-style home, where, starting at age five, he lives almost the rest of his life. Entering this home, one feels like one is entering the nineteenth century. It has high ceilings, dark rooms, dark paintings, dark antique furniture, dark carved-wood cabinets, a dark ancient German piano, and dark antique lamps, all not quite redeemed by a lighter-colored inlaid wood floor. It all has the fragrance of history, like a museum. The home is a living memorial to the father who loved his third son, but who never existed for Pai.

Curiously, one father is actually two fathers. Pai's father was a young, robust, charismatic traveling salesman forging his way through a rugged Brazilian interior. José Augusto's father was a prominent, middle-aged, urbane man of civic affairs. Twenty years can split a man in two.

"*Meu pai* (my father), who was nearly fifty when I was born," José Augusto explains, "never beat me, was never severe with me, and treated me as an adult. He gave me complete freedom. He was calm, highly disciplined, and extremely correct. He was a born gourmet and a bon vivant. He loved opera, food, and red wine. I never saw him tipsy from alcohol."

He was a voracious reader of newspapers and books, especially romance and history. For a time he was a newspaper correspondent from Caxias to Porto Alegre's then major paper, *Correio do Povo*. He was one of several prominent speakers at a ceremony dedicating a new Catholic church in Porto Alegre. He also was a famously powerful swimmer, a gene submerged in Pai, whose childhood lacked sports, but which resurfaced in Sidnei and Daisi.

Surviving into his early eighties, Augusto dies in the late 1960s of irreversible senility. On his death bed he implores his son, "Let me die."

"*Esperou minha visita*" (He waited for my visit). "I approached his bed and asked him, 'How are you, Old Gavioli?' He looked at me, closed his eyes, and died."

The elder Gavioli left this world in the company of his son, the younger of his two Josés, the one he loved.

INHERITANCE REJECTED

"He never helped me in his life, and he's not going to help me in his death!" Pai roars to a stunned inheritance lawyer. Brazilian law entitles Pai, one of two remaining sons, to half of his father's estate. Already dead is the third brother, Rui, whose funeral was paid for by Pai.

"I'll sign any paper you want to remove me from my inheritance," Pai demands, an astonishing order by any measure, fueled by his ancient hurt.

Despite that, the dead live on. Pai's lifeless father continues to occupy free rental space in his head, keeping the lights on and the faucets running, producing a steady drain of psychic energy. Were Pai ever to forgive the dead man, the sole beneficiary would be Pai himself, an inheritance greater than gold.

AN OPEN WOUND

Coincidentally, around the time Pai's father dies, his mother is hospitalized.

Pai brings Amanda home from the hospital to recuperate in bed upstairs. Daisi, then a university student, remembers her grandmother Amanda as big, bony, and angry. Amanda's sister, on the other hand, Daisi's great aunt Marta, is Amanda's opposite. Both women are tall, but the similarity ends there. Marta is soft, kind, and caressing. When Daisi was a girl, she remembers Marta combing her hair, a tenderness Daisi has never forgotten. Amanda, however, is harsh and bitter. Rejected by her former husband and struggling in poverty, she's had a hard life. She comes home from the hospital with one thin leg and one thick leg, which has a bandage wrapped over an open wound that refuses to heal.

Around eleven o'clock one morning, Dona Eva, the Gavioli housekeeper, climbs the stairs to attend to Amanda. She enters the room and finds her lying in bed, mouth open, wounded leg hanging down, touching the floor. She's not breathing. Dona Eva calls downstairs for Daisi, who enters the room, the first family member to see the lifeless Amanda.

As if on purpose, death chooses to visit both of Pai's parents around the same time, each dying in the home of a son. Pai was not especially close to her. She was an iron mother, the anvil upon whom he was hammered into the man he is today. Sarah never liked her. Nonetheless, Pai cared for her in her decline.

Some days later, Daisi dreams about her grandmother. From the far end of a long corridor, Amanda's legs, disconnected from her body—which is nowhere to be seen—slowly walk toward Daisi. The two legs, one of them wounded, grow larger as they come closer. It's a frightening dream, conjuring a woman who was never able to become a whole person.

CALMA, CALMA

While her parents had been poor, Lori—who's married to a well-appointed state judge—is not. She lives high on the food chain yet still feels outrage at a world she believes treats her unfairly. One day, she and her husband, Neco, argue over a cell phone. Cell phones are beginning to proliferate in Brazil, and she wants one.

He says she doesn't need one.

Lori is upset and tense as Daisi, André, and I join her in a walk through her upscale Porto Alegre neighborhood. At one house after another, from behind their iron fences, protection dogs charge us, snarling and gnashing their teeth.

Earlier, Lori had told André, who's now twenty-five and has been living with Pai and Sarah for a year (while Marcus is in Minnesota thinking about applying to grad school), that he would be welcome to stay at her house, which is much closer and more convenient to where he teaches English. Now, however, owing to the tension of the cell phone dispute, it becomes clear this is not a good idea. Realizing that she must withdraw her offer to André, Lori weeps in disappointment.

Daisi, André, and I return to Pai's house by cab at night. Arriving, we notice a man lying in the dark on the sidewalk, his head propped against the fence next to the gate. I hope he's merely drunk and just sleeping. Nervous, I ask the cabbie to wait a minute to see if we can get through the gate safely. "Make sure you have the key ready when we get to the gate," André warns. We run from the cab and I open the gate quickly. The body stirs. We rush inside, my heart pounding. Safely behind the locked gate, I wave to the cabbie, who waves back and drives off.

This incident, together with today's conflict at Lori's house, makes me uneasy.

We go upstairs and Daisi immediately phones Lori, who by now has worked herself into a rage. *"Calma Lori, calma, calma . . ."* Daisi says. André and I sit on a bed, listening. After several agitated minutes, the call ends. Hearing the commotion, Pai gets out of bed and slowly climbs the stairs. *"O que que é?"* (What's going on?), he asks. To avoid agitating him, as one must with Pai, Daisi glosses over Lori's fury. "Lori and Neco aren't getting along today."

His face grows somber. Now he speaks quietly, with biblical solemnity, choosing his words slowly, stepping carefully around family land mines. *"Às vezes, a gente não se entende"* (Sometimes people don't understand one another), he says, deftly describing marriage difficulties.

"André," he declares, "you must think very carefully now. You must decide where you will stay, even if it's not where you want to stay. You already know what Sarah and I think," meaning he's welcome to continue staying at their house.

As I've seen him do before, the gravity of his tone lifts the moment into a ceremonial dimension, as if André's decision is a turning point in Gavioli history. Even if the decision fails to reach historic family importance, at the very least Pai approaches the issue with the caution one needs in dealing with Gavioli family volatility, not unlike the care one needs in stepping over downed power lines.

André readily agrees to stay with his grandparents. Upon hearing this, Pai goes downstairs and returns with a box of chocolates. *"Come isso para se acalmar"* (Eat this to calm down). André, who's calm by nature, is not the one who's agitated here.

For Pai, chocolates are Prozac.

Later, Daisi sees him swallow some pills for his volatile heart.

Two nights later, our last evening before returning home, we're at a family gathering at Sidnei's house, too late in the evening for Pai and Sarah to attend. As usual, Lori arrives late. But my goodness, what a change forty-eight hours can make. Arms waving and eyes blazing, she recounts one hilarious story after another about Gavioli family misadventures. We're all doubled over in laughter. She's the life of the party, performing at the top of her roller-coaster personality, miles above her depths of two days ago. In this, Lori demonstrates that she possesses—more than any of her siblings—the exuberance of her high-spirited father.

Next day, at the airport, for the eighth time, we say goodbye to Pai. And, as he does every time, he weeps, drawing our tears.

Daisi, with her exuberant younger sister, Lori.

MARCH 1998
A Slice of Salami

MARCH 1999
Preserving Patrimony

Daisi and I used to be awakened in the morning by a cock crowing. No longer. What Pai's neighborhood has lost in chickens, it's gained in dogs. Now, instead of cocks crowing, guard dogs are barking, a symphony of yelping and howling that rises and falls and moves across the neighborhood like wind in the trees.

It's been only a year since our last visit. It's just occurred to me that as long as I can remember, Sarah has always called Pai by his last name, Gavioli. She even wrote it on their wedding invitation. This name seems oddly distant for a marriage so devoted. However, she also calls him *filhinho,* meaning "my boy," much more intimate than Gavioli seems to be.

While Sarah sits in her wheelchair in the living room, I take the occasion to ask her about *filhinho*.

"Sou cinco anos mais velha" (I'm five years older), she says, "and I became independent at age ten, while he became independent later, at age fifteen. That's why I call him 'son.'" Their early departure from their parents and subsequent independence is everything for these two.

I can't help noticing the protective touch in her use of the word "son." Sitting right here on the sofa, Pai hears her but says nothing in response, apparently acknowledging his almost filial dependence on her.

Almost before we know it, our eighteen-day stay is over and we're about to take our ninth departure. Sarah sits in the front room, erect and regal in her wheelchair. We share a long embrace. Stoic as usual, she wishes me *"uma boa viagem"* (bon voyage), saying no more than that. This is how she handles our departures. Factually. Realistically. No tears.

The other pillar of the family is outside, on the sidewalk beneath the scrub tree in front of his miniature plot of grass.

"Não vou" (I'm not going). Never before has he refused to go to the airport to see us off. "I try to control myself there, but it's no use," he says, struggling to hold back tears.

After this sadness passes, he tells me, in a solemn tone, as he has already several times during this visit, that by investing in repairs to his three apartment units, he's conserving *"o patrimônio"* (his property, meaning his children's inheritance). This reminds me of how he flatly rejected the inheritance to which he was legally entitled from his father's patrimony. I wonder whether he means he's a better father than the one he had. He goes on, in grave tones, to point out what he and Sarah have managed to acquire in their earthly journey, mentioning their home, their apartment units, their car, their savings, and how they intend to leave it all to their children. In listing his worldly possessions in this way, bravely facing Final Things, he swims in emotional waters too deep for me. I don't have the emotional equipment to reach him at his depth, so I remain silent.

Looming behind his words is the Brazilian currency, the *real*. Ominously, during our brief stay, it lost a staggering 50 percent against the dollar. This is because, several days ago, Brazil's Central Bank severed the *real* from the dollar, to which it had been pegged for five years. It's now a floating currency, cut away from a sluggish world economy in order to stimulate Brazil's economic growth. This sudden inflation is scary, but it may be temporary, because at long last, the *real* has become a stable currency, ending decades of debilitating inflation. Meanwhile, Pai's house and three apartment units—the lion's share of his patrimony—retain their value despite this sudden inflation.

André carefully backs Pai's sedan out of its narrow garage space. Positioning himself on the sidewalk behind the car, Pai holds his arms aloft a foot apart and beckons André to inch backward, as if guiding a Boeing 747 from its hangar. As always, the commander is in charge. Wearing unpretentious shorts, T-shirt and flip-flops, the old man guides the automobile he now rarely drives into the sunlight. He's always guiding, directing, leading. He's the principal energy, emotional force, foresight, humor, generosity, and anxiety forming the glue that holds the Gavioli family together. It's not only me, but also the rest of the family, who declares him impossible to live with, and impossible to live without.

As André drives to the airport, I sit in the front seat, silent, holding back tears, which is what he does to me every departure, all nine times, all nine tortured times. . . .

FEBRUARY 2000

March to Berlin

We're coming every year now. The day after we arrive, Pai wakes Daisi and me at 6:00 a.m. to join him on his morning walk. This is when he releases his inner German soldier. At eighty-five, he's been walking four kilometers every day except Sundays, a regime he started when he suffered chest pains twenty years ago.

This morning, as always, he becomes a German field marshal leading his troops to war. Head locked in a forward position, he sets a punishing pace conducted in iron-jawed silence. His long arms swing like pendulums. His big hands cupped, as if swimming through Brazil's humid morning air. His relentless, mechanical stride suggests a machine assembled back in the industrial age.

White tufts of hair stick out from his cap and bounce in rhythm to his step. Today he wears a T-shirt with the word "ferryboat" in English on the back, reminding me of a Walt Whitman poem about the final ferry that carries us all to the next world.

Pai is not ready to board the final ferry. He's firmly rooted in this world, like the ancient tree roots we encounter that heave up and crack the sidewalk. We march around the roots, holes, rubble, dead branches, boulders keeping cars off the sidewalk, and sawed-off metal posts poking out of the pavement. Porto Alegre sidewalks demand alertness not required on ours, even in winter.

Daisi and I struggle to keep up, like little boats tethered to an ocean liner. I know the route by heart and could take the lead, but Pai is always in charge, always in front of me, as he has been in the thirty years I've known him.

Daisi and I nickname these walks the Forced March to Berlin—Berlin being the name of the avenue on which we begin and end.

Pai always takes precisely the same route, curiously tracing his German, Brazilian, and Italian roots. We start at Berlin, evoking his mother's German ancestry. Then we take Benjamin Constant, named for a leader in Brazil's independence movement. Finally, we turn onto Cristóvão Colombo, honoring the Italian explorer and Pai's Italian paternity.

We barely start the walk and already we pass a semiconscious man with bloodshot eyes slouched on a stool in front of a small neighborhood bar. I recognize him from previous years, a sentinel at its dark door. He waves a drunken greeting to us. Pai, the teetotaler, passes him as if he doesn't exist.

We reach a tiny metal shack the size of an outhouse perched at the curb on the sidewalk. It's owned by a locksmith, one of hundreds throughout this insecure city, keeping residents stocked with keys for their thousands of gates.

Only once did I ever see this locksmith actually grinding a key. One day I saw him leaning against the corner telephone pole, chewing on a toothpick. "How's work?" I asked. *"É uma loucura"* (It's a madhouse), he said. A hand-painted advertisement on his shack announces, *Troca de Segredos,* or "Changing Secrets," meaning he can change lock combinations. This is a country where I guess it's wise every now and then to change your secrets.

Without slowing down, Pai grabs the stool in front of the shack, as he does almost every day, and keeps walking. As if on cue, the locksmith cheerfully yells *"Ladrão!"* (Thief!), and Pai returns the stool. They each smile and Pai pushes on.

We cross the first lane of heavy traffic on Benjamin Constant, reaching a concrete island in the middle of the avenue. The island is home to several imprisoned pine trees that live in the roar of traffic instead of the silence of the forest. I feel wind coming off the lethal river of fast-moving cars, trucks, buses, and motorcycles howling and screaming perilously close to us. Unsteady, I grasp a tree, and with my other hand, I hold my eighty-five-year-old companion's arm to keep him from stumbling one fatal step forward. It feels strange to support the arm of a man who has intimidated me for years.

"Vamos!" he shouts abruptly, and steps off the island—a millisecond behind a passing car—as if it were imaginary, not a ton of high-speed, bone-crushing metal. Caught off guard, I lurch forward after him, trusting this venerable captain to lead me across this deadly river to its other side, life still locked to limb.

Safely across, he shakes his arm loose from my hand, reasserting his independence, the motor that drove him through the Great Depression.

We reach Cristovão Colombo and its nearly uncrossable stream of traffic. A bony-ribbed workhorse wearing blinders drags a cart loaded with cardboard for recycling. The driver, *a papeleiro,* or, "cardboard person," snaps his whip on the wretched animal's sweaty back. Sporty cars snarl impatiently around this plodding piece of Brazil's past.

We're marching again. Pai leads us single file through crowds on the sidewalk, or into the street to get around them, signaling back to us with his arm to stay close to the curb. The field marshal never looks back at us as he leads our charge through enemy territory. I try to make small talk. No response. He's focused on our progress and keeping his troops in single file behind him. *"Ohlem os carros"* (Watch the cars), he warns, momentarily breaking his silence. He's making forward progress, as if mimicking the arc of his life, from poverty to the middle class.

FEBRUARY 2000
March to Berlin

We keep moving. We brush against the chipped walls of decaying two-story dwellings built right to the edge of the narrow sidewalk. We pass beneath small, colonial-style, wrought-iron balconies, from which I imagine a young Juliet a century ago smiling down at a young Romeo, wooing her with his guitar. Farther on, stone faces of Roman deities issuing from the walls, their cheeks streaked black with sooty tears, gaze down at us mortals walking through the current world.

We pass the Cinema Presidente, formerly a grand old neighborhood cinema, now housing one of Brazil's fast-growing evangelical churches. The old movie marquee proclaims: *Salva, Cura, Redime* (Saves, Cures, Redeems).

Pai makes a rare stop. He greets a hotel doorman, an old-timer hosing down the sidewalk against the promise of a hot day. As he does everywhere we go—butcher shop, grocery store, bakery—he introduces me as *meu genro americano* (my American son-in-law). The doorman asks whether I like President George W. Bush, now just one month into his first term. "No," I say. He breaks into a broad smile, shakes my hand, and pounds me on the back with his free hand in the semi-embrace men use in this nation. I'm embarrassed, but gratified that Pai introduces me to people this way, as if he approves my marriage to his daughter.

We pass an old woman clutching a purse to her breast. She gossips with another old woman through the imprisoning bars of a sidewalk gate. We pass other women clutching bags and purses, faces tightly closed, eyes shifting about, alert for purse snatchers. We pass people waiting at a bus stop, all silent, some lost in a dream, others with empty expressions, without dreams. Traffic waits impatiently at a red light, tense as sprinters in the blocks with the starting gun raised.

We walk around a man sleeping in a fetal position on the sidewalk. He has dirty feet. We pass a blind man sitting with his back against a wall, holding out a delicate hand for coins. A young man in dirty clothes sleeps on the sidewalk on newspaper. Two young men are asleep in a driveway, their heads pillowed against a garage door. A family of four sleeps on concrete next to the doors of a bank, not yet open. A young Indian mother, perhaps from the Amazon, snot-nosed baby in her lap, sits begging for coins on the sidewalk with her legs sticking out so people have to step over them.

I've heard that in São Paulo, Brazil's megalopolis, there are homeless families who live under freeway overpasses and yet cling to the illusion of home—setting a table with a tablecloth, propping up a wretched little Christmas tree. Children sit on the curb beneath the bridge, their feet on the pavement only inches from the roaring tires of infernal traffic.

This is Brazil's poverty, a deep well yawning wide open on the cruel sidewalks, streets, and freeways. This is the dark well Pai has worked relentlessly his entire life to avoid falling into. He and Sarah have achieved this, with help from no one.

In a city where assaults at gunpoint or knifepoint are commonplace, Pai has never been assaulted, except a couple of times when boys snatched a cap off his head. Maybe it's because he walks the busy streets, avoiding the vulnerable quieter ones. Maybe he's been lucky. But maybe it's simply that, as in the African proverb, "You don't teach the paths of the jungle to an old gorilla."

One block from home, his pace gradually slows, like a big jet coming in for a landing. He breaks his silence: *"Não se pode falar e respirar ao mesmo tempo"* (You can't talk and breathe at the same time). This pearl is one of many he possesses on an endless string. Some of his other jewels: Wear Clean Clothes. Be Frugal. Drive Hard Bargains. Solve Problems Quickly and Aggressively. Never Quit, Never Quit. These are the tools he uses to confront life in Brazil, which is full of resistance. And he offers these gems to his imperfect son-in-law free of charge, a reminder that life is a moral journey.

TURNING GOLD IN AUTUMN

Bumping and bouncing through the world over time can smooth sharp edges. Even in Pai, one finds an edge here and there that's less sharp. He's stopped striving for wealth, stopped acquiring more things, even stopped eating too much. Having known Excess, he's now accepting Enough. His better angels have finally managed to find a place to sit on his shoulders and pull his strings. He's about as happy as an anxious German-Italian-Brazilian is allowed to be.

Today his angels direct him to go forth into his neighborhood and entertain the citizenry. First stop—just a few steps from his door—is the corner bakery, owned by Nenê, who as a boy was one of the rascals who played the disreputable game of soccer with Davison directly in front of Pai's house. Sitting behind the counter on a high stool is a short, bosomy young female employee named Carmen, sucking on a water bottle.

"Tu tá muito preguiçosa" (You're really lazy), Pai jokes. Then he reaches over the counter and pulls her ear. Her face contorts in mock pain, like a pupil scolded by her teacher. Then, despite three customers patiently waiting their turn behind him, he painstakingly and theatrically counts on his fingers the number of bread rolls he'll need. Carmen sighs and rolls her eyes at the utter tedium of this old man who seems to possess all the time in the world.

Nenê bursts from the back room with a straw basket full of several dozen bread rolls. He pours them into the display case. The back of the case is a mirror, which miraculously doubles the bread like Jesus fed the multitudes. Pai takes his bread and tells Nenê, *"Bota no prego"* (Put it on the nail), meaning to stick the bill on the nail on the wall and Pai will pay it later. Which he always does.

Then, in no particular hurry, he crosses the street to another shop, where he hands a document to a young sales girl for copying. He banters with her over his trivial change of forty-five centavos. Next, we walk a block to a corner grocery called El Kadri, owned by two Lebanese brothers whom he calls *os Árabes* (the Arabs). He teases one brother's ten-year-old daughter.

On our walk back to the house, each of us carrying plastic bags of bread and vegetables, he says, rather out of the blue, *"Graças a Deus que sou ateu"* (Thank God I'm an atheist), one of his standard plays on words, absolving himself of any sins he may have committed with shopkeepers this morning.

After lunch, he gives me a sloppy, succulent mango for dessert. Gobs of delicious orange slime hang from my chin, and fibers stick between my teeth.

"Doutor Jing" (Doctor Jim), he says ironically, pronouncing my name the way Brazilians do, "your manners are shocking, especially here in a Third World country where we expect leadership from a great power like the United States in all things, including how to eat a mango."

He neglects to inform me of the ripe mango's fruity power to place me on the throne several times that afternoon to enjoy its cathartic benefits.

His teasing, bantering, and wonderfully effortless performance in the neighborhood this morning, puts me in mind of how long it takes for people to ripen—some sooner, others later.

Apparently, he's one of the later ones, probably because the garden of his early years wasn't especially fertile. But for all the delay, he's alive and flourishing today.

Even so, as everyone but the young has discovered, life is fleeting. Our better angels can leave us at any time. With no warning, the ferry can carry us off to the other shore. Mindful of this, I simply try to enjoy him for who he is now, a leaf still on the branch, turning gold in autumn.

HIS TRAGIC VOICE

Next day we're packed and ready to leave again. He and I stand beneath his gnarled scrub tree, its roots cracking the sidewalk underfoot, exactly where we first said goodbye to each other twenty-seven years ago.

Because leaving is always more sorrow than sweet, I try to strike a light note.

"Pai, this is your lucky day," I offer. "I'm leaving, which means you have one less loaf of bread to buy. One less mango."

This is our normal banter. I expect him to remind me that I'm his burden, eating him into abject poverty. My role is to act surprised. "Really?" I'd say. "I thought I was part of the family." Then he'd probably say, "No, when it comes right down to it Jim, you're just a freeloader."

At this point he'd start moaning about his disastrous economic situation, hinting that my drain on his budget is also, unfortunately, a drain on Brazil as a whole. I love this theater, playing on a stage where we're equals. It's our separation ritual.

He looks at me directly and says in his tragic voice, for which I have no defense: "I'm going to miss you."

ABruptly, our little imaginary stage vanishes. The playacting is over. Now, here on this cracked sidewalk, I'm on life's real stage.

My throat seizes up. I manage to whisper, "I'll miss you, too."

On life's real stage, I'm a poor actor. My lines disappear from my head. I feel naked, as I do now. The hardest role to play, strangely, is myself. Worse, I'm rarely aware I'm on stage at all. Worse yet, I find myself playing a role that too often I poorly understand. He's different. He plays himself with great assurance. I believe it's because his longer, more difficult, and more troubled journey has demanded authenticity. Evidently, my shorter and easier journey has not.

Buckled up, I'm ready for takeoff. The engine whines. It groans, then spirals up into its deafening roar and orgasm of full power thrust, tilting me backward. I'm airborne.

Then, aloft, the tranquility of a steady drone. Monotony sets in. For ten hours I seem stationary in space, nothing happening. Thoughts of this visit, like sediment sinking to the bottom of a lake, settle into a corner of my mind.

Leaving Brazil for the tenth time, I'm still a potential person, incomplete. Unlike him, who knows who he is, and accepts it. There are others in this category—perhaps Bob Dylan, or Nelson Mandela, or the Dalai Lama—people who have found their better selves, people who fire on all available cylinders. Far down the ladder below these luminaries, the ordinaries, in their charmed moments, sometimes do stumble into focus and occasionally strike the right note. On occasion, not often, they achieve harmony, surprising even themselves. Harmony in compassion, or honesty, or courage. Sadly, these inspired moments are rare. The trick is learning how to make them more frequent, learning how to be more authentic and thus more useful as a human being. I wonder whether, somewhere within me, a better person exists, like the one thriving in Pai, and what it would take to get in touch with him.

JANUARY 2001
A New Wariness

Much has happened since our last visit eleven months ago.

Daisi got a new job.

We moved my mother and father out of their home, where they'd lived for forty-seven years, to a nursing home.

My cancerous prostate was removed.

Marcus started grad school in urban planning.

André married a young woman from Porto Alegre, returned to Saint Paul and bought a house.

We arrive at São Paulo's busy international airport, Guarulhos, a gloomy, cavernous, gray cement fortress with a faint aroma of disinfectant. The airport feels like a grim and humorless holdover from Brazil's twenty-one-year military dictatorship that ended sixteen years ago, in 1985.

For permission to enter the country, I face a stony federal police officer. Wearing a starched gray shirt, he sits behind bulletproof glass in a vertical, steel-gray cylinder that looks like an oversized bullet. His eyes half open, his face cast in emotional lead, he glances at me, then at the photo in my passport, thumbing through it, looking for problems. I'm getting nervous. Abruptly, with a loud bang he stamps it and shoves it back at me, summoning the next suspect to his window with a motion that looks like he's brushing a fly off his ear.

BANKS GET DEFENSIVE

Entering one of Pai's neighborhood banks, his social clubs, feels like getting permission to enter the country. Their former clubby atmosphere is gone, replaced with a cold, hard, hunkered-down posture against armed assault.

I follow him into the revolving door. Imbedded in the glass partition is a metal cup, shaped like a mouth, into which we feed coins, keys, nail clippers, anything metal. Next, we pass through a metal detector. The first human being we encounter is a guard holding an automatic weapon across his chest. He observes me with expressionless eyes. A few feet behind and above him, looking down on us, half concealed behind a curved bulletproof wall covering all but her head, shoulders, and barrel of a shotgun is a stone-faced female guard.

Pai has no complaints about any of this. He cheerfully greets the woman guard, as he does all the many bank employees he knows. She nods back imperceptibly, chatty as the butt of her shotgun.

Vestiges of the former friendly bank atmosphere still survive. A tiny old woman with a bowed back clutches the bars of a teller's window, reciting a long story to the young employee. Waiting patiently in line behind her, unwilling to rush her, are ten people. Her white-haired husband comes up to her and taps her on the shoulder and motions it's time to go. "I'm only telling this young man a story," she says, as if this still were the chummy neighborhood bank of yesteryear.

His business finished, Pai's ready to leave. We push on the bulletproof-glass revolving doors, which hiss and snarl like dogs guarding the gates of hell.

MARCH 2002:
Fathers Poles Apart

My father died of pneumonia nine months ago, at age eighty-nine. The difference between Dad and Pai is immeasurable. To describe my father, it's best to start when I was a boy, and he was a giant.

On a day when I'm about eight years old, Mom takes me to his doctor's office. Dad is wearing a white, priestly smock, which he never wears at home. Hanging from his neck is a shiny stethoscope, a magic charm through which he hears people's hearts whisper their problems. To me, my father is large, strong, and important—godlike—and, in his office, he's as mysterious and distant as the North Star.

When he comes home from the office, I beg him to play catch with me. We toss a baseball back and forth, with not much enthusiasm on his part. When he was a boy, he was nearsighted and not athletic. His father, my grandfather, a small-town doctor and a football player in college, was disappointed in him. Dad is not a rough-and-tumble, physical, down-to-earth kind of father.

No matter. I desperately want to be like him. I recall one evening, when I'm eleven, we're both in the kitchen and Dad is assembling a tall, monumental sandwich.

"How does the heart work, Dad?" I ask. He would know. He's a doctor. If I can get him talking, maybe I can stay up past my bedtime.

"The heart . . ." he says distantly. He's bent over, his broad back to me, staring into the refrigerator. One hand on the counter, the other resting on the refrigerator door, his arms are outspread like the wings of an eagle gazing at his prey far below.

"The heart is a remarkable organ," he says absently, tired from a long day at the office. He finds a jar of mayonnaise. "A-re-mark-ab-le-organ," he intones, examining a head of lettuce.

He slathers mayonnaise on a slice of bread and gently places it as a crown on top of his masterpiece. Holding his creation with both hands, he opens his mouth and I see his gold tooth. When I get big, I'm going to have a gold tooth, too, I think. He takes a big bite, leans back against the sink, crosses his ankles and savors his reward for a hard day of "stomping out disease," as he calls doctor work. I picture him at the office jumping up and down on germs and the nurse coming behind with broom and dustpan, sweeping them up.

I spoon in my Breakfast of Champions and watch him eat his sandwich. Directly behind him is a small kitchen window holding out the night, reflecting the two of us, framing us together, connecting us, as if I were part of him and his greatness.

As I grow older and bigger, Dad grows smaller. I realize that he lives in Mom's shadow. Mom, the family opinion-shaper, is able to criticize him with impunity. Dad brings home the bacon, and Mom makes the big decisions. Dad loves her anyway, because he's a gentle, decent man. But as a father, he's unsure, mostly hands off. It's Mom who mainly raises me and my brother, Jeff.

When Dad misbehaved as a little boy, his father would take him down the basement for the punishment. He'd take a buggy whip and tell Dad to bend over the workbench. Dad would shut his eyes, grip the edge of the bench with his fingers, and feel the whip sting on the back of his legs. The louder Dad cried, the sooner the doctor would stop administering the medicine, leaving red welts. But no blood.

Then one day, when I'm an adolescent, I enter our garage and find Dad bent over his workbench, weeping. "Go away, leave me alone." I immediately leave, feeling hurt and rejected. Now it's clear. Dad's no god. He's merely human.

But instead of appreciating his humanity, I blame him for it. Furthermore, I blame my anxieties, my timidity, my imperfect leadership on the football field or basketball court—on him. It's some comfort to know that these defects are not really my fault.

Then I think, okay, he has his demons. Maybe all men have them. But why must his demons become my own? This is grossly unfair.

Only years later, when I become a father, do I begin to grasp my responsibility for my flaws. The gap between us begins to narrow. I even begin to feel moments of affection for him, including some compassion for the strict, religious, and humorless childhood he endured.

Understanding, like autumn, doesn't come all at once. Now, as I look to Pai for acceptance, I'm dimly aware that I sought the same things from my own father, the one who helped raise me as best he could. He was honest, idealistic, conscientious, public minded, and funny. He loved me in his fragile, distant way. He's my true father, the one so different from Pai.

A SHRUNKEN DOMAIN

The day after we arrive we're already behind Pai on his morning "March to Berlin." He's in good shape, but Sarah has declined. Her hand, trembling from Parkinson's disease, can barely spoon Frosted Flakes into her mouth.

"Estou entrando no tempo ruim" (I'm entering the bad time), she tells Daisi. Her memory is failing. Her right arm hurts. Her eyesight is almost gone, and she can see the old familiar pictures on the bedroom wall now only from memory.

Her right leg barely moves, and her left leg—having endured eight operations since she got polio at age seven—no longer responds. To turn in bed, she pulls on a strap with one hand and grabs her wheelchair with the other.

Several months ago she fell in the shower and broke her leg. Carried back to bed, she insisted on a folkloric treatment—having her leg rubbed with vinegar and wrapped in brown paper.

Daisi can't believe it. *"Mãe, que locura! Por que que tu não chamaste o Sidnei?"* (Mom, that's crazy! Why didn't you call Sidnei?)

"Falta de experiência" (Lack of experience), she replies. "I never broke a leg before."

One day I read her a Brazilian short story to cheer her up. It's about a guy who gets locked out of his apartment with no clothes on. "What a nightmare, to be naked in the corridor outside your apartment door," I say.

"O pior ainda é ficar presa nesses dois quartos" (What's worse is to be trapped in these two rooms), she replies.

They are her bedroom and dining room. They are her diminished space, her realm. This space must be kept clean. It must be perfect.

Tonight she's struggling to control a vital corner of her domain—her bed—which she rules with tyrannical power. She grows hysterical about the position of her pillow. *"Não tá certo!"* (It's not right!), she screams. Other times it's the bedsheet: "It's crooked!" she cries. Sometimes it's the teenage housekeepers whom she berates even to their faces as "ignorant, uneducated, stupid." These are words she had never used before, even up to a few months ago. She's no longer quite the woman she was—caring, composed, stoic.

She's inconsolable. Neither Pai nor Daisi can calm her down. He tells Daisi, *"Isso é que sofro todos os dias"* (This is what I suffer every day). She replies that they should move to an assisted-living facility.

"Tu não entendes!" (You don't understand!), he snaps back. "No one appreciates what Sarah and I have gone through to build this home. I will fight to stay here."

The next morning, light pours in through Sarah's bedroom window. Rested, clean, and freshened up by her teenage housekeeper, Sarah shines with hope and optimism. The Sarah of old is back. If yesterday she was winter, today she's spring. This is the baffling miracle of old age.

At the breakfast table this morning, where she sits in her wheelchair, I mention Minnesota's unusually warm winter. *"Sabe por que o mundo está esquentando?"* (Do you know why the world is heating up?), she asks.

I don't.

"É porque" (It's because), she says, Earth is traveling at five kilometers a year toward a black hole in space. The culprit? The American space agency, NASA.

I gently suggest this is ridiculous.

Oops. This is like tossing gasoline on a fire. Her eyes blazing, she straightens in her wheelchair and wags a trembling finger at me.

"Isso é a verdade absoluta!" (This is the absolute truth!), she declares, and apparently I'm a fool not to see it.

Sarah has a marvelous capacity for producing sweeping, cosmic assertions based on a grain of truth. The grain of truth this time is that eventually all things—including this breakfast table, my spoon, and my bowl of Frosted Flakes—are inexorably moving toward an eventual black hole somewhere in the vastness of the universe. But I'm sure the five kilometers per year is mistaken.

Sarah is deeply suspicious of the world beyond her realm, beyond her home, outside of which she hasn't stepped for years. There's evil out there. One of her favorite evildoers, for example, is our Central Intelligence Agency. The CIA is responsible for Brazil's unexpectedly warm winters and cool summers, as well as tornados and earthquakes, which are commonly assumed to be acts of God, not the CIA. She informs me that the CIA is also buying the Amazon jungle on the sly, which sounds absurd, but impossible to disprove. One day we get talking about Chico Mendes, a courageous Brazilian rubber tapper and environmental activist, who bravely fought to stop the burning of the Amazon rainforest for cattle ranching. Even though he was murdered in 1988 by Brazilian ranchers, and even though Robert Redford once considered making a film about his life, Sarah insists Mendes was an agent of the CIA bent on stealing Brazil from the Brazilians.

Her loathing of US meddling in Brazilian affairs is exceeded only by her passion to argue about it. It's my nefarious government—NASA, the CIA, the State Department, and others—that's at the root of all Brazilian problems. As much as I love and admire Sarah, I find this annoying. Driven into a corner, I feel drawn to defend my country, whose meddling in Brazil and elsewhere—yes—I do deplore, as long as it's honest-to-God meddling. Meanwhile, her ludicrous theories seem unassailable. She can't prove them, and I can't disprove them. Like Pai, she never loses. This frustrates me and delights her.

It's at such moments that Sarah forgets her confinement.

TALKING WITH STRANGERS

For lunch next day, Pai and I pick up some takeout at a neighborhood restaurant. "I'm paying this time," I say, handing him the money. He shoves my hand away.

"De jeito nenhum!" (Absolutely not!) Eyeing me sternly, and speaking from his sentimental Italian depths, he says, "You have no idea how much pleasure it gives me to have you two at our house."

I turn away to wipe my eyes.

It's 111 degrees today, the hottest March day since record keeping began eighteen years ago. It's too hot and sticky to scribble in my journal, or even to think. My shorts cling to me, tug at me. All I can manage is lolling around the house. Pai tries to turn on an air conditioner in Sarah's room, igniting an argument rooted in the heat, her infirmities, and her confinement. Their former summer months at the sea are now things of the past. The seaside cottage has been given to Lori. Sarah and the Old Warrior are now trapped year-round in the hot city.

"Quer sorvete, Jim?" (Want some ice cream?), he calls from the bottom of the stairs. "Yes!" I shout from my bed upstairs, where I'm reading. It's time for our afternoon ritual of ice cream and biscuits at the kitchen table, where even if we sit in silence, our lives touch.

After ice cream, he and I plunge into the beastly heat to obtain temporary swimming passes at his sports club. Because it's too hot to wait for a bus, his favorite transit mode, he reluctantly hails a cab. After some driving around, the thin young cabbie admits he doesn't know how to get to one of the city's busiest streets. Pai administers a tongue lashing, orders him to learn the streets better, and then demands he stop the cab. Pai gets out without paying. The kid seems ashamed, so I pay him something. This displeases the Old Man, who complains that I took the edge off his moral lesson.

He hails another cab. This one is driven by an old black guy who knows the streets, which puts Pai in an expansive mood, engaging the cabbie in political talk. Then I ask him whether life in a cab is dangerous, knowing that it is.

"*A vida é perigosa em todo lugar—num táxi, ou na rua* (Life is dangerous all over—in a cab, or on the street). Young people have lost all respect for others. They'll kill you for five dollars and think little of it."

The next day Pai and I head off to the airport to exchange dollars for Brazilian currency. This time we take the bus, because it's free for people over sixty-five. Besides, on buses he can chat with strangers, his opportunity to connect with the world outside the walls of his house. Old Brazilians are allowed plenty of conversational rope to ask anyone any question anytime, probably because, the thinking goes, they'll be gone soon, along with any shared personal information.

The bus is empty, save for the driver and a young woman who sits behind a little table to take fares and give change. She has high cheekbones, jet-black hair, and caramel-colored skin with freckles. She looks part Indian, part black, and part white. And she's bulging pregnant.

"*Tu estás gravida?*" (Are you pregnant?)

"*Sim,*" then after a pause, "he'll probably be born on the bus."

"*É um menino?*" he asks.

"Sim, it's a boy."

"He'll be his father's pride and joy."

"Sim."

"When will he enter the world?"

"In five months."

"What's his name?"

"Lucas."

She smiles shyly during this exchange, perhaps charmed at revealing so much to her ancient interrogator.

On the return trip, a woman in her seventies, easily ten years his junior, gets on the bus and stands in the aisle next to the empty half of Pai's double seat. He slides out and offers the whole seat to her. She accepts and sits down, while he stands in the aisle out of courtesy. Then he starts a conversation with her and she invites him to sit. I find a seat directly behind them.

"*O senhor notou como passou ligeiro os últimos anos?*" (Have you noticed how quickly the last few years have passed?), she asks.

"*Sim,*" he says.

"When my granddaughter was born," she says, "I never thought I'd live to see her reach age fifteen. Now, wouldn't you know, she's reached it already."

"*Sim.*"

"How swiftly life goes by."

"*Sim,* how swiftly."

Soon we reach our stop and get off.

"Pai, don't worry, I promise never to tell Sarah you're speaking to younger women on the bus."

"Thank you," he says, bowing like a gentleman. Then he says, "I wonder why it took that old woman so long to offer me a seat?"

LOCKING UP

This evening he asks whether Daisi and I plan to go out after supper. No, we say. Good, he says, springing into action, obeying another Rule for the Good Life: LOCK UP AT NIGHT.

He locks the front gate with an ancient key worn to gold. Then he closes the ponderous wrought-iron front door, which groans on its hinges. He secures it with not one but two padlocks the size of cheeseburgers, only heavier. Then he extinguishes the lights, plunging us into near darkness and saving a couple of centavos on his energy bill. Then he rolls down his heavy steel venetian blinds, which rattle like chains on a tin roof. This step seems like overkill, because his windows are already protected by iron bars. But Pai believes in redundancy, because, as in nature, if one eye, ear, or testicle is lost, the other picks up the slack.

Now we're imprisoned but protected from the street, which grows unsafe after dark. The burden, or perhaps the blessing, of all this locking and unlocking is simply living a slower life.

A few years ago, he installed a ten-foot-high iron fence at the sidewalk to keep homeless men from sleeping in his tiny front yard and relieving themselves in a corner. The fence is made of a hundred vertical iron poles, each tipped with an ornamental spearhead, a rather useless medieval touch. Pai's fence is one of scores up and down the cobblestone street, which resembles a riverbed lodged between high banks made of walls and fences on both sides. Burglars have tried several times to break in, and have failed. His safeguards—onerous as they are—seem to be working.

I miss the open yards and windows of Minnesota.

FERRYBOAT CAPTAIN

Soon it's time for us to leave again. I enter Sarah's bedroom. Her ninety-two-year-old head, resting on a white pillow, is surrounded by a halo of gray hair. I lean down and kiss her soft cheek.

"*Boa viagem*" (Have a good trip), she says, affectionately, soberly.

"Same to you," I think—but don't say—concerning her unscheduled final voyage.

Today, Daisi kisses her mother goodbye, without tears. Yesterday, however, she sat on our bed upstairs and wept. She resolved to call Sarah more often, send her more sheets and bedclothes.

Pai has already lugged our bags out front and has placed them beneath the scrub tree, whose roots are still busy destroying the sidewalk. What kind of tree is this? I ask. He doesn't know. Yesterday the city trimmed it way back, he says, to prevent a fungus.

"Pai, I left thirty dollars for our phone bill in your wallet on top of your desk."

"*Mas como?* (What do you mean?) I called the phone company. Your bill is two thousand and thirty dollars."

"Pai, just put the two thousand on our bill and we'll figure it out later."

"*Ah, eu mereço, eu mereço*" (Oh Lord, I guess I deserve this, I deserve this). This banter is the prologue to our departure ritual.

We slam each other in a rough gaucho embrace. I feel his reduced bulk, smell his sweat, hear his weeping. As always, unsaid words of farewell stick in my throat. Once again, beneath the ageless scrub tree, separation brings us closer together.

As our taxi pulls away, he turns his back on us and passes through the iron fence into his shrinking kingdom. He doesn't bother to wave good-bye. The cab turns a corner and starts moving toward the airport and the mechanical bird that will lift us out of Brazil, now thirty-two years after the day I first arrived. As we drive past palm trees and hibiscus flowers, Brazil still seems magical, despite all these years that have fallen on it, fallen on him, fallen on me.

It's Sunday morning. The streets are empty, oddly silent. As the cab moves along the smooth asphalt, I feel the transition I've felt before—leaving one reality for another. Our cab driver is an old man with white hair and wrinkles on the back of his neck. He drives in silence, with effortless simplicity and purity. His big, venerable hands rest easily on his small steering wheel, unlike Pai's white-knuckle grip. However, like Pai, he fits these streets like a key in a lock. And also like Pai, at rare moments such as this one, he seems ancient, as if he, like the captain of the final ferryboat, were piloting me across the hidden river that runs between families, between generations, between nations.

JULY 2002

Temperance

Four months later we arrive on a bright, cold July winter day. The temperature in the house is a chilly forty-six degrees. The forecast calls for thirty-seven tonight.

Like a hibernating bear, Pai sprawls on his recliner in the front room, wrapped in a sweater, jacket, and overcoat. Beneath these layers he wears a white shirt and tie, in honor of our arrival. The Russian fur cap my father gave him sits queerly on his head. He looks ridiculous. I laugh, but he's warm, and I'm cold, with a runny nose.

"*Não te preocupa com as estalagmites de gelo no chão*" (Don't worry about ice stalagmites sticking out of the floor), he says, without smiling.

Sarah is under three blankets wearing three layers of clothing. She and Pai endure Brazil's short winters with no central heating. As do most gauchos. Sarah lies on her side, her ear covered with a pillow. Only her nose and forehead appear. "*O travesseiro me protege da dor de ouvido*" (The pillow protects me from ear aches).

She looks better than she did in the heat last March, but her left hand shakes more violently than ever.

The winter sun is low on the horizon and pours in through the bedroom window, lighting up her covers in a blaze of color. Sunlight passes through the bedroom doorway and lights up the first two steps leading to her room containing her dolls, paintings, and phonograph records, a room she's not entered for years. The sun also illuminates the normally dark nook at the center of the house, where the heavy black telephone sits proudly on its tiny table. It also brightens the fading newsprint photo on the wall of President Franklin D. Roosevelt.

That evening, Daisi and I join them in the small bedroom. Sarah is comfortable beneath several covers. Pai lies nearly horizontal in his chair at the foot of her bed, his eyelids at a drowsy half-mast behind his thick glasses. He's wearing a brown, heavy, wool gaucho poncho. Now eighty-seven, he recalls the day at age fifteen when he entered a church to renounce smoke and drink.

"*Desde então* (Since then), I've never violated my pledge," he intones. Sarah stares at the ceiling, half listening to her lifetime partner. "Temperance became habit, habit became lifestyle, lifestyle became health in my old age," he drones. He counts on his fingers the virtuous behaviors that have forged what he now describes as his temperate life: no smoking, regular walking, less red meat. I can't help but recall the prodigious amounts of red meat the Twilight Moralist—a term I use in all respect—used to consume. But tonight, in this rambling, impromptu autobiographical fragment, he portrays himself just two degrees shy of Gandhi.

The Moralist drones on, recalling a cold winter night in which he triumphed over intense social pressure to drink at a bar with colleagues from his sports club.

"*Eles tomavam uísque, enquanto eu tomava café preto com açúcar* (They drank whiskey, while I drank black coffee with sugar). Among them was a respected doctor, who told them that my choice of drink was the best one. He said I'd stay warmer with my sweet coffee than they would with their whiskey!" Pai stretches out the tale, doubling back and repeating the most praiseworthy parts where he conquers temptation, always with the implication that it would be wise for me to imitate his exemplary life of moderation.

I guess he'll be like the health nut who one day ends up dying of nothing.

At some point during the soliloquy, Sarah falls asleep.

Stopping for a while to gaze at his sleeping life partner, he breaks the silence to say that when he was young, he never expected any good would come of his life. At one point, he says, he even despaired of life itself. I've never heard him say this before. But then, he says, good things began to happen. He met Sarah. They married. They had children. They bought a house. *"Até comer sorvete era uma maravilha"* (Even eating ice cream was a marvel). Only years later, he says, when all his children had graduated from college, did he know his struggle had finally borne fruit.

I change the subject. I ask him why Lula, head of the Workers' Party, and who's running for president, is ahead in opinion polls at 40 percent.

Brazilians are familiar with Lula. They know his life story: raised in poverty, didn't learn to read until age ten, quit school after the fourth grade to shine shoes and sell things on the street to help his family. I'm curious about Pai's opinion, this proud member of the middle class, who also started life low on the ladder, and who in the 1940s, around the time Lula was born, worked to help form unions when they didn't exist in Brazil, a time when bosses could stretch out the workday at will and deny vacations.

"*Ele está na frente porque tem mais pobre do que classe média* (He's ahead because there are more poor people than middle class). The minimum wage has risen for the working class, but the middle class has been sacrificed. Besides, the middle class is tired of the current government of Fernando Henrique Cardoso. Brazil wants something new. And that something new is Lula—even though he's already run for president three times and lost every time."

We don't talk about George W. Bush, who has the distinction of being the least popular US president in the history of Latin American polling.

SLEDGEHAMMER

On his morning walk the next day, Pai wears his poncho and Russian fur cap. Walking slower than last year, and not as far, we thread our way on busy sidewalks through schoolchildren and people going to work. As we walk past storefronts, the uneven sidewalk keeps changing—brick, tile, concrete, stone. Porto Alegre's sidewalks, which are privately owned, are a patchwork made of whatever its owner wants.

After the walk, we start the day with a breakfast of hot milk poured over powdered coffee and sugar, plus French rolls, cheese, and salami. For supper, same thing. Everyday food at Pai's house is simple and symmetrical.

He buys bread at a bakery several blocks away, not at Roberto's corner bakery, only a few steps from his house.

Roberto, whose nickname is Nenê, or Baby, is an amiable guy with slumping shoulders and a nose shaped disarmingly like a miniature dinner roll. Pai and Nenê have known each other for more than half a century. As a boy, Nenê played soccer barefoot with Davison and other mischief-makers on the cobblestone street in front of Pai's house. When Nenê grew up and took over the bakery, Pai regularly bought bread and pastries from him, often without paying, saying, *"Bota no prego"* (Put it on the nail), meaning, poke the bill on the nail on the wall with all the other unpaid bills.

This afternoon, Nenê is taking a break. Wearing his white apron, he's sitting on a wooden chair in front of his bakery. I approach him on my way to catch a bus. We know one another from my several visits, so he leaps up to greet me, throwing an arm around my shoulder.

I ask him what's going on between him and Pai. *"O velho me ignora* (The old man ignores me). He walks past my bakery every day. Nothing I can do about it."

This Cold War began several years ago, shortly after Nenê had borrowed Pai's sledgehammer. That's when Nenê made a grave mistake. He loaned it to the locksmith on the corner. The locksmith, who Nenê later discovered was a cheat, loaned it to someone else. Pai's sledgehammer eventually evaporated into the neighborhood.

But then Nenê did the right thing. He gave Pai a new one. But because the new sledgehammer was not the battered and beloved original, Pai refused to accept it—on moral grounds. Nenê's unpardonable sin was loaning Pai's property to another without asking permission. Thus began Pai's excommunication of the unfortunate baker for this unspeakable transgression, a punishment Pai administers in a slow, grinding, relentless boycott, walking past the bakery, head high, eyes forward, resolutely unconscious of the baker's existence.

I ask him what else is happening. *"Estou fugindo das balas* (I'm dodging bullets) from bandits below and government above." As he says this, he bobs and weaves, like a boxer, demonstrating how, as a small businessman, he's besieged from all angles.

"My shop has been assaulted twice already this year. The economy is stagnant. Economic injustice is rampant. Fifty thousand wealthy Brazilian families control 70 percent of the economy."

He launches into a denunciation of criminals, taxes, crumbling morals, and the thickly greased palms of corporations, the media, and the *governo corrupto*—which he calls the Machine. *"Nada pros pequenos"* (There's nothing for the little guy).

During his rant, his hands are in constant motion, tapping my chest, touching my shoulder and ribs, holding my arm—pressing home his urgent

The baker, Nenê, with his wife.

PAI GAVIOLI
Thirty-six Years of War and Finally Peace with My Impossible Brazilian Father-in-Law

thoughts. This fleshy contact pulls me in, and before I know it, I'm telling him intimate things about myself, my marriage, the Gaviolis, and things maybe I shouldn't. But this is Brazil, the land of spontaneity, affinity, and candor, a land where glacial Scandinavian reserve melts away.

Then he gets personal. His family life is getting worse. His twenty-one-year-old daughter has an eighteen-month-old child, but the father is gone. Young people, he says, change spouses as if they were cars. The growth of drugs is fearsome, destroying young people, pulling their parents down with them.

His laundry list of woes draws his face into an imploring, haunted, frightened look. This startles me, but there's nothing I can do to help. As I'm about to pull myself away from his misfortunes, I receive another arm wrapped around my shoulders, and a hand squeezing the back of my neck. This is not improper. This is Brazil. Be they bakers, butchers, or candlestick makers, these affectionate, touch-happy Brazilian shopkeepers amaze me. As I take my leave, he shouts, *"Tchau, Jimmy."*

VENUS

Sitting alone on his front step this evening, I write in my journal. I pause, surveying his tiny, hopeful plot of lawn at my feet and his iron-spear fence marking where his grass ends and his broken sidewalk begins. Dusk is growing. Soon I can barely see the page. A crescent moon, tipped slightly backward, hangs lovely in a soft, gray-blue sky. Venus shines on the far side of an electric wire leading to Pai's house. I write a couple more sentences, then look up. She's moved across the wire toward me. I gather that the Earth, though I can't feel it, is rolling smoothly on its axis beneath me, sending Venus on her preordained course across the city. A few moments later, the Earth has moved such that I can no longer see to write. On her silent, unstoppable path across the sky, past the gnarled scrub tree, and past his little lawn, the evening star soundlessly traces Pai's journey, and seems a distant expression of it.

Perhaps she traces mine, too.

SLUM DRAMA

That night, I sit with them in Sarah's bedroom, watching local TV news. There's a live report of a SWAT team, wearing helmets and carrying automatic rifles, running through a *favela*, one of the city's slums. They're after someone who is reported to have machine-gunned a ten-year-old child going to school. Running behind them is a TV reporter named Tony Gomes, followed closely by a dozen excited children and barking dogs.

We witness this chase from above, filmed by a TV helicopter, accompanied by a studio reporter's breathless narrative lavishly praising the aggressive search by the SWAT team and courageous reporting from Gomes.

The team stops. They pull a man from his shack and pat him down. Then they run on. He's not the one.

It's a gripping drama, a foray into one of Brazil's urban jungles. The suspect is described only as a *marginal,* someone outside the perimeter of normal society, probably poor, jobless, a drug abuser.

No one is apprehended.

We are reminded that this sensational live footage is provided by no other station. Then we're told we'll return to this spectacle right after these commercials.

Watching this, one wants to be sure all windows are shuttered and doors securely locked. One wants to look with care and suspicion upon strangers—the jobless, the poorly dressed.

Startling to me, but likely not to Pai, are images of the favela itself—its tin roofs, dirt paths, ditches running with raw sewage. To his credit, the studio reporter tells us this drama has many roots, but he doesn't say what they are. Probably because Brazilians already know them—lack of proper food, decent housing, clean water, good education, jobs, health care, security—the building blocks of a healthy nation.

"Isso é triste" (This is sad). I wonder what he means. What's sad? The child's murder? The slum? The fear? The drugs? The sensationalism?

Probably all of the above.

Earlier today, Daisi and I were downtown. As we strolled through an outdoor market, she abruptly said, "We shouldn't walk here. It's too dangerous. We should stay outside the stalls, not between them." Holding hands like Hansel and Gretel in the forest, we managed to find our way out of there.

HERE IT IS!

This morning I make the mistake of wondering aloud how to get to a particular restaurant this evening. Pai lurches out of his easy chair, opens a map of Porto Alegre, and spreads it over the dining room table. He leans over it, peering through his thick lenses at the city whose streets he once knew like a cab driver. He bends closer to the map. Strands of white hair float out from the sides of his head like little antennas. He locates his house, and places the tip of his index finger squarely on it as our starting point. Now he looks for the restaurant, mumbling street names. He's getting impatient.

He finds it! Great. Looks like he's got it. He lifts his finger off his house and places it on the restaurant. Oops, now he's lost our starting point.

Frustrated, he grabs the map and whips it about 180 degrees, aligning the city with the map in his mind. Upon closer examination, he discovers street names are upside down. Muttering an oath, he spins the map another 180 degrees, bringing us back to where we started. After more fingers placed on houses and restaurants, and fingers sliding along wrong streets, and more twisting of the map, abruptly he sweeps it off the table, sending it zigzagging to the floor like a falling autumn leaf.

He stalks off to his desk for his phone book. We're moving on to Plan B.

This weighty publication, three years out of date, battered and curled at the edges, looks like something salvaged from a solid-waste landfill. He opens it to a city map, its thin paper smudged and wrinkled from earlier searches.

With mounting anxiety, as if time is running out, even though we have all morning to do this, he rushes forward in the hunt. He looks for his house again. Doesn't find it. Tiny beads of perspiration appear on his brow. He's getting jumpy, as if on a mission to defuse a ticking time bomb.

Then he finds his house.

Whew, what a relief! Finally, we're getting somewhere. To nail down this starting point on the map, as if for the next thousand years, he thrusts his thick finger down on top of his house with such force that he rips the page.

"*Pai, calma, calma,* let's just cool down and wait a minute," I say. As I slowly and deliberately tape the page back together, he stands close beside me, watching my every move. I can feel his impatience, like heat off a radiator.

Then, with grim determination, the Ancient Warrior rushes back into battle. Meanwhile, I'm getting exhausted. This is taking too long. My mind wanders. I drift off. Then I'm jolted back to consciousness, seeing him trace with his finger the streets connecting his house to the restaurant. Over and over, his finger traces and retraces the route, nearly erasing names of the streets between the two points.

"Jim," he shouts, his little finger covering his house and his thumb crushing the restaurant, he raises and shakes his free hand in triumph, "*É isso aqui, Jim! Isso aqui! Olha o jeito de chegar!*" (Jim, this is it! Here it is! This is the way to get there!)

I grab his hand and shake it vigorously. He's victorious. We're both delighted. He's carried the day. It's taken only two hours.

Once again, I'm reminded that no matter how trivial or complex the job, he never quits. He just never quits. Never quits.

TO REMEMBER IS TO LIVE

It's hard to get him out of the house now, away from his lifelong companion, even for a few hours. But this afternoon, his struggle with the map behind us, Daisi and I manage to take him downtown—by bus—his favorite, and cheapest, transportation. The goal is to give him a break from his cares by showing him a photo exhibit.

The exhibit is housed in a lovely colonial-style bank building, now a museum, on the *Praça da Alfândega,* or Customs House Square, the heart of old Porto Alegre. The former bank is a jewel among several colonial-style gems preserved in the city's core, no longer the commercial and cultural nerve center it once was, its vitality drained by new shopping malls away from downtown.

He shows little interest in the photos, century-old images of downtown Porto Alegre. They show horse-drawn carriages on cobblestone streets, bearded men in dark suits and tall hats going about their now-forgotten business in front of two-story buildings made of brick or wood. There are also images of grander, more ambitious stone buildings, one of which we're standing in now.

Some photos are on a computer screen. To see them, one must operate a mouse. Pai has never used a mouse. I take his meaty hand and place it on top of one, his thick fingers covering it completely. This is a hand shaped by the ax, which decades ago helped carve a path through jungles and over plains, opening the way for the then-new telephone technology. It's a hand friendly with a sledgehammer, but not a plastic mouse and the alien technology flowing through its tail. He quickly loses interest.

He's more interested in the building we're standing in. We stop in front of a massive bank vault. He passes his large hand across the surface of its cold iron door that once held the city's wealth. Then he slowly climbs the delicate spiral staircase, curved like the inside of a nautilus seashell. At the next landing, he stops and gazes at stately, slender pillars that support the ceiling with their leafy stone outcroppings. The pillars, like petrified trees, rise from the stone floor, beneath which their invisible roots spread into the city's past.

Placing his hand here and there on timeworn stone and iron, his eyes widen in wonderment. The architecture seems to reach out from the past and touch him. He appears to know this place. Perhaps he's been here before, when he was a messenger boy delivering money or documents, a job nearly obliterated today by the Internet.

We follow him as he wanders across the smooth stone floor. He pauses. Then he drifts in a different direction. He seems to be looking for something. My eye, caught in his slow-moving rhythm, is drawn to what he looks at—the stone pillars, the spiral staircase, the mighty vault. They seem to loom out of the past, with an unseen pressure behind them. The past—not dead and gone as it normally seems—is alive, enveloping me. The ordinary present moment seems to have drifted off like smoke, clearing the air for an older time to come into view.

We leave the bank and descend its broad steps into the *praça*, or square. More lovely old stone structures present themselves, and, like the mouse, each has a long tail connected—not to the new technologies, but to the old days. There's the stately revenue building. There's the noble post office. Over there's the larger-than-life statue of Atlas, thick with straining marble muscle, his back bending under the weight of the world. And, of course, next to me, is Pai himself, bearing his long train of years, which like the mouse tail, fastens him to a past I cannot see, but can almost feel.

The customs house, after which the square is named, is also here, on the bank of the wide Guaíba River, lifeblood of the city. The building still receives shipments from Uruguay, Argentina, Europe, and other points on Atlas's globe. Upstream, the Guaíba is fed by smaller rivers that drift past towns in the state's interior. One of these upstream towns is Montenegro, where Pai was born eighty-seven years ago, upstream in time, where his maternal grandfather, Senhor Finger, operated a riverboat to Porto Alegre. *"Eu me lembro* (I remember) when the Guaíba flooded past the customs house, through the square, up to *Rua da Praia* (Beach Street). I had to row a boat to get around."

We walk along one side of the square past a narrow street market, where men are yelling, *"Vale! Vale! Vale!"* (Tokens! Tokens! Tokens!), selling black-market bus passes. Others yell, *"Corte de cabelo!"* (Haircuts!), and others, *"Compro ouro!"* (I buy gold!) Still others hawk things made from cattle—cowhorn rings, key chains, cowhide rugs, leather purses—together with wooden necklaces made by Brazilian Indians. There are T-shirts displaying icons Pai surely recognizes, like the intense face of Che Guevara, who helped lead the only successful socialist revolution in Latin America, as well as the dreamy face of John Lennon, an icon probably beneath Pai's radar.

It's cool today, and he's wearing a coat. But his head is bare. He keeps his Russian fur cap clutched in his hand, so it won't be snatched off his head. I stay close, lightly supporting his elbow at curbs. He walks slowly, looking from side to side, possibly seeing what's gone, as if it's not really gone at all.

Today the square, colorless and gloomy, rests beneath an overcast sky darkened even more by towering Amazonian trees, their smooth gray skin covering hardwood muscle. Their massive and exposed century-old roots swoop gracefully into the earth, like buttresses to medieval cathedrals. At the foot of one majestic tree, a dozen men play checkers with bottle caps, surrounded by jobless slackers and roughs with nothing better to do than to watch.

Nearby, four men play dominoes on a concrete table. Others watch in silence, with no apparent desire to go anywhere, do anything, achieve anything, or satisfy any ambition other than to watch the flow of the game. These are men who know how to wait life out.

This area seems unsafe for strolling. We're often warned of muggers and pickpockets who would find us easy pickings—an old man, his daughter, and her gringo husband well into his defenseless years. Let's not get too close to the checkers players.

Curiously, I feel immune to assault. This is crazy, I know, yet I feel protected by his venerable presence here, in this time-honored location, the ancient heart of his city. It's as if he has a right to be here, an esteemed emissary from an earlier time, around whom is cast an aura of security protecting even those near him.

"Para cá" (This way), he says, turning down a sinister-looking sidewalk leading directly into the heart of the square. Walking beneath the Amazonian trees, we pass a heavy, white-haired old black man asleep on a bench. Pai picks up the pace. He's in charge, as usual. Where are we going? We encounter two elderly women, arm in arm, evidently not yet assaulted by thugs. This is reassuring. We pass a large, black, iron statue, a colossal gaucho warrior astride a powerful horse with blazing eyes and flaring nostrils. This fiery icon of gaucho manhood towers over a small man at the foot of the monument, his face pinched like a mouse. He sits astride a tiny wooden stool, reading the local newspaper, while an old black shoeshine man rubs some small distinction into his shoes.

Moments later Pai stops. He points to a spot from which he says he once ran errands as an office boy. This would be back in the day when he once returned to a cashier money he'd been given by mistake. He's pointing directly to a McDonald's restaurant. He seems to be looking right through it—as if it were made of air—to an earlier day, upriver in time, a day brighter than the dark and shabby one in which we're standing now.

Pulled by his undercurrent, which has been gathering intensity since we left the bank museum, I feel oddly invisible. Drawn under his spell, seeing partly through his eyes, I'm carried away from the idlers, the gloom, the downtown decay, to the brighter, fresher, dynamic days of his youth that built this once-noble city.

In a faraway voice, eyes fixed on the McDonald's he doesn't actually seem to see, he says, *"Jim, recordar é viver"* (Jim, to remember is to live).

THE LAST PIECE OF BREAD

Years ago, when I first met him, I thought he was old. As time passed, he didn't seem to change. When he reached his mid-seventies, he still seemed fifty-nine, frozen in time. Today, even though I know he's eighty-seven, on a whim I ask him, "Pai, how old are you?"

"Estou chegando aos setenta (I'm pushing seventy), getting on in years. But I've still got lots of time left to irritate people, just as they've irritated me," he says, with a face that doesn't seem to be kidding.

Daisi and I are now spending lazy, unscripted hours with Pai and Sarah, hours in which nothing in particular is happening. The highlights of our days are lunch and supper. They take place in a long, dark, windowless corridor, which a remodeling a few years ago turned into a walkway between the kitchen and the rest of the house.

On one long wall is a shelf holding his collection of German beer mugs. They're decorated with jovial, well-fed villagers in lederhosen raising their steins in a jolly toast to health and vigor, an idealized version of Pai himself, without the beer.

On the opposite wall hangs a gaucho lasso made of rawhide. At the ends of each of its three braided cords is a stone the size of a tennis ball wrapped in a tight leather sack. This is the instrument that gauchos, galloping on horseback, swing about their heads and let fly, entangling a steer's legs, bringing it crashing to earth. I'm pretty sure there's a tough, rawboned gaucho cowboy living somewhere in Pai.

At lunch, Sarah sits in her wheelchair in her usual place at the head of the table, which, like the room, is long, dark, and heavy. In a surprising moment, from the kitchen behind her, a sunbeam touches her and brilliantly brightens the outline of her form into a full-body halo.

Pai and I sit across the table from one another. The meal moves slowly along in the comfortable silence of old people who've seen it all, heard it all, and find little more to say about it all.

I offer him some grapes. *"Obrigado"* (Thank you), he says,

uncharacteristically subdued. "I want to accept, but because I must save every penny, I must decline."

I smile at this whimsy, mindful that he's a man who knows something about saving pennies.

Another day, at the same lunch table, Daisi, Sidnei, and his wife, Maria Eunice, are talking more than eating. Pai leans over and whispers, *"Jim, deixa eles falarem* (let them talk). That means more food for us."

"Pai, I'm full. I can't eat any more,"

"Jim," he says, pressing me, "three people economizing on my food is enough. Go ahead and eat."

It feels good to be on his side against others, as if he and I were equals.

Then he points to a half-empty bowl of chopped fruit. He looks at me, gloom spreading over his face. "This was supposed to last all week," he laments. The corners of his mouth droop. He slowly shakes his head in dismay.

On another day, we share a light supper at the heavy table, whose time of groaning under the weight of big family churrascos is only a memory. I pick up a plate and offer him its last piece of bread. He looks at me, eyes filling with sorrow. He puts his elbows on the table and buries his face in his hands.

"Não, não, Jim, I can't accept," he murmurs, "because, well, you know, we need to economize here, and, well, there's no bread for tomorrow, so, well, you know, there's really nothing left, therefore, well, to get to the point, I was saving that piece for you."

I gaze down at the last piece of bread. Then look up at him. He shrugs his shoulders, holds out upturned palms with nothing on them, all joy drained from his face, as if, lamentably, nothing can be done. I decide to accept his selfless offer. Just as I reach for this last morsel, Sarah announces, "There's more in the kitchen."

Pai seems hurt. "Sarah, you didn't have to say that. We're just playing!"

This is merely the most recent in his litany of endless calamity. A collapsing household economy . . . insufficient food . . . hard times . . . guests (Daisi and me) eating him out of house and home. In this melodrama of scarcity, misery, and despair, he approaches Shakespearian heights.

ALWAYS ECONOMIZE

The next day, he follows Daisi around the house, extinguishing light bulbs that she leaves burning. Later I find him sitting at his disorderly desk paying bills.

"Pai, is it okay for me to run the ice-cold water to warm it before I take a shower?" Actually, I have no intention of taking a shower.

He drops his pencil, throws his head back and raises his arms like a sinner at a Baptist prayer meeting. Rolling his eyes heavenward, he cups his hands in prayer, begging help from the Lord. I remind him that tomorrow is our last breakfast before we leave for Minnesota. Again, his eyes drift heavenward, palms touching in pious prayer, thanking God for this miracle.

Seeing bills scattered on his desk, I ask: "Pai, how are your household finances holding up?"

His lower lip trembles. His mouth tightens into a tiny hole. His head slumps and his shoulders droop.

"Lamentably, there's no more food for me. For you, Jim, perhaps, but for me . . . none. Economize, Jim. That's the lesson. Always economize."

His acting is so real that for a moment I wish I could trade childhoods with him—my comfortable one for his deprived one—allowing me to acquire his priceless, hard-won wisdom about survival and economizing. Then the wish evaporates.

Morning comes and we're ready to leave. Sarah looks great. She sits erect in her wheelchair, sun streaming through her bedroom window. Her hair, freshly cut in a Dutch boy, is straight around the back of her neck, like a bowl turned upside down. She looks young, as good as I've seen her in months. With characteristic stoicism, she wishes me a safe trip, and to greet my mother, my brother Jeff, and our sons.

Old people are unpredictable, changing like the weather.

JULY 2002
Temperance

Pai greets Daisi at the
airport in December, 1990.

Eyeing me sternly,
and speaking from his
sentimental Italian depths,
he says, "You have no
idea how much pleasure
it gives me to have you two
at our house."

I turn away to wipe my eyes.

DECEMBER 2003

A Year of Losses

A brilliant orange sunrise explodes over the green Amazon jungle, which I behold through the window of the aircraft. Seventeen months have passed since our last visit. My mother, my lifelong mentor and hero, died eleven months ago, just shy of ninety-six.

She was a lot like Pai, forever taking charge. Like the day on the Minnesota farm where she grew up, when her brother, age seven, was kicked full force in the face by a horse. He was unconscious, blood sinking into the barn's dirt floor. Her mother was hysterical and her father was beside himself. Finally, a doctor arrived.

"I had to take charge," Mom said. "I brought the doctor hot towels."

"How old were you then, Mom?"

"I was three."

Years later, she was a young nurse, handing scalpels to a surgeon. Unexpectedly, in mid-operation, the doctor grew faint and had to lie down. Mom knew the procedure, so instead of calling in another doctor, which was the rule, she stepped in and finished it. "They gave me a real talking-to," she said proudly.

Jeff and I were subjected to her heroic stories over and over, tales in which I lived vicariously. Like Pai's, hers were laced with moral lessons. Like when she and other farm kids trudged through fields of snow in bone-chilling cold to their one-room schoolhouse. When the wind hit their faces and froze their eyelids shut, they walked single-file holding hands, she said, so in their blindness they wouldn't get lost and freeze to death.

Like Pai, Mom was generous with advice. Do this. Don't do that. Don't wear white socks. They make you look like you grew up on the farm. Stop thinking, just do it! Stand up and fight for yourself! Her advice gave me courage, but scared me at the same time. I could overcome any obstacle, she said—even be a United States senator—probably because she knew I wasn't cut out to be president.

Like Pai, she was a hard worker, with drive and self-discipline. Whenever I whined or complained, she'd quote President Harry Truman: "If you can't stand the heat, get out of the kitchen!"

In her middle years, she began painting. She poured acrylics on horizontal canvases the size of large coffee tables. Painting became her passion. She wanted to exert a "loose control" on the colorful puddles, she said, dabbing them with sponges, fingers and brushes, but mostly letting them "wander on paths of their own." She expected her canvases, like her sons, to be free and assert themselves.

Too little control invites chaos, she'd say. Too much imposes deadness. Good art, she'd say, lies between too little and too much. While painting, she'd whisper, "Don't dominate it," all the while fishing for joy, vitality, mystery. Occasionally, beauty would happen.

This is how she painted, and how she tried to live. I loved listening to her talk about creativity, which she considered to be at the heart of life. And which was, by the way, how I should live. These talks, like sermons from the mount, were exhilarating, inspiring, and regrettably beyond my reach. They left me discouraged, feeling as if I were wasting my life.

Two days before she died, I visited her in the nursing home. The curtains were drawn and the room was dark. By this time, she had pretty much stopped eating, and was frighteningly thin. I approached her bed.

"Mom, how are you doing?"

She looked at me for several seconds. She slowly raised her hand, swiped it quickly across the top of her head, as if brushing away a fly, and said in a faint whisper, "Comb your hair!"

She never gave up on me.

Six months to the day after Mom's death, my only brother, Jeff, one month shy of sixty, has a heart attack and abruptly dies in his sleep. This happens at a time when we've been growing closer, returning to our childhood brotherliness, no longer trying to shape the other in our own image.

His death rings through me like a sad bell, tolling for him, and because I'm older, for me. My own death is something I never consider. Perhaps I should. Philosophers recommend it as a lesson in life's fragility. Jeff's death is a blow, jolting me awake to my need for people—Daisi, Marcus and André, my American and Brazilian families, and my friends. I'm reminded that I'm a social animal.

As if all this isn't enough, Cenira, Pai's valued housekeeper and attendant to Sarah, lost her sixteen-year-old son yesterday, two days before Christmas, murdered in a shooting. Today, incredibly, she's here working, and weeping. I'm humbled to see her here, sweeping the floor, a stark reminder of how work is survival. She reawakens me to how housekeepers, and those for whom they work, live in parallel worlds.

DECEMBER 2003
A Year of Losses

Despite all this bad news, nature moves along without noticing us. Spring is in the air. The old scrub tree in front of Pai's house is in surprising bloom, releasing an intoxicating fragrance.

A MILESTONE

On this visit, Daisi and I pass a milestone we've dreamt about for years. We buy a condo in Torres, a seaside resort 115 miles north of Porto Alegre, three hours by bus. We're just two blocks from the ocean, which we can see by leaning over the balcony.

Like Daisi's parents, who spent summers at their retirement cottage in Santa Terezinha, we hope to spend Minnesota winters here. It's time to put more Brazil into our lives.

Most of the year, Torres is relatively small, with a population of thirty-three thousand people, mostly lower-middle class. Its fifty hotels, bars, and restaurants are closed. But in January and February, Brazil's summer vacation months, it mushrooms nearly six-fold to 180,000, filling with new middle-class vacationers—families, surfers, rock-concert-goers. With this influx, the city has lost its former aristocratic charm. The very wealthy now go north to lovelier beaches in Santa Catarina.

Two short blocks from our condo is a miniature town square shaded by an immense, thick-leaved fig tree. Surrounding the square is pretty much everything

Daisi, around eight years old.

we need: a coffee shop, ice cream shop, butcher shop, pharmacy, post office and outdoor market full of cheap stuff from China. Groceries and movie rentals are three blocks farther. A band shell in the square sometimes has music in the evenings. What's not here we don't need.

Torres gets its name, "towers," from three cliffs facing the sea. The middle one, resembling a small, sawed-off mountain, has a spacious grassy top, wonderful for strolling. Its vertical face, looking to the sea, is a sheer drop-off of 120 feet. There's no railing. At the bottom, the sea hammers the rock day and night, opening several cavernous mouths. They swallow incoming waves with a thud, and hurl them back with a hiss.

One evening at sunset, strolling the beach, Daisi uncharacteristically says she enjoys being with me, even loves me. I'm speechless. We're not accustomed to using the "L" word out loud to each other.

"I hope I'm not too boring," I reply weakly.

"You are, and so am I."

This exchange brings to mind what Daisi has brought into my life: her family, their language, their city, their nation, our sons' Brazilian citizenship—and the greatest gift of all—Daisi herself. Unlike the Swedish farmer, who loved his wife so much that one day he almost told her, I say, with all sincerity, "I love having you beside me."

We've been lucky. Divorce has never been an issue. If it were to come, God forbid, it wouldn't be the tranquil Scandinavian one, the one where they smile at one another, sign a couple of papers, and shake hands. No, ours would arrive accompanied with plates and cups smashing against walls, and I'd be carrying their shrapnel the rest of my life. Even good marriages need incentives.

As we continue walking along the beach, the light fades, and with it, a large, luminous, peach-colored full moon noiselessly rises out of the sea, as if pulled up by an invisible hand. Gazing out to sea, we witness this unhurried birth of a beautiful something out of nothing.

Back in Porto Alegre, I make Pai a proposition. I suggest Daisi and I sell our Torres condo and buy the tool shed behind his house and spend our winters with him there. Naturally, we'd use his bathrooms and kitchen and upstairs bedroom, and basically live in his house and eat his food. This would save us and the family lots of money.

DECEMBER 2003
A Year of Losses

Inexplicably, for the first time in our thirty-three years of banter, Pai has no comeback. It's a stunning upset victory for me. The score is now: Pai, five-thousand; Jim, one.

This is followed by another shocker. Pai's ceremonial hour of cafezinho migrates from three o'clock to four in the afternoon.

This is radical. I had no idea he was capable of such flexibility.

Other things, however, don't change. He continues buying bulk food wholesale. His forays into discount stores include amassing half a dozen jars of instant coffee, a dozen boxes of cookies and chocolate bars, scores of soft drink bottles, and hundreds of paper cartons of unrefrigerated milk. It's like buying breakfast cereal in the form of grain from barges on the Mississippi. And it's all for the grand total of three people: Sarah, who eats nearly nothing, a housekeeper, and himself.

JUNE-JULY 2004

Quietness

As our cab approaches, I fear Sarah may be in poor health.

Instead, we find Sarah in the center of the living room, proudly erect in her wheelchair, dressed as if ready for church, which she doesn't attend. She's dressed up for us. She greets us happily, as in the old days. She looks clean, fresh, and beautiful. The cut of her white hair suits her perfectly. She looks decidedly healthier than when we left six months ago, before a mastectomy performed in January. Today she looks five years younger. Maybe ten.

Tonight, however, unable to turn herself in bed, false teeth removed, shaking with Parkinson's, she looks frail again.

Little is happening in the house. Sarah is usually sleeping. There's little to do. It's so quiet, even the ticking clock holds a certain fascination. Daisi lounges in Pai's recliner in a corner of the living room, which thirty-four years ago was their bedroom, the very spot where he officially admitted me into the family. Today, however, I'm on the sofa, straining to read in dim natural light, because Captain Austerity has removed the bulb.

He sits in semidarkness at his disordered desk, doing his monthly budget with a flat, thick-leaded carpenter's pencil with no eraser. He whispers numbers to himself, counting on his fingers, as he did before the dawn of the hand calculator, but quite a while after the abacus.

His desk is strewn with piles of bills, receipts, bank statements, folders, and envelopes, a disarray comprehensible to him alone. Between the piles is a sea of scattered screws, nails, hooks, padlocks, keys, ballpoint pens whose ink dried up years ago, and pencils with erasers petrified to stone. We've given him new notebooks, new pens, and new pencils. However, fearing they'd walk away in the pockets of his housekeepers, he's shut them behind lock and key, never to be touched in his lifetime. Also stowed away, for the same reason, are nineteen boxes of chocolates in an upstairs cabinet secured by chain and padlock.

In this manner, Pai journeys life's bumpy road day after day, like an old horse in harness and blinders, once vigorous, but still hauling through the world his cart bearing food, water, electricity, gas, medicine, insurance, apartment units, housekeepers, health care workers, and the one he lives for, Sarah.

ABANDONMENT

After supper, Daisi and I sit on the sprawling sofa that dominates the small living room. Sarah is comfortable, asleep in her bedroom down the corridor. Leaning back in his chair and thinking of her, Pai reminisces on how they've been together for sixty-eight years, and—as always—how they started with nothing. Except their will to survive.

When his children were young, he says, the phone company gave him a temporary, and better-paying, assignment in Curitiba, a city 340 miles away, in the state of Paraná. He'd be gone for several months. Daisi knows this story, and grows quiet.

I've heard this one before, too. Like some of the others, it comes dressed in moral clothing with a scent of sweat, regret, and nostalgia. He's told this one again and again, probably because it contains something he wants to hear, or his children to hear. They've heard his stories and are disturbed by some. These are the darker ones, the ones that are part history, part autobiography, part catharsis. When these stories surface, his children try to change the subject.

Nonetheless, tonight he forges ahead and recalls the time when he was a young father, struggling to balance the two things he clings to for dear life—work and family. As this story unfolds, his voice drops a notch. His words come slower, more measured. He's sinking into his mournful Italian self, the one I can't handle. Raising his eyes, searching the dim upper corners of the room where memory appears to be stored, he says that after six months away, he returns home from Curitiba, "with more money for the family."

He pauses here. I know what's coming. Sidnei, his eldest, recognizes him and runs to greet him. Daisi, however, is too young. *"Ela não me reconhece. Ela está com medo de mim"* (She doesn't recognize me. She's frightened of me).

His head drops to his chest. His shoulders slump. He begins to weep. He looks very alone.

It's painful to see this in a tough, eighty-nine-year-old man. His story, providing for his children by temporarily abandoning them, touches a deeply buried live wire. It's a story that wants to be out, wants to be told, wants to be heard, and wants to put a big lump in my throat. Which it does.

> *I believe there is a special figure in men who leads them down into one of their great strengths—the power to grieve. . . . yet in our culture a man gets very little permission to grieve.*
> –Robert Bly

"Pai, this is ancient history. Let's forget it," Daisi says. She's trying to change the subject.

"*Sim,* it's old history," he replies, "but it leaves a scar, one I can never rub out."

I admire his courage to touch this old scar. I guess I must have a few scars by now, small ones probably, scars I rarely take the trouble to visit.

How different our lives are. I was raised in Minnesota. He was raised in Scarcity Nation. I have a tragedy-free past. I don't believe he can say the same. Our childhoods were baked in different ovens. Mine was slow, warm, and comfortable. His was quick and hot, forming a hard crust and sense of danger.

DISTANT THUNDER FROM VENUS

We visit Torres for three days. Torres has a history that mirrors that of Brazil itself. Five hundred years ago, one of its city streets was a path carved through jungle by two Indian tribes who used it to trade with one another. In 1500, the three rock outcroppings facing the sea attracted Portuguese ships, whose merchants proceeded to use the Indians' own path to capture them and ship them north to São Paulo as slaves. In 1777, a time when Spain sought to colonize southern Brazil, the Portuguese built a fort on the northernmost cliff. It was never attacked, and there's no trace of it today.

Under protection of the fort, Portuguese settlers, originally from the Azores Islands off Portugal, arrived from villages in the state immediately north, Santa Catarina. German and Italian immigrants arrived a short fifty years later. Fifty years after that, in 1878, the settlement was incorporated as a city.

After World War I, Torres became a seaside retreat where Porto Alegre's elite could "take the waters." Fast-forward to 1960, when Daisi, as a teenager, visited Torres as a guest of a friend, and found it to be an enclave of snobs. It's lost most of its elitism today.

Sidnei ceremoniously hands me the key to lock up our newly acquired condo. I confess to him that I feel fraudulent, a guest in a home that's not ours. This is because for the past six months, he and Maria Eunice have driven here many times, to fix, clean, hang paintings, move beds and desks, and generally create a light, airy, beautiful space. As such, I feel it belongs more to them than to us.

That night we all walk two blocks to the beach. The moon pierces a thin veil of clouds, illuminating white crests of waves rolling slowly in, long chains of pearls. They deliver a soft hiss and rumble, like distant thunder from Venus. The sand is soft underfoot, and the heavens are soft above. Softness below, softness above. It's beauty I don't feel I deserve. It is, however, a door to a new beginning in Brazil.

An aircraft lifts us out of Porto Alegre and, only hours later, drops us in Saint Paul. Our house feels small. Our bed seems unfamiliar. Our rooms feel remote, unreal. I wake the next morning to the distant rumble of engines and tires on the freeway about a mile away, not unlike the ocean's soft thunder in Torres. But Saint Paul is not Torres. Today I have to pay bills, mow the lawn, fill the tank with gas, and buy groceries. This is beauty of a lower rank.

MAY 2005

No One's Home

Our cab stops at the old scrub tree on a cool, autumn day in May. Pai emerges slowly from the front door, more carefully than I remember. His hair is whiter and thinner. It needs a trim. So does his tiny plot of grass, which is weedy. A tile on the front stoop is broken.

"*Ninguem tá em casa*" (No one's home), he announces, a joyless joke, light years from the bear hug and tears of welcome years ago.

Next day we go shopping, stopping at the corner grocery owned by the two Lebanese brothers. One of them launches into a familiar anti-government litany. Government workers, he says, behave as though they're doing you a favor, forgetting that you, the taxpayer, are paying their salaries. Americans are more efficient, he says, working under organized systems, while Brazilians improvise and figure things out on the fly.

Then he complains about the growth in petty thievery, which he says has forced him to close his fruit and vegetable stands on the sidewalk earlier, at 8:00 p.m. Pai's neighborhood seems to be in decline.

Later I accompany him to a small supermarket, where he proudly introduces me as *"o americano"* (the American). *"Que maravilha"* (how marvelous), says the woman manager, in a flat, unimpressed tone.

Traffic is intense on Benjamin Constant, the main street one block from his house. Motorbike delivery boys live dangerously, weaving in and out between cars and trucks. I saw a movie recently about these opportunistic *motoboys,* in which one kneels before his bed at night and prays: "Dear God, I wasn't able to kill myself today, but I promise to do it tomorrow for sure." Just yesterday, I saw a motorcycle delivery boy scraped off the asphalt of Benjamin Constant and shoveled into an ambulance. Traffic on that avenue is a hungry lion, waiting to rip into anyone who weakens.

TOUCHED BY THE STARS

Sidnei and Maria Eunice drive us into the mountains for a few days, including one night at a rustic farm. Here, the country night sky is black, huge, and teeming with stars. The Milky Way glitters with astounding clarity. We see the Southern Cross, smaller than the Big Dipper, and a brilliant Venus. Some stars appear close, others distant, revealing the immense depth of the universe, and how I'm just a grain of sand, though unaccountably a conscious one. These silent, ancient fiery bodies are blinking and winking, as if sharing with me a cosmic joke. The punch line hits when, feeling my way along a wooden fence in absolute pitch darkness, my shoe sinks into a warm cow pie.

Next day, we walk an empty gravel road through gently rolling hills. Pebbles underfoot glisten in the sunlight, some broken open like eggs to reveal hollow crystal interiors forged in volcanos long ago. I hike alone for a while, looking for things to photograph, like these gargantuan million-year-old boulders. Like the stars last night, they emit a palpable silence, broken only by the diamond gravel crunching beneath my shoes.

I begin to feel absorbed by the pebbles, the road, the boulders, and the surrounding hills and valleys. I remember having this sensation when I was a child, a sense of a space opening around me in which I could go anywhere and do anything. As a boy, I took great pleasure in the kinetics of simply walking, running, or riding my bike, in any direction I chose to go. I don't know why this feeling has come over me now. Perhaps it's last night's stars nudging me from their inky space. Or perhaps it's from two weeks ago, when after forty-three years of work, I retired.

THE RAIN THAT NEVER COMES

Pai is stretched out on his recliner this evening, staring out of his office window through its bars, across his tiny front lawn, through his spear fence, into the street. He rarely leaves the house, preferring to stay near Sarah, who is alive thanks to a feeding tube. These days it seems that what the tube is to her, she is to him.

She's cared for tonight by a male nurse, Valdomiro, a cheerful guy whose face resembles that of a young Hubert H. Humphrey. Suddenly, from her bedroom, come choking sounds. Pai springs from his recliner. He sweeps the corridor curtain aside and rushes with astonishing speed down the hall toward her bedroom. I follow him.

Sarah's feeding tube has become detached. A section of it is sticking deep in her throat. Breathless, whimpering and wringing his hands, Pai stands helplessly at the side of her bed.

Valdomiro bends over Sarah, his fingers deep in her throat. She's turning blue. Something momentous seems to be happening. I lean against the door jamb, forcing myself to watch. My lower back feels soft and tingly. Valdomiro manages to grasp the tube and pull it up out of Sarah's throat. It's surprisingly long. While we watch, he skillfully reattaches the tube, inserts it back down her throat, and reconnects it to a food pouch.

Feeling dizzy, I can't watch anymore. I return to the living room, where Daisi has stayed. I put my head between my legs to keep from passing out.

Slowly, Pai returns to the living room. He's weepy, agitated, and breathing hard. He apologizes for the state he's in, as if it's somehow disgraceful. He leans against a wall at an odd angle, looking very alone.

"Sarah e eu ficamos juntos setenta anos" (Sarah and I have been together for seventy years), he begins. Daisi sees what's coming, a lament about their hard lives. She interrupts and tells him to sit down, trying to head off this familiar story, which to hear again, now, would be unbearable.

"Prefiro ficar de pé" (I prefer to stand), he says stubbornly. She insists he sit. He persists on standing. This is how Gaviolis deal with each other: one insists and the other resists.

Finally, he sits on the sofa. He looks up to an empty place where the wall meets the ceiling. Irresistibly, he launches into the old refrain: *"Não tínhamos nada . . .* (We didn't have anything . . .) We did everything together . . . No one

I am consoled to learn
that it isn't just me—
and not just his children,
or his housekeepers,
or neighbors, butchers,
bakers, and candlestick
makers—who feared
him. Everyone did.
Had God appointed him
disciplinarian in the Garden
of Eden, the Fall would have
been avoided, and we'd all
be living in perpetual bliss
now.

could do alone what we did together . . . She gave me a family . . . Now the time has come for me to stay by Sarah's side."

As he rambles on, in the wake of the fright moments ago, it occurs to me that I've never heard him speak the word *morte*, or "death." It's as if the appearance of this sinister word would open a door for the Grim Reaper to walk through.

For a long time, we sit in silence. As day ebbs away, the room darkens. The air is still. A sea of sadness fills the living room. A good life, an honest life, a long and useful life, seems to be coming to its end. I feel my throat tighten.

Down the corridor, Sarah is quiet, having narrowly escaped asphyxiation. This is the same corridor, which on my very first day in this house, I imagined would lead into the mysteries of Brazil. Now, sitting only a few feet from this same passageway, I grow aware of a wonderful privilege, something that would seem to be no privilege at all. I am witnessing the unraveling of two lives. Lives laced together seventy long years ago, forming a strong cord, braided into a marriage of strength, endurance, and dignity. Bearing witness to their union in my various visits to their home has been a gift. One I can never repay.

The following morning, I hear steps slowly mounting the stairs to our bedroom, where I sit on the bed reading. Daisi is folding and putting away clothes. Like a ghost, he enters slowly, stopping just inches in front of me, gazing out the window over my shoulder. He seems not to know I'm here. For several moments, he looks out at a gray blanket of clouds covering the city from horizon to horizon. Then his eyebrows slowly lift on his heavy face, which seems to take great effort, and he says softly, *"E cadê a chuva que nunca vem?"* (And where's the rain that never comes?)

The question seems rhetorical. Another long pause. Then he says, *"O pessoal da assistência esta me matando"* (The nursing-care people are killing me). I've stopped giving him advice on what to do about this.

Another lengthy pause. He continues to stand directly in front of me, looking beyond me at the gray day outside. Then, to nobody in particular, "I can't live without Sarah."

Daisi sees another tragic mood coming.

"Pai," she says, in a practical, unsentimental tone, "if you need money to cover nursing costs, you can sell my apartment unit." This is the property he has given her in his will.

He rejects this as absurd, as he does all advice from the family now. *"Estou fazendo tudo sozinho, como sempre fiz"* (I'm doing it all alone, as I've always done), he contends, with a maddening mix of independence and self-pity.

LOOKING FOR CAPTAIN CORNUCOPIA

Next day the weather turns cold. That evening, Pai plunges into the dark night to buy bread for supper. Wouldn't it be best for me to buy it? Wrong. In his ninety-year-old mind, he's the one who must bring home the bread.

At least couldn't he buy bread at the well-lit corner bakery, a mere twenty-second walk from his door? Wrong again. This is too simple. He must continue his one-man boycott of Nenê the baker, now well into its sixth year, for the Sledgehammer Sin.

I go out looking for him. I pass the bar and its fallen men drooping over their little tables, pass Nenê's bakery, and turn right onto Benjamin Constant, which at this hour is a menacing river of headlights flowing in both directions. I look for him at El Kadri, the corner grocery. One of the Lebanese brothers tells me Pai bought cheese and lunchmeat a few minutes ago, then headed to a bakery several blocks farther on.

I follow his trail, then spot him. He's trying to get through heavy traffic on Benjamin Constant. He lurches into the street on unsteady legs, plastic bags of bread dangling from each hand, headlights screeching to a stop just inches away. When he reaches my side of the street, I silently take his venerable arm, and escort him home over a broken sidewalk.

I don't scold him. I don't remind him to please try to stay alive. I don't rebuke him for his suicidal trip to buy bread. I do none of these things, because reprimands don't fit my role in our drama. A scolding by me would mean our roles have reversed, that he's become my inferior. This will happen only when the sun stops rising in the east.

THE BITTER TIMES HAVE NOT YET ARRIVED

Cafezinho, a Gavioli ritual as unfailing as the rising sun, is no longer prepared by Sarah, who's now bedridden. The honors are carried out by Jana. She's the latest in a long parade of housekeepers whom Pai keeps hiring and firing. With Jana, he gets lucky.

A married woman in her early thirties, with long black hair and a missing front tooth, Jana is one of those rare helpers who complete their work quickly then look for more. Her day is full. She starts by fixing Pai and Sarah a simple breakfast. Then she washes dishes. Then makes all the beds. Then washes clothes, including ours. Then hangs them to dry. Then cooks several dishes for the main meal at noon. Then cleans the dishes. Then irons clothes, stacking them neatly on our beds. Then cleans bathrooms. Then washes floors on her hands and knees. If there's nothing left to do, she pushes a little mechanical duster over a rug. Or reorganizes a kitchen shelf. Or cleans windows. Then she fixes a simple supper. Then does the dishes.

On weekends, she goes home to a difficult life with several children and a difficult husband.

She does her work willingly, apparently taking pleasure in helping him. Perhaps this comes from her reading of the Bible, in which fear of the Lord is a form of wisdom that gives her perspective on her own troubles. She's a religious woman. Before going to sleep on a sofa bed in the dining room, she sits, with her knees up to her chin beneath a dim forty-watt bulb, reading the Bible. This is one bulb he allows to stay in its socket.

Jana shows remarkable compassion for Pai at his stage in life and anticipates his needs. Take *cafezinho*, for example. She carefully arranges it on the kitchen table at the appointed hour with no less care than a priest preparing the Eucharist. The consecrated elements she places before him include a tin of dry crackers, a jar of freeze-dried coffee granules, another coffee jar filled with sugar, a small saucer, a tiny spoon, and a tiny cup. Into this cup she carefully pours boiling water. With attention equal to hers, he watches his cup fill, instructing her when to stop, always at the usual spot, near the brim. She spoons in authorized amounts of coffee, then sugar. He stirs it himself.

She doesn't sit at the table with him. She leans against the sink, a dish towel over her shoulder, watching him, mostly in silence, content to wait when he's finished, so she can tidy up.

Pai's cafezinho has taken on an austere quality. I notice he never shares this intimate ritual with any of his domestic help, including Sarah's caretakers. He pretends they are not here, retaining a wall between his life and the lives of those he pays to work in his home. They are not his friends. They are not his guests. They are his employees and will remain such, especially during cafezinho. I'm uncomfortable with this inequality, which seems to come in sharper focus during cafezinho, a communal moment in an otherwise scattered day. But in his house, the sharing of wafers, strong coffee, and companionship is restricted to family only, which includes me.

In this, he's guided by another of his Iron Rules for Living: DON'T GET CHUMMY WITH PEOPLE WHO MIGHT GROW MEDDLESOME. This rule is prerequisite to another: INSIST ON SUPERB WORK FROM PEOPLE YOU PAY. These rules, which are immutable, help hold his life together.

Refusing to share his coffee and wafers also could very possibly be an absurd attempt to stock up for what he calls *"os tempos amargos"* (the bitter times). I told him I thought these are his bitter times. No, he said, the bitter times have not yet arrived. Like the camel that goes a month without water, Pai, his steely stoicism forged during the Great Depression, can endure remarkable amounts of discomfort. It's almost as if now, in his declining years, he welcomes the return of his old friend, Deprivation.

His home, now virtually a nursing facility for Sarah, is still his castle. He rules it with an iron fist rusting at the joints. He spends evenings compulsively locking doors and window shutters and spends mornings opening them, only to start all over again the next evening. He's continually turning off lights, or unscrewing bulbs not needed for basic survival—like reading lamps near our bed or the living room couch.

One day he shows me a small electronic black box installed next to his upstairs phone. It's a control box that prevents housekeepers and Sarah's caretakers from calling out and driving up his phone bill. They're obliged to use their cell phones. While this is normal, it means I must ask his permission to make a call. This means he must laboriously mount the stairs, insert not one, but two separate little keys in the phone security box, then turn them to award me a dial tone. It's similar to security systems employed to prevent an accidental nuclear missile launch.

When I looked skeptically at the box, he says, *"Se a vida fosse simples, não teria graça"* (If life were simple, it wouldn't be any fun), with a face quite free of fun.

PULLING OARS

At breakfast I try to cheer him up. "Hey Pai, how's it going?"

His face darkens. *"Puxando os remos"* (Pulling on the oars).

I wonder what this means. Pulling oars is heavy work. The boat doesn't seem to move much. Being old must be like this, rowing through heavy waters. Or maybe he simply means surviving in Brazil, starting poor, with little schooling, struggling upward in a world that wants to hold him down. Rowing in these waters requires strength and determination. Years of it.

I'm reminded of the bright-blue oars crossed like an X over the fireplace in his cottage in Santa Terezinha. I can imagine Pai and Sarah in a little boat on the open sea, he pulling his oar, she pulling hers. Their children, in smaller boats trailing behind, are attached with ropes to their parents' boat. When I arrive, a long rope attaches my little boat to theirs, too.

He's not one to let his oar drag loose in the water. But when living gets choppy, and the oar might slip from his grip, Sarah is right there to return it to his hands.

"We're going forward! We're not giving up!"

This is fact. Daisi has heard her say it.

SEPTEMBER 6, 2005
The Phone Rings

Back in Saint Paul, Daisi is busy at work writing a funding proposal. My brand-new retirement is busy with walking, reading, journaling, playing the piano, and taking photographs, things of no importance to anyone but me.

As usual, on September 6, 2005, we prepare for bed. The telephone rings. Daisi answers. It's Sidnei. What he has to say arrives like lightning from a cloudless sky. Daisi is stunned but not surprised. At age ninety-five, Sarah has finally let her oar slip into the sea.

Death is well known, and yet no matter how expected, it catches us unprepared. It's as if, floating along on life's stream, our busy lives unexpectedly strike a submerged rock, which has been waiting for us.

Sarah is buried the very next day, according to Brazilian custom. We're told it's an intimate and touching ceremony led by a mendicant Capuchin friar, who, in my imagination but not in reality, is wearing a brown hooded habit and a plain rope around his waist honoring the simplicity and austerity of Sarah's life.

Davison, who can't bear to see his mother's coffin, stays at home in São Paulo.

The loss of a mother, the one who brought us into the world and who, for Daisi, has been so far away for so long, takes time to sink in. Several long-distance phone conversations occur over the next two days, and Daisi learns that many of her friends attended the funeral. Hearing this, she finally grieves and weeps for the first time.

Sarah was my main Portuguese teacher, crawling upstairs on all fours to the baking-hot attic, dragging me into a grammatical jungle. A woman of great dignity and determination, she was the family's true north. She'd wait until the right moment to express her often-decisive opinions. She was deeply suspicious of government, hers and mine. She left behind a legacy of paintings done in a simple, primitive style, often with vibrant color. They express a joy that her somber personality did not.

In another call from Sidnei, we learn that Pai is becoming unmoored. He's more forgetful than ever, phoning Sidnei sometimes ten times a day, repeating his questions again and again. He sets appointments then forgets them. He shouts refusals then does precisely what he's refused to do. And because he's still the patriarch, chief of the Gavioli tribe, much of what he declares, dictates, and demands, is delivered in imperious tones. With Sarah gone, he's rowing with one oar, and his boat is going in circles.

For years Sidnei and Maria Eunice have physically and morally supported Pai and Sarah, as well as Aunt Cecilia. Now they're exhausted. They need relief.

It's decided that I'll go to Porto Alegre for six weeks. My task is to move Pai from the family home to the apartment directly across the street from his house. Cecilia, who owned the unit for more than thirty years before recently moving to a nursing home, has willed the apartment to him, the one who managed her affairs all those years.

Daisi plans to arrive three weeks after I get there to clean out the family home. This exhausting job falls to her by default and, because she's lived more than half her life away from home, she wants to help any way she can.

OCTOBER–NOVEMBER 2005
The Wreckage

I arrive a month later in a spring rain. Pai greets me at the door with a perfunctory embrace. He looks weary, older. He's lost weight. His once-firm arm muscles sag like a shirt on a hanger. *The years do not fall on the ground but on the body,* says an African proverb.

The living room, dining room, and entire inside of the house look like the end of a play when the stage set is torn down. The big corner sofa is gone, leaving an empty space. Paintings hang crooked on walls. Chairs, desks, and tables are either gone or askew. Nails, screws, wires, tools, dust balls, and odds and ends are everywhere.

Wandering into the dining room to survey the wreckage, I get a sharp blow to the head from a ceiling lamp hanging by a wire. It seems to say, "Where have you been?"

My reply is that eighteen hours ago I was in Minnesota. My body's here but not yet my brain.

Minutes later, he loses his set of keys. He paces anxiously from room to room looking for them. *"Estou perdido* (I'm lost), lost without my keys." Jana and

I look everywhere. Then he finds them on his dresser, where he always puts them.

"*Whew, que susto!*" (What a scare!)

He's found his keys, but he's lost his wife, and now he's working on losing his home, along with his memory. I wonder how I can possibly help.

That evening, while Jana is washing dishes, I sit at the kitchen table and ask her what happened the night Sarah died. With a towel over her shoulder, leaning back against the sink, she says Pai had gone upstairs to bed that evening. At about ten thirty, Sarah died peacefully, "*. . . nos meus braços*" (. . . in my arms), she says.

While she's talking, I notice something behind her. It's the shadow of a large rat calmly walking along the wall just outside the window that overlooks the back patio. I'm startled, but say nothing.

Jana says she dreaded waking Pai with this heavy news, fearing it might break his erratic heart. So she called a doctor. He would give Pai the sad news.

Just then Pai enters the kitchen. He demands to know what Jana has just said. Frightened, she quickly exits the kitchen. I hesitate, then confess it was about the night Sarah died.

"Don't talk to me about this!" he shouts, his voice rising to a pitch I've never heard before. "I don't want to be thinking about this!"

Suddenly he looks unsteady, as if he might collapse. I reach out to keep him from falling, but he grabs the back of a kitchen chair. I've never seen him like this before.

He sits down. After a long silence, he starts speaking slowly, searching for words. He recalls the days long ago when he was gone from home, sometimes for months. This is when, he says, Sarah taught high school, cared for the children, sewed dresses for Daisi and Lori, and managed their small income.

His red-rimmed eyes scan the ceiling, searching for memories. "She was a great companion in our struggle."

Next day, thinking about the large rat, I go out the back door and cautiously poke around the patio behind the kitchen. This area, about the size of a pickup truck, is where Jana hangs the wash. At the back of the patio is a tool shed. This is where he stores his chisels, saws, and other tools that hang from nails in Germanic order. Pai hasn't been here in months, maybe years.

At the base of the shed door is a small opening in the shape of a half-moon, chewed by rats. Directly beneath it, the concrete has taken on a shiny beige color from thousands of bellies squeezing under there. Apparently a thriving village of rats has taken ownership of the shed, using the patio as their front yard and play area. They've made themselves at home and are free to shop around for food, start families, care for their young, and live in tranquility—except when Jana invades to hang the wash.

One day when she was hanging the wash, a fearless thrill seeker ran directly across the top of her bare foot. Another time, she tried to shoo away *"um grande senhor"* (a great big fellow). Eyeing her with brazen defiance, this warrior wouldn't budge.

"Aren't you afraid of rats?" I ask.

"Tenho horror (I'm terrified). But I need this job, because I have six children between the ages of four and twelve, and my husband is out of work. He was drinking every Friday, Saturday, and Sunday night with friends. I told him he had to choose between his friends and his family. Thank God he made the right choice."

I say nothing, moved by her courage.

On the evening of my third day I mount the stairs, flip on the bedroom light and see sprinting diagonally across the floor a big cockroach. I charge and nail him with one lucky stomp.

Catching my breath, I figure where there's one, there's a hundred more. And another thing. Bedbugs in my mattress are feasting on me. Last night, they sketched on my rump a line of welts that looks like the map of Brazil.

Before bedding down, I brush off my pillow little granules, like grains of sand, fallen from termites in the ceiling. I lie down and turn off the light. In the darkness, I can hear them nibbling wood panels directly over my face. I fear that as I sleep, dreaming that Daisi will soon be here, crumbs will fall from their banquet into my open mouth.

I wake at 4:30 a.m. and can't get back to sleep. My thoughts wander. Yesterday I told him about the rat infestation behind the kitchen. *"Isso fica por último na lista"* (This is last on my list), he told me. Yeah, right. I doubt he has any list at all. I wonder where to put poison. I wonder whether a big one might run up my leg. I wonder whether rats and bugs will inherit this place.

In the distance, soft thunder explodes, like boulders rolling on heaven's floor. A light rain begins to fall. I'm reminded of the warm rain that soaked me thirty-five years ago as I first set foot in this house.

This morning he can't find his identity card. The three of us, including Jana, search the house everywhere. His agitation is growing. At last, he finds an old card he can use temporarily. Then, fumbling around on his messy desk, he loses track of it.

"*Ah, meu DEUS!*" (Oh, my GOD!), he says, shaking his fists above his head and looking upward, as if blaming the stars. "*Isso é impossível! Impossível!*" (This is impossible! Impossible!) Then he pauses, collects himself, turns to me, and confesses, "This is how I am now, Jim, very forgetful."

We spend all morning looking for his ID card. I'm trying to keep my distance from his anxiety, but it's radioactive, and it's blowing in my direction. I feel awkward and unprepared for him and the work ahead. I'm not sure how long I can last.

We spend every day together now. We eat together, talk together, and work together. What seems best is to let go of myself, follow his orders, and simply be a tool in his hands. This way, there's no conflict.

At night, I sleep upstairs with the termites, and he sleeps a few steps away in the room that used to be Sarah's study. We share a bathroom between our rooms.

Today we spend nearly all afternoon at his apartment in what will be his smaller office, visualizing where to put things. From some big sheets of brown wrapping paper, I've cut out six shapes, each representing his desk, cabinet, chair, couch, music player, and speakers. There are only three ways to arrange them in the office space.

I spread them out in the first configuration. Okay, now he wants to see the next arrangement, so I move the sheets of paper. Now the third, so I move the papers. Then he wants to see the first one again. Now let's see the second. Now let's see the third. For a full hour, I move the sheets from one position to the next, as he doggedly puzzles over them again and again, always forgetting what the two previous arrangements look like. He will not be hurried. He will not be forced. I struggle to be patient. Jim, Jim, be calm, I say to myself. I take deep breaths to relax. This is simply who he is now. Just be his tool.

Finally, he tires of the effort and goes back across the street to take a nap. When he's fatigued, he's a hundred years old. But when he wakes, he's fifty, sparring and joking in deadpan style. His age goes up and down like the sun goes in and out of clouds on a windy day.

Between his house and the apartment is a street we must cross. At the curb,

I offer my arm, as if helping an old woman. He jerks his arm away. But I persist, because he's under my care now, and I cannot have him stumble and fall in the street. The Gaviolis would never forgive me. After a couple of days of offering my arm, he relents and takes it, but only when crossing the street. At all other times he's a rock-ribbed individual doing everything himself, as he's always done.

An even more frightening place is the smooth set of indoor steps needed to reach his apartment, which is on the second floor. There's no handrail. These stairs are pitiless, possessing an alarming power to shatter the bones and brains of anyone who stumbles. Going down, I always place myself directly in front of him to break any tumble. He takes each step one at a time, his hand sliding along on a concrete ledge. We never discuss this peril.

Little problems crop up. One is his new portable, push-button phone. Sidnei arrives, for the third time, to teach the new phone to his father, who years ago helped bring the telephone to Rio Grande do Sul. Pai's face grows pinched and tense trying to understand new features—redial, memory, pause—features I don't even use myself. As a frustrated Sidnei goes through the explanation, Pai opens and closes his big hands again and again, as if trying to grasp the nature of this digital tool that's beyond his reach.

Later that day, I tell Sidnei about the rats. He calls an exterminator, a man named Sergio, who comes to check things out. Sergio has low eyelids that cover the top half of his flat, leaden eyes and a metallic voice that sounds like a chain saw—perfect for a rat exterminator. He says he'll need to make several assaults on the creatures.

On Saturday I take a break from Pai and stay overnight at Sidnei's house. Sunday morning, Sidnei, Maria Eunice, and I return to pick him up to attend a monthly mass for mourners that Pai has marked in his calendar. He's waiting for us at the curb, bareheaded in a cold, gray drizzle, wearing a light jacket and a bereaved expression on his face.

It takes us an hour to reach the cemetery. A fine rain comes and goes every few minutes, like grief breathing. We locate Sarah's grave, which in the month since she was buried September 7, is almost completely grown over with wet grass.

Then we're told there is no mass today. It was held yesterday.

Pai is inconsolable. He grips the edge of the door to a small chapel, gazing out at the wet, misty rolling hills containing Sarah's remains. *"Fiquei confuso"* (I got confused), he moans, over and over, to no one in particular. I drape my arm over his broad shoulders. He doesn't even notice. He's grieving completely alone, somewhere far away from me. The silence is broken only by rain dripping from the eaves. I gaze out at the grassy slopes. All is silent out there, too, except for the quero-quero birds, crying sharply, *"Quero, quero"* (I want, I want).

Housekeepers are now writing their own paychecks for his signature, because, he says, his hand trembles. I doubt whether he remembers how to write a check, but I don't dare ask him. His weekend housekeeper, Mara, just filled out her two-day check for roughly eighteen dollars.

Pai signs his checks with great flourish. His signature, "Gavioli," begins impressively with a large, graceful G, like an egg tipped on its side. Then he rushes headlong through the letters, flattening them like an iron on a wrinkled shirt. By the time he reaches the end, he's moving so fast that the final letter, *i*, is distorted into an *o*. Then he abruptly changes direction and swoops backward, slashing a dramatic underline beneath his name, serving as a pedestal upon which to rest his creation. The final touch is to dot the final letter, the *i*, done in such a rush that it lands as a lonely speck in a far-off orbit, like the dwarf planet Pluto, completing a work of art that ranks among the world's great signatures.

At supper, he, Mara and I discuss Brazil's racial mix. Mara proudly says her mother is Italian, her father is black, one grandparent is Brazilian Indian and another is Portuguese.

"Os imigrantes italianos," Pai says, "mingled easily with other Brazilians, but German immigrants stayed to themselves." Germans are intransigent, he says, *"com fogo na roupa"* (with fire in their clothes), shaking his fist with frightening authority. I suspect his German-bred mother, Amanda, must have been a holy terror.

Five days later, a wooden board turns up missing. It belongs to a sofa he took apart to carry to the apartment. We hunt for it in my bedroom upstairs, where the sofa used to be. *"Está aqui! Sei que está aqui!"* (It's here! I know it's here!), he cries, his voice rising. The room fills with tension. He appears to be blaming me.

His fists are clenched as if brawling with an invisible enemy. His face is red, on the verge of tears, as if possessed. Then, gaining a toehold on self-control, he shouts, *"Olha, Jim! Olha como estou tremendo!"* (Look, Jim! Look how I'm shaking!) This is how I am now!" he cries. "This is how I am!"

At last, we find the board in a closet, where he must have put it.

Today four of us—Pai, Jana, a skinny guy hired to help with heavy stuff, and I, are working hard on the move. Eating lunch in the kitchen, the skinny guy, Jana and I get into a lively discussion about Brazilian racism, which we all condemn. Just as we're warming to the subject, Pai cuts us off.

"*Come, não fala!*" (Eat, don't talk!), he orders. "This talk has nothing to do with why we're here, which is to eat."

We go silent. Our exchange of views censored, we're reduced to a crew of sullen, thought-deprived grunts. Maybe not unlike those laborers of yesteryear laying telephone lines in the forest, men led by a tyrannical foreman who's in charge at our table right now.

After lunch he and I return to his apartment, where he orders me precisely where on his cabinet shelves I must position decorative plates, cups, silver, and Sarah's ethnic dolls. "Not there!" he shouts imperiously. I move them. "Not there!" he shouts louder. Resentment rears up in me and I'm on the verge of shouting back that he can do it himself. Instead, I bite my tongue, take a deep breath, and remind myself why I'm here. Just stay with him. Don't get blown off course.

Next day he has the corner locksmith replace a lock. This is the same locksmith to whom Nenê the baker loaned the sledgehammer, which subsequently vanished. Pai holds no grudge against the locksmith. He reserves it all for Nenê.

The lock is for an iron, cage-like outer door to Pai's apartment, a second door to safeguard against break-ins. In order to walk from his house to his apartment now, we need seven separate keys to unlock six doors and two gates. More numerous the barriers, greater the security, slower the job.

The following day, Rat Man Sergio removes eighteen corpses from the rodent colony in the shed. A few days later he returns for a follow-up attack. Before distributing the poison, he points to a pile of several hundred red clay tiles on one side of the patio, leftovers from the exterior of Pai's house.

"*O que que eu faço?*" (What should I do?) he asks. "There might be a nest in there."

Take them, I reply. He loads them in his VW van and is about to drive off, when Pai sees what's happening.

"*Jim, o que que você está fazendo?*" (Jim, what are you doing?), he cries. "Is he taking away my tiles? You can't do this! This is impossible! What if a tile on my house breaks? Where will I get a replacement? I won't find tiles like this anywhere in Rio Grande do Sul! I won't find them anywhere in all of Brazil!" Once again, he's going ballistic. He can't bear to let go of a single spare tile for the house he and Sarah built.

"Pai, it's my fault. I told him to take them."

"*Não!*" he shouts. "This is not your fault. The exterminator knows better! He knows what they're worth! He must return them!" he cries out, eyeing Sergio, who stands only a few feet away, as he would a thief.

Unfazed by everything Pai just said, Rat Man calmly unloads all the tiles and rebuilds the pile.

A week later, one of his four neighborhood banks calls to say they've blocked his checking account. The problem is the check his weekend housekeeper Mara had filled out for him. It calls for a withdrawal—not for the equivalent of eighteen dollars, the original amount—but for the extraordinary sum of *six-thousand* and eighteen dollars.

In near panic, the ninety-year-old pushes his way through four blocks of crowded sidewalks to the bank. He returns a couple of hours later, white around the mouth. He phones Mara. A few minutes later he confronts her, right there on the broken sidewalk beneath his wrinkled scrub tree. She claims innocence. He calmly fires her on the spot.

Firing housekeepers is nothing new. He does it with regularity, like an athlete staying in shape.

CALL THE MANAGER

That afternoon, he and I trudge six blocks through heat and traffic to a supermarket. Shouting over traffic's roar on Avenida Benjamin Constant, I defend the housekeeper he just fired. "Pai, someone else could have altered the check after she countersigned it. Firing her is unfair."

He doesn't budge, insisting she's guilty—and maybe guilty of something even more disturbing—missing chocolates from one of the nineteen boxes he hides in a chained and padlocked cabinet, chocolates he probably forgot he had eaten. People who forge checks for an extra six thousand dollars are perfectly capable of stealing chocolates, his thinking goes.

We enter the cool air of the supermarket armed with a grocery list prepared by Jana. Pai stops in his tracks, astonished by the wondrous cornucopia of goods. Then he grabs a cart and plunges into the products.

Great, we'll be out of here in no time.

We enter the first aisle and he stops dead. He picks up a colorful package. *"Olha aqui"* (Look at this), he says, turning it over with childlike wonder. "What could this be?"

"Pai, that's not on the list," I say, impatient. "We don't need it. You can put it back." I gently take it from his hand and return it to the shelf. He moves forward, stops, and picks up another brilliant package, turning it this way and that as if admiring a stone from Jupiter.

When we get to something we actually need, detergent, he chooses the jumbo size to save money, and then picks up three more jumbos to save even more money. I reach into the cart to put the extra ones back on the shelf. He grabs my arm, steps between me and the cart, and wordlessly bounces me out of the way with his hip.

Captain Consumption is back in charge.

"Jim," he commands, pointing to the list, "go find this." The problem is I barely understand Jana's handwriting, which is wider and freer than our self-contained style in Minnesota. Jana's hand disguises an *a* as an *o;* the *1* as a *7;* and the *7* becomes a backward *F*. When I do manage to read something, it's often a brand I don't know, like *Omo*, a detergent. Actually, I do know that one. Still, I'm beginning to feel stupid again.

I'm performing below expectations, so he summons reinforcements. He catches the arm of a bosomy, matronly floorwalker who knows where everything is. He asks her for this and that in his scattershot style, sending the poor woman helter-skelter here, there, and everywhere. Soon she's rolling her eyes in exasperation. This is comforting. It means I'm not the only one becoming unhinged. She abruptly snatches the list from his hand, and quickly finds everything on it.

We reach checkout. When everything is paid for and placed in ten plastic bags—far more stuff than we need—he demands to see the store manager. No explanation. This is disquieting. The manager arrives, a thin, mousy-looking creature. Now Pai demands to see the matronly floorwalker. We wait some more. She arrives, looking frightened. Now what? My stomach tightens. This guy is living in a different orbit, barely intersecting with this store, and somehow it's my job to bring him back to planet earth. Another thing not taught at Harvard.

Standing at full attention now are the mousy manager, the rattled floorwalker, a subdued checkout girl, three slack-jawed bag boys, and me. The audience is assembled and ready. I take a deep breath. The footlights dim, the curtain parts, the Brazilian Shakespeare turns to us, and . . .

"*Eu quero lhes informar*" (I want to inform you all), he says, his booming oratory reaching innocent shoppers all the way back to the vegetables, "that the service I have received from this employee"—sweeping his arm in a dramatic flourish toward the flustered floorwalker—"has been outstanding." Hearing this, delivered before her supervisor, she glows like a fresh tangerine. The checkout girl and bag boys are all smiles. The rodent manager is relieved, then delighted, then jubilant, vigorously shaking hands with Pai, who, with this bit of theater, has blessed a good employee with the simple gift of appreciation.

I exit the store, grateful to see trees, traffic, and a normal world.

TRANQUILITY

The day's work done, Jana, Pai, and I gather after supper upstairs in his bedroom to watch television news. Reception is poor. Ghosts move slowly from left to right across the screen, like mysterious forces at work behind the day's events.

After the news we call it a day. Outside doors are locked and metal shades are rattled shut. We go to our respective beds—Jana downstairs to her sofa bed, I to my upstairs room, and he to his room, our doors open between us. I read, aided by a bed lamp he now permits. He shuffles quietly about in his room, preparing to bed down for the night, his simple ritual bringing the day to a close. A pleasant tranquility spreads throughout the house.

"*Boa noite, Jim.*"

"*Boa noite, Pai.*"

The house is quiet. From outside, I hear a neighbor's voice, then a distant chorus of barking dogs, then the plaintive whistle of a lone guard patrolling dimly lit streets, then frogs calling out their question, always in English, "Why, why, why?"

Maybe they're asking why he's losing things. His identification card, his keys, his chocolates, part of his sofa, his ability to mount a curb, write a check, read his calendar, use a telephone. He's wearing down, that's why. And there's no good answer for the frogs, who I assume also will be wearing down some day. Perhaps it's simply the price he must pay for his long journey, starting long before the day he generously declared his family my family, his house my house. Now his troubles are my troubles.

This morning I called Daisi. She asked whether Pai had moved out of the house yet. Not yet, I said, things are moving slower than expected. She said she wants him moved before she arrives to clean out the house, an order delivered in an imperious tone inherited from her father.

PICKLE JARS

Today is Sunday, Jana's day off. Pai needs to arrange his pills for tomorrow—under my supervision. I've got to get them right, Jana said, because the medicines are strong. She gave me a list of the pills, and when to take them, penciled on a scrap of brown paper. Her undecipherable handwriting, plus the inscrutable drug names, makes the list useless.

Pai takes pills in the morning from one pickle jar, and in the evening from another. One is labeled "8 Horas" (8:00 a.m.), the other "20 Horas" (8:00 p.m.). Jana stocks the jars each evening for the next day from a shoebox where he stores eight bottles and boxes of pills.

To begin organizing, he dumps pill bottles and boxes from the shoebox in a jumble onto the seat of a chair. One of the pills is for anxiety, but I don't know which one. I could probably use it right now.

Now he's taking some tablets from their containers. He's fiddling nervously with them. He decides to arrange them on the chair in two lines, one for each bottle. This looks promising. He rushes one line of pills into one of the pickle jars. Oops, now he's pausing, eyeing the jar suspiciously. He's unsure. He grabs the jar and overturns it. The little demons tumble back onto the seat of the chair. He's fumbling with them. He's mumbling to himself. Now he's starting over. This is nerve-wracking.

His big hands are fidgeting with the tiny devils, dropping them on the floor, picking them up, and rearranging them on the chair in positions I don't understand. Abruptly, he scoops some up and drops them in a jar. Now he picks up the other jar. He dumps its contents back on the chair. He's like a magician, moving beans around under cups in quick and confusing motion. I'm getting dizzy trying to follow this.

He keeps consulting the brown scrap of paper for direction. Wait a minute. He's got a new tactic. He picks up each tablet one by one, examines its shape, whispers its name to himself, and then forgets where it belongs—in a jar or somewhere back on the chair, now in chaotic disorder. This is crazy. I'm feeling useless, probably worse than useless, an accomplice to a drug disaster.

At last, I'm beginning to recognize some of them. I start to call out their names, guessing whether they belong in one jar or the other, or back on the chair for reshuffling all over again. Frankly, I have no idea. After half an hour, we maneuver the little fiends into what I pray are their proper pickle jars. I'm exhausted.

Like poison gas on a battlefield, his confusion is seeping into my foxhole.

THEY'RE TAKING MY LIGHTS

Daisi arrives, enters the house, glances about and takes in the disarray of a life uprooted.

"Why isn't Pai moved to his apartment?" she wants to know. "This is what you were supposed to do in your three weeks here with him."

She's angry because wants to clean out the house without Pai looking over her shoulder. I understand that. Meanwhile, the warm reunion I expected between us is now out of the question. Her face is full of determination. She's dreading the prospect of digging into the remains of her parents' lives.

"Daisi, calm down. I *have* been helping him move, but it's taking more time than I thought." I'm feeling defensive.

She's in no mood to hear what the past three weeks have been like. Such as the companionable days the old man and I have been spending together, the pleasure of working under his agendas, at his rhythm, at his measured pace. Neither he nor I have wanted to spend our nights apart, he alone in his apartment and me alone in his house. We much preferred sleeping near one another, like friends, doors open between us.

Daisi is agitated and anxious to start. She's gripping us like a pair of jumper cables. The woman is definitely made in her father's image.

The next day, summoning the grim determination at which Gaviolis excel, she attacks the pieces of her parents' lives: furniture, appliances, utensils, clothes, books, even underclothing. For what she decides is worthless, she's going to be a human broom and dustpan.

For three days, with marvelous help from Jana, Daisi advances through the house room by room, coming to grips with everything. A cabinet and a table go to Sidnei. An ornate serving cart goes to Lori. Pai's barbecue oven, the heart of spirited family gatherings, goes to no one. No one needs it. Piece by piece, she's breaking up the family home.

She delves into old photos, old letters, old phonograph records, a small journal her mother had kept before marriage. She sifts through her mother's personal care items, not finding the new nightgowns, clothing, and sheets Daisi had sent over the years. They've been quietly removed by housekeepers, who are poor people. Daisi understands this, yet is saddened by it.

She finds Sarah's Portuguese-English dictionary, a wreckage held together by a string, as if gift wrapped for someone. She opens a drawer and discovers more of her mother's oil paintings. Some are painted on recycled cardboard, some on paper originally used for something else—art created in scarcity. Her books, her paintings, her journal—they're all pieces of her mother's soul.

She digs into her father's thirty ties, some stained, some torn, some with holes, some wide and colorful from the sixties. She sorts them in triage: some to keep, some to clean, some to toss. She does the same for his five suits, ten sweaters, ten jackets, and numerous shoes. Then she discovers his remarkable collection of caps and hats. They are saved. Also saved is his yellow vest, weighted down with bronze medals honoring his leadership in his Lions Club.

Nothing she touches is dead. Everything is alive, charged with a voltage of memory. Struggling to resist echoes, undertones, and even fragrances, she works quickly, putting a stone over her emotions, a trick learned from someone I know. She forces herself to become ruthless, turning things saved for years into trash. At one point, when Pai sees the old pans he used for frying potatoes about to disappear, he objects. The old food-making tools are hard to let go. This is precisely what Daisi feared, and why she wants him out of the house. Thankfully, he backs off, lacking stomach to stand around and watch.

"I'm the villain, willing to take the heat," she says bravely.

This evening, through the bars of his front window, he watches a man step down from a horse-drawn cart and scavenge through bags Daisi left on the curb for trash pickup. The scavenger examines a curious pair of old lamps made of seashells the size of cantaloupes. He places them in his cart—along with electric cords, pots and pans, and other fragments of a life. His horse takes him down the street out of sight.

Seeing this, Pai, the once great acquirer of things, says quietly, almost to himself, *"Eles até estão levando as minhas luzes"* (They're even taking my lights).

TRIUMPH

On a clear blue morning, birds chirping in the trees, I accompany him to a luncheon at Grêmio Náutico União, where he's not appeared for over a year.

We take a ferryboat owned and operated by the club into the broad Guaíba River to *Ilha do Pavão* (Peacock Island), which five months shy of one hundred years ago is where the club began. It was in this river, and from this island, that Daisi and Sidnei first trained to be competitive swimmers.

We enter a large and noisy dining hall containing three long rows of tables dressed in white tablecloths, and a huge keg of beer in one corner with a young black guy operating the tap for a crowd of men.

Several men immediately surround Pai and greet him with vigorous handshakes, powerful hugs, backslapping and boisterous shouting in the vigorous gaucho style. He embraces them all, laughing and joking. Suddenly, he's reborn as the witty, fast-talking, animated, Italian life-of-the-party I remember from years ago. The transformation is stunning.

No one knew he was coming. Arrangements are quickly made to seat him at the head table and formally present him to the two-hundred-plus members in the room, almost all white men. His introduction, as the oldest living former club president, produces an explosion of hurrahs and applause, sending a thrill down my spine. He rises to his feet, accepts the ovation, then dramatically throws both arms aloft, triumphant, as if just elected president by a landslide. More hurrahs. Then he fires off a clever remark, which I don't catch, but which draws loud laughter. He's stealing the show.

After lunch, men in their fifties and sixties, some well-established as civic leaders, approach me and acknowledge, with nostalgia, how as boys they feared their formidable club manager.

"Quando Senhor Gavioli vinha, a gente calava a boca" (When Senhor Gavioli arrived, we shut our mouths), one says.

Pai, the oldest living former president of the sports and social club, Grêmio Náutico União, arrives unannounced at a club luncheon and is welcomed as a returning hero.

PAI GAVIOLI
Thirty-six Years of War and Finally Peace with My Impossible Brazilian Father-in-Law

A paunchy, balding man in his fifties recalls one morning before dawn when he and his buddies dove into the cool, dark waters of the Guaíba. They swam several hundred meters to the island, where they planned to execute some mischief. Who should meet them at the dock, powerful arms folded, righteous indignation burning brighter than the sun just now dawning over the river, but the fierce authoritarian, Senhor Gavioli.

"*Ele era fogo na roupa*" (He had fire in his clothes), a hefty, gray-haired admirer says. Obviously, Pai had a talent for sending the fear of the Lord into pranksters and slackers.

Hearing this story, I am consoled to learn that it isn't just me—and not just his children, or his housekeepers, or neighbors, butchers, bakers, and candlestick makers—who feared him. Everyone did. Had God appointed him disciplinarian in the Garden of Eden, the Fall would have been avoided, and we'd all be living in perpetual bliss now.

On the ferry back to the city harbor, I reflect on how today, the ferryboat has brought me into this great river, reminding me once again, as if I didn't know already, that he's a warrior. He was a tough teacher, inflicting his brand of wisdom on young boys, some now occupying positions of influence in the city. For those who knew him then, he's a living legend now. As for me, it's been a privilege to witness the lionization of a lonely old man.

DEFEAT

This morning's sun gives way to a cold rain this afternoon. I find him in his apartment searching for records of his monthly pension. Without these records, he fears the government will slash his payments in an upcoming reform.

He sits on the edge of his vinyl sofa, his thick fingers leafing through a dozen three-ring binders strewn about his feet. They contain yellowing documents going back to his wedding and beyond. Reaching the end of the binders, he starts the search all over again.

I have no idea what the document looks like. It would be easier to decipher the Dead Sea Scrolls than comprehend this heap of officialese in Portuguese. Furthermore, I dare not ask, fearing a volcanic explosion. His anxiety is filling the room. My lower back tightens like a drum. I'm having trouble breathing.

His German doggedness, his relentless capacity to stay on task until all barriers are smashed and all enemies are overwhelmed—paramount among his virtues—is now backfiring. He can't stop looking for what isn't there.

Abruptly he slams a binder to the floor, claps his hands sharply and yells,

"*Não adianta, Jim! Estou perdido! Estou ralado! Estou liquidado!*" (It's no use, Jim! I'm lost! I'm skinned! I'm liquidated!)

His anguish is too painful to bear. I can't take it. I need a break. I leave and walk back to his house. Grief, the state he's in now, is a cruel country, one I fear getting too close to.

Two hours later I return to find him calmer, but still shuffling endlessly through the binders, repeating over and over, "It's lost, Jim, it's no use. It's lost. It's lost."

Only a few short hours ago, in a sunny morning on a lovely island in a great river, he was a king, bathed in glory, lifted by thunderous ovations honoring his lifetime of service. Now, bent over on a small sofa in a small apartment, the king is humbled, lost in the tangles of his dimming memory. The wheel of fortune turns from jubilation in the morning to torment in the afternoon.

He's like a spinning top that's slowing down and beginning to wobble. He's losing his balance, letting go of things even against his will. Regarding his will, I'm awed for the hundredth time by his tenacity, his resistance, his determination and readiness to throw himself into the struggle. He doesn't give up. He simply Does. Not. Give. Up.

One cannot expect him to slide gently into eternity like a worn key slipping smoothly into its well-oiled lock. A friend of ours once knew an old black woman who was familiar with adversity. The secret of this woman, who had never gone to school, was simple: "I cooperates with the inevitable."

For Pai, the inevitable is optional. Sometimes he cooperates, sometimes he doesn't. This is a big part of his charm. But his power to shape the inevitable is ebbing. Now his boat has only one oar.

Next morning all his anguish is gone, as if it never happened. His pension documents are mercifully forgotten. I'm struck by the volatile and fickle nature of his suffering, which seems almost childlike. I tell Sidnei his pension papers are lost. Pai doesn't need them, he says. The government has his records and would honor them.

Ten days pass. One morning I return from the dry cleaners with his raincoat and dark-blue business suit. He thanks me. Later that morning, as I assist him across the street, he thanks me for helping arrange his apartment furniture. This is unexpected. Among Gaviolis, favors are assumed, verbal thanks are unnecessary. They're woven into the family fabric. This morning he allows me to touch his elbow as he lifts his leg from the cobblestone street onto the granite curb, an intimacy and permission that to me feels like a gift. Perhaps helping him in this trifling way, I manage to remove a grain of sand from my mountain of indebtedness.

HARD BARGAINS

Early next morning, we cross the treacherous Avenida Benjamin Constant, whose cruel rush hour awakens thoughts of mortality. We take a bus downtown to buy a refrigerator.

We enter the vast, quiet department store showroom of *Lojas Colombo*. We're the day's first customers. We look at several models and find one, for $650, that fits his small kitchen perfectly. Yet he keeps looking at bigger ones, which match his prodigious food needs of yesteryear.

"These bigger models don't fit your small living space," I tell him. He keeps looking. Then I tell him again. He keeps looking. I tell him a third time.

Now he drops a plastic ice tray on the floor, clattering and shattering the showroom serenity. Salesmen heads turn his way. He doesn't seem to notice.

I think he's slipping out of orbit. My lower back stiffens. What should I do? Maybe I can divert his attention, like giving a rattle to a child who's poking his finger in a light socket. No, this would be demeaning. And it wouldn't work. Let's just buy the darn thing and get the heck outta here.

Our salesman is José Machado. He's a short, stocky, cheerful young man wearing a starched white shirt and flamboyant tie. He offers us seats across from his tiny desk. Then he begins filling out a mammoth purchase order, including phone numbers for three personal references. With José Machado's head buried in paperwork, Pai launches into one of his Rules for an Excellent Life: DRIVE HARD BARGAINS.

Interrupting José Machado's paperwork, Pai says he wants a discount. José Machado shaves off eight dollars. Pai wants more. José Machado raises the warrantee from two years to three. Pai notices his ballpoint pen and wants it as a gift. José Machado says it's his only one.

Finally, lengthy paperwork completed, José Machado takes it to his manager for approval. Pai leans over and whispers: *"Fala baixo para não estragar o negócio"* (Speak softly so we don't queer the deal). Evidently he believes he's about to make a killing, even without getting José Machado's pen.

José Machado returns with everything in order. Pai demands to see the manager. José Machado is startled. The manager arrives, eyebrows pinched, mouth tight. Pai slowly and theatrically rises from his chair and positions himself directly in front of the two merchants, like a sharpshooter at an execution. I stand back to avoid getting blood on my clothes.

"*Senhor,*" Pai loudly addresses the manager, the old man's booming grandiloquence bouncing off refrigerators throughout the cavernous showroom. Summoning all the power and glory of formal Portuguese, he proclaims, "Senhor, I am obliged to inform Your Excellency, that contrary to all expectation, the attention rendered to me by this young employee, José Machado, has been, in every possible respect, exemplary."

The manager's face melts from dread to delight. He grins broadly, tilts his head to one side, opens his arms wide and grips Pai in a powerful gaucho hug. The three of them—Pai, José Machado, and the manager—burst into a boisterous banging and pounding of one others' backs, congratulating themselves on this marvelous turn of events. Sweet cafezinhos are sent for to seal the deal and celebrate this superb victory.

Watching this gaucho ritual, it occurs to me that if I were in Minnesota, and needed a refrig, I'd simply sip a cup of coffee and buy it online. Not here. With Pai, it's pure theater. Here you must leave your home, go out into the world and climb onstage. You must join the other actors and perform. You must take risks. You must face conflict head on, feel your pulse quicken, your back stiffen. You must look your adversary in the eye and engage him. You must maneuver. He must look you back in the eye and execute a counter maneuver. You must be cunning and try a third maneuver. He must be brilliant and try to block you. This is not about a refrigerator, which has been long forgotten. It's about drama. The play's the thing. And, in the end, harmony is restored. Hey, it's a comedy! Why didn't anybody tell me?

The Brazilian Shakespeare does it again.

FAREWELL TO THE KITCHEN

Punctually at four o'clock on Tuesday, as we do daily now, he and I share cafezinho at the kitchen table. A soft late-afternoon light slants in through the open windows overlooking the back patio. He's strangely quiet. Then he breaks the silence with a familiar refrain, how Sarah was a wonderful companion. His grief is still raw. She left him only two months ago.

My chair feels hard on my backside. I'd like to get up and go do something, but there's nothing to do at the moment. The kitchen faucet is dripping into the stainless steel sink—plink, plink, plink. Absentmindedly, I place my fingers beneath the faucet to catch the drops. I feel useless, restless.

He seems tired. His large hands, with their muscular fingers and veins like little rivers, drape like paws over the back of a chair. There's history in these hands. His skin sags beneath his jaw. History there, too.

He glances around the kitchen. *"Nada,"* he says, shaking his head, "Nothing . . . we started with nothing. I even had to sleep on the ground." This is new. He hasn't mentioned sleeping on the ground before.

He's not speaking to me. He's addressing his ancient warhorse of a refrigerator, his proud aluminum oven, his loyal wooden table, his honest dish towel hanging at the open window. They all listen patiently. They are his worthy companions that, for more than half a century, have helped put his stomach out of its misery. In silence, he seems to be bidding them farewell.

With heavy eyes, he looks up at the pale light from the window. Sarah taught school, he says, saved money, and sewed clothes for Daisi and Lori. Then he repeats her words: "We're not giving up . . . we're going forward." More silence. Then, "She opened her heart to everyone." He chokes back a sob. He seems to be saying farewell to her, too. I feel a knot gather in my throat.

"Esse foi o caminho" (This was the road), he barely says aloud. He recounts milestones along this road: staying in cheap hotels on work trips to save money . . . his thirty years at the telephone company . . . his service to Grêmio Náutico União. His words come slowly, one by one, like drops from the faucet. He seems to be bidding farewell to the long road itself.

I dislike farewells. My chair feels really hard. Maybe I should get up and go take a walk.

But I stay.

He goes quiet again, so quiet you could hear a heart break. The kitchen waits for him with infinite patience.

I don't know how to comfort him. I simply listen to these fragments of his journey, these single notes in the seemingly endless symphony we've been hearing from him over the years.

"This was the road, Jim . . . this was the road." He compresses his life into these four simple words. Another silence. I imagine his road . . . spending a hardscrabble childhood in Montenegro . . . working as a youth in downtown Porto Alegre . . . marrying his Portuguese teacher . . . buying this house . . . erecting telephone lines . . . fathering four children . . . reaching the middle class . . . becoming president of União and his Lions Club . . . retiring near the sea . . . . All these events—chosen freely at the time, except for his childhood, which was determined by his parents—are now fixed, locked into history, appearing, as one looks back at them, to be the thread of destiny.

Pai as a young man, seemingly reflecting on twists and turns in life's road.

Remarkably,
he absorbs adversity,
digests it, then converts
it into vitality, alertness,
vision, an anger-energy
of the soul that drives
him forward even harder.
There's something fierce
in choosing a road.

The so-called destiny forged in the stars didn't determine Pai's road. He and Sarah chose it themselves, accepting all its penalties of hard work, self-restraint, endurance, intense focus on goals, absence from children, drudgery, defeats. Remarkably, he absorbs adversity, digests it, then converts it into vitality, alertness, vision, an anger-energy of the soul that drives him forward even harder. There's something fierce in choosing a road.

A relaxed, peaceful expression spreads over his face. He appears satisfied with the path he chose. Or maybe the path chose him. Maybe they chose each other.

> *Walker, your footsteps*
> *are the road, and nothing more.*
> *Walker, there is no road,*
> *the road is made by walking.*
> *Walking you make the road,*
> *and turning to look behind*
> *you see the path you never*
> *again will step upon.*
> –Antonio Machado

"*O mundo é engraçado,*" he says softly. The world is funny/strange. His eye darts about the kitchen, as if seeing proof of this. It must be an odd and marvelous thing to be old and look back, from the great height and distance age provides, upon one's entire life compressed.

Drops keep falling on my fingers, rolling off my fingers into the sink. One by one, they form at the faucet's mouth, like past events in liquid form.

"I was put here on earth to torment others," he says. "Otherwise, life would lose all joy." I smile. He doesn't.

Yes, he's a tormentor all right—with a gift for shaping people up and straightening them out—as I can attest.

"*Sabe, Jim*" (You know, Jim), "sometimes I don't feel like doing anything. People have no idea what I'm going through."

This must be true. His seventy-year partnership with Sarah is gone and has no substitute. Without her, he's stepping into an entirely new world, forced to become a different person.

Be kind, we're told, because within every person there's a great struggle. Seems there's little I can do now, other than just sit here with him. Just be here and listen to him. Be a companion. Nothing more.

No, we're more than companions. We're bound together, like father to son, son to father. We need each other, my need probably the greater.

I remember that first day in his home thirty-six years ago when the curtain covering the corridor fell over my head. I was temporarily blinded. And then, as the curtain lifted, I remained blind in a deeper way, unaware that I was on stage with him. Unaware that I was an actor, free to better understand my lines, free to play a better role. Meanwhile, he played himself with great authority, creating ceremony out of events around him, understanding that life is theater and the world is a stage.

I wondered then what secrets lay hidden behind the curtain. Now I know. The main secret, the one that has been gradually revealing itself over time, is our bond. It has gradually opened, like a curtain, discovering him, his family, his nation, him, and even me.

The raw destruction of his home, and then the letting go of its pieces, is an immense loss. It's a loss that has not been recognized in any formal way. Perhaps these moments here in the kitchen—shaped by his words and the long silences between them—resemble a farewell ceremony. A ceremony unplanned, unannounced and, except for the two of us, unattended. He has ceremony in his soul.

As the pastel light fades and the kitchen grows dim, he's quiet, done saying goodbye. He seems changed. He's calm, as if restored, without agitation or fear. His demons, for now, are gone. His face, usually so full of purpose and determination, is relaxed. He appears to have the self-possession of a star, or an old scrub tree that has the right to be here. Despite his native flaws, and the wounds life has carved into him, he is fully who he's meant to be.

A week later, Daisi and I prepare to leave. In my six weeks and her three weeks we did what we could. His home is cleaned out and he's in his apartment. He's still strong, ornery, and ever more confused—a perfect recipe for tormenting others, which keeps his life from losing all joy.

MARCH-APRIL 2006
If I Were to Die This Morning

I wake before dawn in Torres and walk two blocks to the beach with my camera. It's strange to see no one on the street, probably normal for a predawn hour. I reach the broad stretch of beach just in time to see the sun behind a bank of clouds perform its daily miracle of giving birth to itself. All at once everything turns blue. The sky turns light blue, the clouds go dark blue, and the sea is an in-between blue.

I'm not the first one here. At some distance away a fisherman tosses his net into the shallows. White egrets are here, too, with their long, slender necks, jabbing at fish in the shallows left by waves that slide back to the sea, hissing in retreat. As always, the sea leaves its gifts of long, foam necklaces on the sand. The life of a necklace is short—only a couple of minutes—until its billion bubbles burst. Here comes one now, rolling along the sand. I aim my camera, shutter cocked, waiting for its peak moment of beauty. *Click*. Nope, I missed it. Moments later, another necklace arrives, then another, all sent in the measured rhythm of the ever-generous sea.

Seagulls are here, too, shorter and stouter than the elegant egrets. So are the skittish quero-quero birds, crests on their heads, always in faithful pairs. And there go the comical little sandpipers, tiny sprinters dashing in beelines across the sand like wind-up toys.

Suddenly everything brightens. The sun flares brilliantly at the top of a cloud bank, turning the sea a robin's-egg blue.

I wade into the surf, picking my way among black glistening-wet boulders. They're victims of the ever-pounding sea, dislodged from high rocky outcroppings. In very slow motion, Torres' three cliffs are gradually crumbling. Centuries from now, the restless sea will have battered them into sand.

Clinging to the boulders, like wet hair, is a brilliant green moss, which in the dawn's horizontal light, take on a stunning emerald color. Minutes from now, the sun will lift and the green will turn ordinary. Months from now, the moss will probably be dead and gone. An hour from now, the blue sea will probably turn gray. Moments from now, those purple clouds probably won't be purple anymore. The light-blue sky will turn deeper blue.

Everything is changing too quickly for my camera. To catch peak loveliness, I'm either ahead or behind. A wave explodes on a rock, arching into a white spray. I raise my camera—far too late. Necklaces slide gracefully along the sand in perfect order, like birds in parallel flight. *Click*—oops, too soon. An egret stands in a glassy pool, its noble neck and head mirrored in perfect profile. I raise my camera. Just then a wave shatters the mirror and the egret darts at a fish. Everything's moving. Nothing waits for me.

Wading deeper into the warm shallows, I approach another egret, careful to stay just outside its fright zone. If I keep walking, moving, joining the rhythm of his world, he accepts me. If I stop dead, he leaps into the air. My stillness spooks him. I wonder how long he'll live.

Egrets die, but sun and sea live forever. Well, not really. Even the sun will cool, and the sea will freeze. Even they have lifetimes, albeit cosmic ones, beyond imagination.

I reach one of the towering rock outcropping for which Torres is known and named. Its wide, black stone face, seen from this angle just after dawn, burns a bright orange, as if on fire. I climb a path along its base for a while, then stop, catch my breath and look down. Far below, waves are crawling in thin parallel lines. Plumes fly off their crests, like snow blowing off the brow of a snowbank. Waves live only minutes, from their birth hundreds of yards out to sea to their crashing death on the sand.

Click. I fail to catch their peak. Just as I fail to capture the optimum beauty of birds, necklaces, and even those low, bulging clouds, sun fire glowing deep in their bellies.

A lone fisherman looks out to sea. *Click.* Maybe I got him, not sure. Waves explode against the cliff beneath me. *Click.* Not sure. Below me, low houses huddle tightly together at the edge of the beach, all bathed in golden light. I aim the camera. *Click.* Nope, they go dim under the shadow of a fast moving cloud.

Impermanence is everywhere, but it's more noticeable here where sea meets land. Small changes over time can add up to big change. Torres, for instance, today still young, was created by the Portuguese five hundred years ago. It became an official city only a hundred and thirty years ago. In the last two years it's been growing like an adolescent. What will it be in twenty years? Fifty?

I reach the top of the cliff, a wide, flat, grassy plateau. I approach three men fishing at the very edge of the precipice, their lines dropping 120 feet to the sea churning and thudding below. They're fearless. I stay back.

I keep walking along a path near the edge. A few feet beyond the precipice, clinging to the face of the cliff, appears a slender rock, like a finger pointing to the sky. It beckons to me. I approach it, nearing the edge. I brace my sandal against a clump of tall grass near the lip and peer into emptiness below. I move a step closer. I can almost touch the rock finger. I point my camera at it. Abruptly, a cloud obscures the sun, plunging all in shadow. I lower my camera.

It's brevity that gives life value. The pursuit of loveliness, such a momentary thing, is what keeps me going. Were I to join eternity now, in this beautiful spot, falling into the ever-moving sea, I shouldn't complain. The top of this rock would be the last, farthest and loveliest point in my little journey. But this would upset Daisi. Everything here—the rock, the sea, the sand, the birds, the fishermen—they're all gifts from Daisi. Torres is a gift I hope will keep rolling into my life for years to come, like necklaces from the sea.

I've seen enough beauty for one morning. Stepping away from the edge, I head back to the remainder of my life.

A TORN CAPE

Pai doesn't like his new companion, an elderly housekeeper who listlessly cooks and cleans. She may not like him, either. With nothing to do, he needs something to worry about. He telephones Sidnei several times a day about rent collection from his three apartment units, which Sidnei oversees.

This morning he and I take a walk. He's wearing white socks, white tennis shoes, white shorts, a blue polo shirt, and a baseball cap. He could be heading to the first tee at a country club. He wouldn't fit there. His sporty outfit is a costume, a breezy leisure-class disguise. The truth hangs on his face, a wary, lonely expression, strangely at odds with his jaunty cap. He's still the Man from Want.

Far from our vigorous marches of only five years ago, our walks are now so slow that as we inch along I count my steps, just for something to think about. The more I fall into his poky pace, the slower time becomes. Scenery drifts sluggishly by, as if seen under water through the eyes of languid whales. Again I'm drawn into his orbit by the gravitational force of all his years. These are the years he hauls behind him, a large swath of gaucho and Brazilian history, like a royal cape several miles long dragging on the rugged sidewalk.

Embroidered on the cape are ninety years of experience, starting in a tiny German-immigrant river town. It's a handsome cape, in some ways even a beautiful cape, except it's torn where the weaver began, at its first fragile threads.

The laceration occurred years ago, when traveling salesman Augusto returns

Pai walks slowly now, hauling his years behind him.

PAI GAVIOLI
Thirty-six Years of War and Finally Peace with My Impossible Brazilian Father-in-Law

home to his lonely wife Amanda and discovers she's seeing another man. He makes a big mistake. I am not, he says, the instrument of my wife's pregnancy. He rejects her and his unborn child, never to be the father he actually is.

The infant, suspected illegitimate, becomes an object of Gavioli contempt, an untouchable, the product of alleged adultery. The infant is an offense against the Gavioli family, its lineage, its honor, and its property. He is shunned.

Yet all evidence points otherwise. Pai's resemblance to his father is affirmed by his half brother, José Augusto. "If I miss my father," José Augusto has told the Gaviolis, "all I need do to see him is look at my half brother."

These torn threads, ripped from the Gavioli family, become the wound that never heals. This wound is Pai's greatest weakness, and his greatest strength. The wounded know the world in ways the unwounded don't. This is the great difference between us.

LEAVING HIM

A big event is about to uncork in Minnesota—the arrival of our first grandchild—Pai's first great-grandchild. Only two days after we'll get home, Marcus's wife, Karen, is scheduled to give birth to a baby girl. Daisi's excited. Pai takes little notice.

He's been losing weight and complaining about pain in his stomach, that great organ whose hunger he's spent years putting out of its misery.

Sidnei takes him to a doctor. X-rays show nothing wrong.

The day before our scheduled flight, he starts vomiting. It's probably a virus that's going around. To avoid it, we don't visit his apartment to say goodbye. Besides, only two days ago we spent a pleasant evening with him at the home of his half brother, José Augusto. Pai seemed fine, although quiet, not his style.

The next afternoon at the airport, our bags checked, Daisi calls Sidnei from a pay phone. He says Maria Eunice checked on Pai today and found him dehydrated. She called an ambulance.

When Pai arrived at the hospital, Sidnei said, he could barely lift his arms. He asked a nurse to move them for him. *"Nunca"* (Never), he said, "have my arms felt so heavy."

They connected him to a bunch of tubes. He quickly improved. He's awake now, Sidnei said, alert, comfortable, and teasing the nurses.

The old Pai is back. The man has many lives.

"Should I stay?" Daisi asks her brother.

"There's nothing you can do here. He'll have stomach surgery tonight. Stick with your plan, fly home in time for the birth of your grandchild."

Daisi hangs up. "Do you think he'll die?" she asks me.

"Daisi, he's strong. He'll bounce back, as he always has."

Our flight to São Paulo is overbooked. After an hour's delay, two hundred of us are rushed chaotically onto the aircraft. No time to assign seats. Grab one anywhere.

Two hours later, we hit the runway hard, wings bouncing and flapping like a bird. The Brazilians burst into applause.

Because we're late, our gate is occupied by another plane. We all crowd into the terminal through a small service door. It's already 10:30 p.m. and our Minnesota flight is to leave in a few short minutes.

We hurriedly ask a woman in uniform the way to the international terminal. She has no idea. Someone shouts, *"Pega a direita!"* (Go to the right!) We jog along a corridor for several minutes. "This is the wrong way!" someone yells. We turn and jog back, out of breath, too old for this.

We barely catch our flight home.

Fifteen hours later, we land in Saint Paul. Waiting for us at baggage claim is our son André. Daisi tells him that when we left, Pai was sick.

André clears his throat, looks carefully at his mother's face. Visibly holding back tears, he says, "Mãe, he died last night."

This is the last photo of Pai, here with Daisi. He died two days later, one month shy of age 91.

PAI GAVIOLI
Thirty-six Years of War and Finally Peace with My Impossible Brazilian Father-in-Law

Daisi's stunned. Then bursts into tears. They embrace a long time.

I stare at the luggage carousel, slowly rotating with indifference. Bags slide down from a black hole, bouncing clumsily against a railing.

He died at ten thirty last night, April 26, 2006, amid our chaotic rush for the plane home. He was one month shy of ninety-one.

His death seems remote, like a great tree falling in the forest, landing without a sound. It seems unreal that the man who for thirty-six years had teased, badgered, and challenged me has left so quietly. This is not his way. This is not the boisterous, exuberant, irrepressible man I remember.

We wait for our bags. They don't arrive.

He waited until we left him before he left us. I want to believe this. He spared us the agony of a final, melodramatic, Italian goodbye, for which I'm grateful. Only people with emotions made of cast iron could endure such a farewell. Among Gaviolis, such people don't exist.

The quietness of his death is wrong. It's as if one were in a theater, deeply absorbed in a long symphony, when suddenly, with no warning, it ends abruptly, followed by stunned silence, the audience barely realizing the music is over and applause can begin.

BURIAL

I'm told he didn't suffer in death. Good—he had enough of that in life. The disease that undid him—either a tumor or other intestinal obstruction—started in his formidable, hard-working belly, a region of emptiness he'd spent his life trying to fill.

The next day, nineteen hours after he died, on a lovely autumn afternoon, Pai is buried. His remains are laid to rest above Sarah's in a separate compartment within a double vault. Years ago he had purchased two burial sites, one for Sarah and one for her sister, Aunt Cecilia. He made no plans for his own burial.

For someone who loved acquisition, he takes nothing with him. Except for two things. His wedding ring, which was impossible to remove from his finger, as if he refused to let it go. And his blue business suit, reflecting the rank into which he rose. These simple things, a ring and a suit—emblems of love and labor—represent the twin pillars of his life.

Honoring its fallen warrior, Grêmio Náutico União, the club he helped grow into one of the largest in Brazil, presents the family with its flag.

Emblazoned on it are two crossed oars, like those enshrined above the fireplace in his cottage by the sea, representing, in my mind at least, the oars he's pulled to row his boat—towing many behind him—not always gently down life's stream.

One more thing goes with him: a Minnesota Twins baseball cap. It was a retirement gift to me last year. He liked it, so I parted with it, reluctantly. It's the last in his collection of seventy-seven hats. Maria Eunice placed it with him as a remembrance of Minnesota. I'm touched and honored.

This tiny gift to him, however, is dwarfed by his two immeasurable gifts to me. The first was unintentional—his daughter—who married me before he could pass judgment. The second was intentional—his family. There are no greater gifts than these.

And yet, my life with him wasn't always easy. Imagine me, for example, as a young tree, growing at the edge of a field, a tree rubbed and irritated by a barbed wire fence. Over many seasons, the tree grows and gradually absorbs the wire, accepts it, and gains stability from it. As time passes and the fence posts grow soft in the earth, the tree embraces the barbed wire, eventually growing to love it.

FEBRUARY 2007
They Belong to the Grass

On a balmy February summer day ten months later, Daisi and I return and visit the cemetery. Except for the wind and the birds, this is a quiet, grassy open space, surrounded by gentle hills beneath an immense sky.

As we approach their graves, quero-quero birds sharply defend their nests, dive bombing us and shrieking in unmistakable Portuguese, *"Quero! Quero!"* (I want! I want!) These birds live in pairs, always together. Pai and Sarah would appreciate them.

All gravestones here are identical—small rectangles flush to the earth. Bolted to each flat stone is a simple metal plaque, inscribed with a name, date of birth, and date of death. The stones express simplicity, equality, universality.

There are no grand columns here, no sculptures of heroes adorning the deceased in glory. These simple flat markers depart from traditional Brazilian cemeteries, where vertical stones huddle together, resembling a crowded cityscape, each stone proclaiming its rank, power, and prestige. Here, however, vanity is missing, in character with Pai and Sarah.

Also missing are the city sounds of multitudes and howling engines. In their place, the wind breathes through the trees. This is where a tranquil earth accepts the remains of a selfless woman and a dynamic man. An ordinary man, thoroughly un-Minnesotan, he was one of the most extraordinary ordinary men I have known.

It's strange to look upon this grass and know they are down there, while the world up here remains. Especially the Brazilian world, which they left better than they found it. Brazil's large poverty has been shrinking, while its former small, middle class has been growing, some say to more than half the population. They played their part. While building a family, they helped build a nation.

Now they rest in an afterworld where I suspect all are the same, far from the broken sidewalks and inequities of the living. Here they rest under green pastures and spacious skies. They belong to the grass, the trees, and the stars.

> *Time, like an ever-rolling stream,*
> *Bears all its sons away;*
> *They fly forgotten, as a dream*
> *Dies at the opening day.*
> —Isaac Watts

They will be forgotten, as will we all, but they are worth remembering until memory fails.

EPILOGUE

There is one more gift. Four days after he departs this world, his first great-grandchild enters it. Zadie Evelyn Martin is born to Marcus and Karen. "Zadie" is the diminutive for "Sarah," her great-grandmother's name, which in Hebrew means "princess." Within her short early years, this little princess already shows auspicious signs—exuberance, stubbornness, love of family, willfulness, caution, managerial tendencies, a weakness for chocolate, and the roar of a lion. In these sparks, passed down through two generations, Pai lives on.

And now her brother, Nico André Martin, has arrived, a little guy who many say is physically a dead ringer for his great-grandfather. Lastly, two more great-grandchildren have arrived, Raphael Gavioli and Beatriz Valentina Martin, still too small to know what part of him they will return to the world. When they are old enough, and if I'm still here, I hope to remind them of two people who have gone before, who are part of who they are, and who are still with us.

END

APPENDIX I

Rules He Lives By

- Make friends with bankers, butchers, shopkeepers, doctors, and lawyers
- Don't get chummy with people who might grow meddlesome
- Put more food on the table than can possibly be eaten
- Insist on superb work from people you pay
- Solve problems quickly and aggressively
- Fear hunger as you would the Lord
- Earn the trust of supervisors
- Never embarrass the family
- Always be right in advance
- Educate your children
- Don't smoke or drink
- Drive hard bargains
- Argue aggressively
- Work relentlessly
- Make sacrifices
- Be watchful
- Be frugal
- Never quit

PAI GAVIOLI
Thirty-six Years of War and Finally Peace with My Impossible Brazilian Father-in-Law

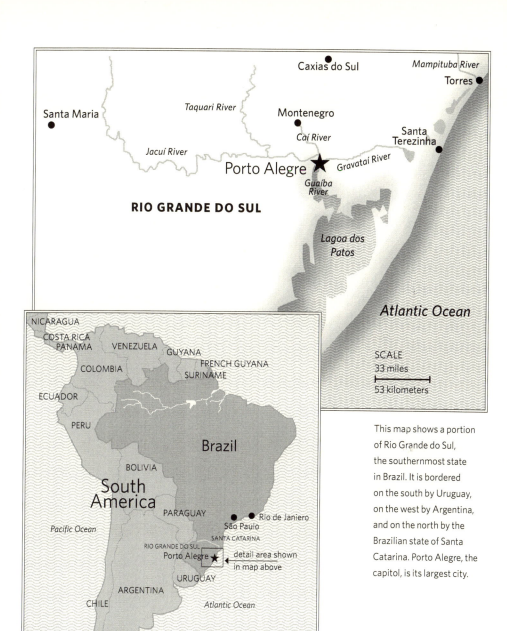

This map shows a portion of Rio Grande do Sul, the southernmost state in Brazil. It is bordered on the south by Uruguay, on the west by Argentina, and on the north by the Brazilian state of Santa Catarina. Porto Alegre, the capitol, is its largest city.

APPENDICES
Map

APPENDIX II

Chronology

Mid-1800s
Pai's grandmother, Rosa Leibnitz, immigrates to Brazil from Germany. She marries a German-Brazilian, whose last name is Finger, and settles in the German colonial village of Montenegro, Rio Grande do Sul.

Pai's mother, Amanda Finger, is born in Montenegro.

1881
Pai's grandfather, Felix Gavioli, immigrates to Brazil from Modena, Italy. He and his wife, Marietta, settle in the Italian colonial village of Caxias, Rio Grande do Sul.

1880s
Pai's father, Augusto Gavioli, is born, the eldest of five children.

1890s
Felix dies of malaria and is buried in Caxias.

1910
Sarah Medeiros is born on March 29 in Cananéia, São Paulo.

1912
Amanda Finger and Augusto Gavioli are married.

1915
Pai's parents separate while Amanda is pregnant with Pai.

Pai is born on May 25 in Montenegro.

1917
At age seven, Sarah gets polio, affecting her legs and feet.

1918
Sarah's father, José Augusto de Medeiros, dies of influenza. Sarah's mother, Maria Simões de Medeiros, dies one or two years later of typhoid fever.

1922
Augusto moves from Caxias to Porto Alegre and becomes co-owner of a clothing store.

Amanda takes Pai and his older brother Rui to São Paulo, where she finds work cleaning people's homes.

1930
At age 15, Pai leaves São Paulo and moves to Porto Alegre seeking work. He shares a boardinghouse with Rui.

Pai asks his uncle, José Gavioli, a pharmacist, for a job, but is refused.

Pai finds work as a messenger boy in Porto Alegre's downtown financial district.

1932
Augusto Gavioli ends his 17-year separation from Amanda, and marries Aracy Godoy Gomes.

1935
Pai studies business and accounting at night school. His Portuguese teacher is Sarah Medeiros.

Augusto and Aracy give birth to a son, José Augusto Godoy Gavioli.

1936
Pai and Sarah are married at *Igreja Esperança* (Church of Hope) in Porto Alegre.

Late 1930s
Pai starts working for American Telephone & Telegraph (AT&T). Sarah teaches high school math and Portuguese.

1939
Sidnei is born.

1940
I am born.

1943
Daisi is born.

1946
Davison is born.

1951
Lori is born.

1955
Pai becomes treasurer of a private sports and social club, Grêmio Náutico União. He continues working at AT&T.

1962
I graduate from Harvard College and join the Peace Corps, teaching English for two years in Niger, West Africa.

1965
Daisi graduates from the Federal University of Rio Grande do Sul.

Pai is elected president of Grêmio Náutico União.

1967
At age 52, Pai buys his first car.

Late 1960s
Pai becomes manager of Grêmio Náutico União. He retires from AT&T, ending his 30-year career.

Pai's father Augusto dies. Entitled to inherit half his father's estate, Pai refuses to accept it.

Amanda dies.

1968
I meet Daisi, who is on a work-study program in social work in Saint Paul, counseling troubled teenage girls.

Our first date is at Mickey's Diner in Saint Paul.

1969
Daisi and I are married on June 7 at Unity-Unitarian Church in Saint Paul.

1970
We spend four months mostly hitchhiking through Mexico, Central America, Colombia, Ecuador, Peru, and Bolivia before reaching Porto Alegre on Oct. 1. We live in Daisi's parents' home.

1971
Four months later, we move into a small, two-bedroom apartment unit that Pai bought for us.

Daisi's Aunt Cecilia has a stroke, paralyzing her right side. She comes from São Paulo to live with Pai and Sarah and later moves to an apartment across the street from their home.

I teach English literature part-time at the Federal University of Rio Grande do Sul. Daisi returns to her former social work position.

Marcus is born on May 25th, Pai's birthday.

1973
Daisi, Marcus and I leave Brazil and move to Saint Paul. My parents purchase a triplex and rent us the first floor.

I teach English at a private school in Minneapolis. Daisi recruits volunteers to tutor disadvantaged children.

1974
André is born on September 24th.

1975
We buy a home in Saint Paul.

1976
Pai retires and buys a summer cottage in Santa Terezinha, a seaside village two hours by car from Porto Alegre.

1988
Marcus attends his junior year of high school in Porto Alegre, living at the home of Daisi's brother Sidnei.

1991
André attends his junior year of high school in Porto Alegre at Sidnei's home.

1997
Sarah is hospitalized with a stroke. She is assisted by Dr. José Augusto Gavioli, Pai's half-brother. The brothers begin a relationship.

1998
Sarah begins to use a wheelchair.

2004
We buy a condominium unit in Torres, a seaside town three hours by car from Porto Alegre. We plan to spend winters there.

2005
I retire at age 65.

Sarah dies peacefully at home. She was age 95.

I go to Porto Alegre to help Pai move across the street to the apartment owned by Cecilia, now in a nursing facility. Daisi arrives later to clean out her parents' home.

2006
Pai is honored at an annual Grêmio Náutico União luncheon as its oldest living former president.

Pai is hospitalized on April 26 and dies that evening, while Daisi and Jim were flying back to Minnesota. The next day, he is buried next to Sarah. He was age 91.

2007
Daisi retires at age 64.

2008
Cecilia dies on July 8. She was 91.

APPENDICES
Chronology

APPENDIX III

Six Generations: the Gavioli-Medeiros Families

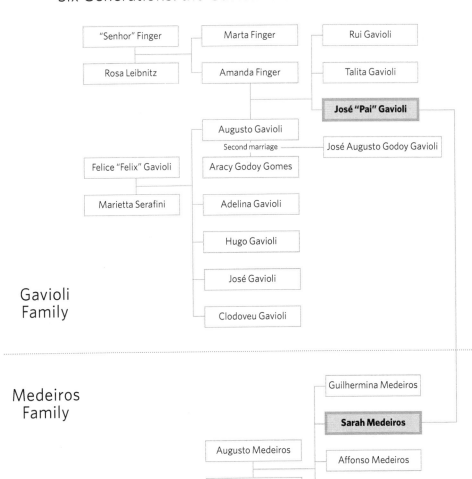

PAI GAVIOLI
Thirty-six Years of War and Finally Peace with My Impossible Brazilian Father-in-Law

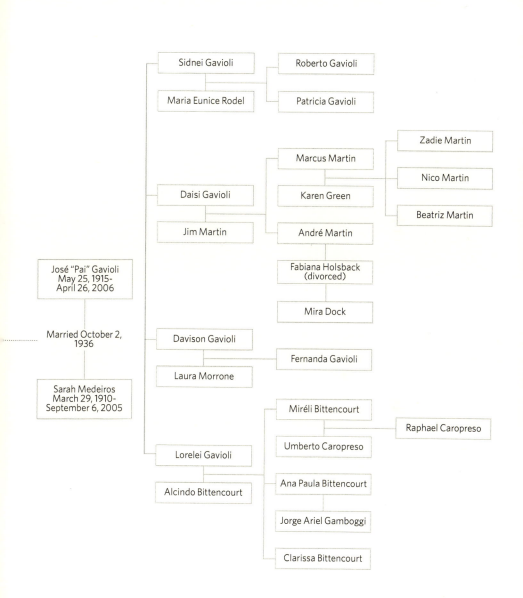

APPENDICES
Six Generations: the Gavioli-Medeiros Families

APPENDIX IV

Index

A
Amazon, 15, 44, 48, 76, 137, 150, 158, 159, 178
Argentina, 51, 171, 227, 233
Aunt Cecilia, 21, 68, 77-78, 99, 118, 195, 223, 229

B
Bly, Robert, 9, 90, 110, 130, 184
Bolivia, 22, 27, 227, 229
Brazil, 13, 15, 45, 47-48, 51, 62-64, 76-77, 82, 98-99, 112, 117-119, 126, 147, 159, 164-166, 184-185, 225, 227

C
Cardoso, Fernando Henrique, 126, 133, 165
Caxias, 43, 57, 63, 69-70, 142, 227-228
Churrasco, 34-36, 51, 52, 88, 141, 174
Collor, Fernando de Mello, 118-119
Colombia, 22, 26, 27, 227, 229
Cooper, Bernard, 9, 60, 99

D
Dona Eva, 31-33, 39-42, 45, 47, 143

E
Ecuador, 22, 27, 227, 229

G
Gaucho, 29-30, 34-36, 47, 51-53, 55, 57, 64, 70, 96, 98, 102-103, 115-116, 119, 136, 139, 162-163, 172-173, 208, 212, 220, 234
Gavioli
  Amanda, 57-58, 63, 69, 91-93, 98, 102, 131, 141, 143, 200, 221, 228-230

Augusto (Pai's father), 57-58, 63-64, 69, 93, 100, 102, 141-142, 220, 227, 228-229
Beto, 33, 110
Daisi, 9-10, 15-22, 23-26, 34, 42-43, 60-61, 67, 71, 72-75, 79-80, 83, 84, 106-7, 108, 116-117, 143-145, 162, 168, 176, 180-181, 184, 190, 195, 206-207, 221-223, 228-229, 231
Davison, 33, 42, 59-60, 66, 68, 71, 77-78, 84, 107-108, 133-136, 151, 165, 194, 226, 229
Felix, 69-70, 137, 141, 228, 230
Fernanda, 133-134, 231
José (Pai's uncle), 64, 69, 163, 230
José Augusto (Pai's brother), 9, 135, 138, 140-142, 221, 228-230
Laura, 133-134, 231
Lori, 33, 41, 51-52, 66, 71, 108, 135, 143-145, 159, 196, 206, 213, 228, 231
Maria Eunice, 33, 46, 111-112, 174, 185-186, 195, 199, 221, 224, 231
Pai
  AT&T, 104, 108-109, 228-229
  Birth, 57, 110, 131
  Childhood, 57, 105, 130, 132, 142, 157, 184, 213
  Death, 222-224
  First impression of, 11
  Grêmio Náutico União, 105-106, 109, 133, 207-208, 213, 223, 228, 229

  Marriage, 98, 121, 133, 136, 144, 146, 190, 206
  Retirement, 90, 129, 180
  Rules he lives by, 36, 54, 59, 95, 99, 112, 120, 126-127, 132, 161, 192, 193, 211, 226
Pati, 111-112, 231
Rui, 57, 61, 63-64, 92-93, 131, 142
Sarah
  Childhood, 38, 88, 134
  Death, 194-196
  Described, 33, 38-39, 50, 62, 65, 68, 87, 88, 103-104, 133-135, 137, 140, 146, 157-159, 163, 175, 182, 187, 190, 194, 196, 228, 229
  First impression of, 38
  Health, 38, 62, 88, 104, 134-6, 157, 175, 182, 187
  Her study, 42, 50, 198
  Painting, 87-88, 134, 140, 163, 194, 207
  Polio, 38, 50, 62, 87-88, 134, 157, 228
  Pregnancy, 103
  Stroke, 135-136, 140, 229
  Teaching, 38-40, 97, 103, 194
  Wedding, 97, 146, 209, 223

PAI GAVIOLI
Thirty-six Years of War and Finally Peace with My Impossible Brazilian Father-in-Law

Sidnei, 11-12, 33, 62, 71, 76-78, 103, 105-108, 110-112, 135, 137, 142, 157, 174, 183, 185, 186, 194-195, 199, 206, 208, 210, 220-221, 228, 229, 231

German, 10, 29, 49, 55-58, 68-70, 75, 80-81, 93-94, 102-103, 129-130, 136, 139-140, 142, 148, 151, 173, 184, 196, 200, 209, 220, 228

Gomes, Aracy Godoy, 141, 228, 230

Great Depression, 3, 17, 56, 65, 96, 98, 120, 127, 141, 149, 193

Guaíba River, 31, 44, 91, 110, 133, 171, 207, 209, 223, 227

Guatemala, 26

Harvard, 14, 55, 110, 204, 228

I

Inflation, 12, 89, 118-119, 126, 147

Italian, 29, 46, 49, 55, 58, 69-70, 72, 80-82, 90, 95, 102-103, 117, 136-137, 148, 151, 159, 177, 183-184, 200, 208, 223, 228

J

Jana, 191-192, 195-198, 201, 203-206

L

Latin America, 26, 165, 171

Leibnitz, Rosa, 57, 69, 228, 230

Lions Club, 12, 93, 108-109, 137, 207, 213

Lula, 93, 118, 164-165

M

Martin
André, 9, 83, 85, 93, 114, 116-117, 144-145, 147, 154, 179, 222, 229, 231
Beatriz, 225, 231
Dwight, 14, 23, 48, 49, 59, 64, 92-93, 96, 110, 155-156, 163
Evelyn, 23, 49, 65, 110, 156, 178-179
Jeff, 23, 74, 82, 156, 175, 178, 179
Karen, 221, 225, 229
Marcus, 9, 73-5, 81, 83, 85, 87, 114-116, 144, 154, 179, 221, 225, 227, 229, 231
Nico, 225
Zadie, 225, 231

Mexico, 22, 24, 26-27, 229

Middle class, 23, 24, 34, 39, 40, 56, 59, 83, 89, 96, 99, 101, 106, 109, 111-112, 118-119, 149, 164, 165, 180, 213, 225

Minnesota, 4, 10, 13, 23, 26, 34, 35, 43, 46, 48, 52-3, 61-62, 65, 67-68, 71, 79, 81, 82-85, 87, 90, 93, 115, 117, 130, 162, 178, 184, 195, 203, 212, 224

Modena, Italy, 69, 141, 228

Montenegro, 57, 63, 171, 213, 227-228

P

Paraguay, 51, 227

Peace Corps, 9, 14, 56, 114, 228

Peru, 22, 27, 227, 229

Porto Alegre, 9, 10, 13, 21, 31, 44-45, 63-64, 68-69, 91, 112, 117, 130-131, 141, 144, 148, 165, 170-171, 227, 228

Portugal, 69, 79, 184

Portuguese language, 10, 12, 15, 31, 33, 34, 39, 43, 45, 46-50, 54-5, 74, 82, 85, 102-103, 137, 140, 194, 207, 209, 212, 224

Poverty, 23-25, 27, 45, 56, 59, 66, 79, 83, 89, 105, 107-108, 116, 143, 149, 151, 153, 164, 225

R

Rio Grande do Sul, 4, 9, 13, 35, 44, 45, 51, 53-54, 57, 64, 69, 70, 99, 100, 102-103, 199, 202, 227, 228-229

S

Saint Paul, 10, 13, 14, 15, 17, 19, 22, 24, 54, 83, 110, 154, 185, 194, 222, 229

Santa Catarina, 88, 180, 184

Santa Terezinha, 86-88, 91, 94, 112, 114, 126, 130, 133, 135, 136, 180, 194, 227, 229

São Paulo, 53, 63, 64, 68, 84, 91, 110, 131, 133, 150, 154, 184, 194, 222, 226, 227-229

Scandinavian, 9, 13, 53, 58, 62-63, 68, 81, 82, 85, 90, 95, 133, 167, 181

South America, 13, 17, 18, 25, 34-35, 102, 107, 130, 227

Spain, 69, 184

T

Thoreau, Henry David, 97, 127, 132

Torres, 180-181, 184-185, 217-219, 227, 229

U

Unitarian, 20, 22, 81, 129, 229

Uruguay, 51, 141, 171, 227

V

Vargas, Getúlio, 64, 99

Venus, 17, 167, 184-186

Veríssimo, Luis Fernando, 9, 62

W

Work ethic, 56, 80, 83, 108

We slam each other in a rough gaucho embrace. As always, unsaid words of farewell stick in my throat. Once again, beneath the ageless scrub tree, separation brings us closer together.

PAI GAVIOLI
Thirty-six Years of War and Finally Peace with My Impossible Brazilian Father-in-Law